WHAT THE BIBLE **REALLY**
SAYS ABOUT SLAVERY

WHAT THE BIBLE **REALLY** SAYS ABOUT SLAVERY

This and other information on the issue of slavery as it applies to history and religion

Elreta Dodds

Press Toward The Mark Publications
Detroit Michigan

What the Bible REALLY says about Slavery

Copyright © 2000 Elreta Dodds
Revised Second Edition—Second Printing
Published by Press Toward The Mark Publications
P.O. Box 02099 Detroit Michigan 48202
First Edition published by Winston-Derek Publishers, 1996*

Scripture taken from the HOLY BIBLE, 1611 KING JAMES VERSION.
Scripture taken from the HOLY BIBLE, NEW INTERNATIONAL VERSION®. Copyright © 1973, 1978, 1984 by International Bible Society. Used by permission of Zondervan Publishing House. All rights reserved.
Scripture taken from the NEW AMERICAN STANDARD BIBLE®, © Copyright The Lockman Foundation 1960, 1962, 1963, 1968, 1971, 1972, 1973, 1975, 1977 Used by permission.

Throughout the text of this publication, the abbreviation NIV is used to indicate scripture taken from the New International Version. The abbreviation NASB is used to indicate scripture taken from the New American Standard Bible. No abbreviation is used for scripture taken from the 1611 King James Version.

Acknowledgements as cited in the first edition:
A very special thanks to Joan Haith Hussey, research assistant. Special thanks to Pastor Emery Moss, Jr., and Jerome H. Smith for their written critiques and letters of endorsement. Special thanks to Jerome H. Smith for pointing me in the direction of my publisher. Special thanks to Joan Haith Hussey and Marisela Melendez for their written critiques. Special thanks to Rev. Nicholas Hood III for his letter of endorsement. Special thanks to Paul Campbell for teaching me how to use a computer and to his wife Aneita for putting up with all the midnight phone calls to her husband. Special thanks to Joshua Cheek and Audrey Gunter-Mabins for their attempts at soliciting my material. Special thanks to Toni Holmes and Carl Davis for the books they loaned me. Special thanks to Phillip M. Chalk, Ovella Maples-Davis, Carl Davis and Paul Campbell for their verbal critiques. Special thanks to Ed King for helping me decide which topic to select. Special thanks to Dennis Herwig of channel 56 Detroit for giving me his last 1990 Civil War Timeline Poster. Special thanks to Noreta Dodds-Dennard, Octavia K. Dodds, Alfred Cameron and Elaine Askew for listening to me talk about this project on many occasions and for their undying support. Also, for all their support, additional thanks to the aforementioned, as well as to William A. Dodds, Jr.

ISBN: 0-9660390-1-7
Library of Congress Catalog Card Number: 99-93470

Editor: Noreta Dennard
Cover: Barb Gunia

---

* First Edition entitled, *Slaves Obey Your Masters: What the Bible Really says about Slavery*
Copyright © 1996 Elreta Dodds

THIS BOOK IS DEDICATED
TO MY BELOVED SISTER

NORETA DENNARD

WHOM I LOVE WITH ALL MY HEART
AND THANK GOD FOR

ASIDE FROM JESUS, SHE IS MY BEST FRIEND

ACKNOWLEDGEMENTS.................

Shouts of praise and a resounding "Thank you" to Jesus Christ, Lord and Saviour, who has given me the fortitude to take on such an endeavor.

A Very Special Thanks to my Editor, Noreta Dennard.

Special Thanks in alphabetical order to Minister Toni R. Buxton, Noreta Dennard, Derek Maurice Grigsby, and Pastor Emery Moss Jr., for their written critiques.

Special Thanks to Pastor Emery Moss Jr., Jerome H. Smith, Joan Haith, and Marisela Melendez for their first edition written critiques. Special Thanks to Joan Haith for her research assistance during the writing of the first edition. Special Thanks to Paul Campbell for his transferring of computer systems data. Special Thanks to Octavia Katrina Dodds (my beloved mother) for all of her support. Special Thanks to Barb Gunia for her cover design.

See publisher's page for entire first edition acknowledgments.

Table of Contents

INTRODUCTION: WHY THIS BOOK?

While growing up in Detroit, I would hear people say things such as, "the Bible is the white man's religion," "the Bible was written by a bunch of men," "white people are blue eyed devils," "white men tampered with the Bible," and so on. These sayings were very prevalent in the black community and discouraged me from reading any of the Bibles that were in my home. In my twenties, when I became a Christian, I remembered these sayings and they haunted me because I came to understand that Christianity is a religion for everyone and not just for the white man. I knew that those who wrote the books of the Bible were not just a bunch of men who had written some kind of esoteric philosophy but that their writings were inspired of God, and I knew that the Bible had not been tampered with.

I eventually began to feel that God was leading me to write literature aimed at dispelling the "white man's religion" myth. Although, I had heard all of the "white man's religion" sayings that had been pitted against the Bible, I didn't know from what source they initially sprouted. Before I could begin writing anything, I needed to know who had originally propagated these lies and why. The agony I felt at the misinformation being funneled into the black community came to a head when in 1991 or thereabout, I happened to be watching the *Oprah Winfrey show*. The focus of this particular program was homosexuality. Of course, during the show, there were various views expressed as to whether or not homosexuality is a sin. But when a Christian woman in the audience stood up and cited biblical scriptures that specifically labeled homosexuality a sin, Oprah replied by saying something like, "Don't talk to me about the Bible. Isn't that the book that says 'slaves obey your masters?'" This hit me hard. I realized that Oprah must have heard the same negative things about the Bible that I had heard all of my life. The only difference was that she had the ability to influence millions of people towards her way of thinking. I didn't have that ability, but I figured I would do my best to even the playing field.

Yes, indeed, the Bible does instruct slaves to obey their masters. This is found in Ephesians 6:5. There's no way of getting around it. It is this scripture, as well as others that were erroneously used as a catalyst to justify the atrocities of slavery imposed upon blacks during the slavery era in America. However, the Bible says so much more about slavery, that once a thorough investigation is conducted on the subject, the command to obey one's master is no longer seen in the oppressive context that many biblically unstudied blacks (and whites for that matter) might take it.

During my research, I soon discovered that black nationalist Bible-bashing had rooted itself from the seed of the *slavery* issue, an issue which has never been fully resolved in the United States. The enslavement of blacks somehow led to a tarnished image of the Bible in the American black community. But how and why?

The vicious enslavement of blacks was the catalyst for America's greatest tragedy: racism. But racism, whether consciously or unconsciously expressed, is considered contemptible, even by those who fall into its snare although they often times repress the knowledge of its evil. A strong *need* for justification creates the need for *strong* justification. Justification by religion is one of the strongest tools a person can use to defend his or her beliefs. Consequently, many antebellum[1] era whites misused and misinterpreted the Bible in an attempt to justify what was the brutal enslavement and mistreatment of blacks. Unfortunately, many blacks began to buy into and promote this justification which resulted in their belief in the accusations that Christianity is a white man's religion and the Bible is the white man's gospel. Blacks were also encouraged to believe that the Bible teaches that all black people are cursed to be slaves. With this, many blacks began to turn away from the Bible, thereby endangering their very souls.

When looking further into the matter, one surmises that there are two pieces to the puzzle. Both whites *and* blacks have had a hand in feeding the "white man's religion" lie. As stated before, during the American antebellum years, pro slavery whites were able to set the tone for this kind of thinking by accepting and misinterpreting the biblical account of the curse of the Canaanites to mean that all black people were cursed and therefore inferior to whites. Since blacks were seen as inferior they were also seen as people who could be enslaved and treated like animals.

To make matters worst, religious groups such as the Mormons were very instrumental in developing racist theological doctrine against blacks all in the name of the church and Jesus Christ. In addition, the Ku Klux Klan held up the banner of white supremacy, lynched blacks, castrated black men, beat, whipped, and tortured blacks all in the name of Christianity while the American government let them do it. It was this same government that instituted Jim Crow

---

[1] The slave era years in America before the Civil War.

laws similar in scope to the apartheid laws that existed not too long ago in South Africa.

In their book, *What Color is Your God?*, Columbus Salley and Ronald Behm explain why so many blacks in America are disillusioned with Christianity:

> ....the enslavement of Blacks was justified in the name of Christianity. Blacks were made to feel cursed in the name of Christianity. Blacks were excluded from White churches in the name of Christianity. Blacks were [and are] excluded from the benefits of American life in the name of Christianity which blesses the status quo.[1]

They went on to say that:

> Any society which deliberately singles out a group of people for a particular type of negative treatment based on an unchangeable factor [e.g., skin color] is, in effect, telling those people that they are not fit to participate in the benefits which naturally accrue to those living in that society. The overwhelming majority of Blacks in America during the segregation period were made to feel a profound and inescapable sense of personal inadequacy and political and economic impotence. The tragedy of the black experience during segregation was that Blacks perceived 'Christianity' as the chief support for the forces of racism that shaped these negative intrapsychic attitudes and social deprivations. [2]

As a result of these things, and keeping in mind that America identifies itself as a Christian nation, its no wonder that a predominant number of black people began to believe that Christianity was indeed a white man's religion. Unfortunately, there were some prominent black leaders who began to cultivate this falsehood. Noble Drew Ali was the first to do just that.

Noble Drew Ali was born as Timothy Drew in 1866. When he was 47 years old he began what he called the Moorish Science Temple. He felt that salvation for black people in America was impossible unless they discovered the origin of their heritage. He also believed and taught that each race should have its own religion, that Christianity was the white man's religion, and that Islam was the religion of the black man. Marcus Garvey, who in 1916 began the Universal Negro

Introduction

Improvement Association, took things a step further. He encouraged separation of the races, taught that Jesus was the white man's God, and said a white God could not serve a black race. Garvey delivered speeches on the street corners of America and despised white people to the point where he taught that biracial blacks couldn't be trusted because they had too much white in them. He also pushed the idea of racial segregation that led him to organize a back-to-Africa movement that eventually collapsed. Wallace Fard, original founder of the Nation of Islam (organized in 1930), took things even further. He was the first to call white people blue eyed devils and called himself the supreme ruler of the universe. Elijah Muhammad, the successor to Wallace Fard, when passed the baton, wrote *Message to the Black Man in America,* published in 1965. In his book he taught that Christianity was nothing more than a black-slave-making religion.

As stated earlier, many of the atrocities committed against blacks during the American slave era and beyond were done so in the name of Christianity. However, the teachings of the Bible do not condone the mistreatment of human beings for it was Jesus that told us to love our neighbors as ourselves (Matthew 22:39). It is the Bible that tells us not to oppress a stranger (Exodus 22:21). It is the Bible that tells us that the fruits of the Spirit are love, joy, peace, patience, kindness, goodness, faithfulness, gentleness, and self control (Galatians 5:22-23). Therefore, the Bible certainly can not be used to justify the brutality that was imposed upon blacks during the slavery era in America.

And when it comes to the question of whether or not the Bible condones racism we have but to look at Malachi 2:10 which asks the questions, *"do we not all have one father? Has not one God created us? Why do we deal treacherously each against his brother so as to profane the covenant of our fathers?"* We have but to look at Acts 17:26, which says that God has made all nations from one blood. This being so, there is really no such thing as race besides the human race. Man has created racial identities, not God. We have but to look at Acts 10:34-35 which says that God is not one to show partiality but in every nation the man who fears him and does what is right, is welcome to him. We have but to look at Colossians 3:1 coupled with verses 9-11 which says *"If then you have been raised up with Christ, keep seeking the things above, where Christ is, seated at the right hand of God. Do not lie to one another since you laid aside the old self with its evil practices, and have put on the new self who is being renewed to a true knowledge according to the image of the One who created him—a renewal in which there is no distinction between Greek and Jew, circumcised and uncircumcised, barbarian, Scythian, slave and freeman, but Christ is all, and in all."* In other words, those of us who are in Christ are all the same. This being the case, God makes no distinction between race and nationality, nor does he make a difference between a slave and a free man. Consequently, white supremacists and black supremacists who misrepresent the Bible to convince others that there are those who are racially superior are convincing those who are unread and unstudied. If the latter would read the Bible for themselves they'd see that the only Supreme Being that the Bible talks about is God.

Slavery is what set in to motion the tide of racism, discrimination, supremacist views, civil rights infractions, and poor race relations in America. It was the trigger that led some whites to use the Bible as a spiritual scapegoat for justification of racial bias. Because of this, I felt Led of the Lord to write a book that investigates what the Bible *really* says about slavery in order to aid in annihilating the bad reputation that Christianity has gotten over the years concerning these things.

Part One of the book gives a brief look at Christianity with Chapter One addressing what Christians believe. Chapter Two explores the reasons why Christians believe what they believe. Chapter Three briefly examines the history of slavery in America and abroad as well as the history of the involvement of Islamic nations in the past and present enslavement of Africans. Chapter Three also takes a brief look at what the Koran says about slavery. Part Two of the book gives an exhaustive look at what the Bible says about slavery. Chapter Four discusses the biblical perspective on slavery, kidnapping, and oppression. Chapter Five gives a complete scriptural investigation of what the Bible says about slavery scripture by scripture. Chapter Six addresses the myth of the black curse and examines the miracles of the Civil War. The Epilogue follows.

This book was specifically written for those who reject the Bible based on their belief that the Bible supports slavery and, therefore, promotes racism against blacks. It was also written for Christians who are not sure what the Bible says regarding slavery, and therefore, avoid the subject altogether. We all have preconceived notions about things. Many have preconceived notions of what the Bible says about slavery and oppression. However, if those notions have a direct effect on how one behaves, how one thinks, or what one believes, then it is best to make sure those notions are correct, especially when one's eternal soul is at stake. The foregoing pages dispel spurious notions that surround the subject of what the Bible

Introduction

says about slavery and were written to be used as one of many tools to defend the Christian faith.

PART ONE

CHAPTER ONE

♦

WHAT DO CHRISTIANS BELIEVE?

♦ The Bible is the word of God ♦ The absolute authority of the Bible ♦ Jesus Christ as Lord and Saviour ♦ The Deity of Christ ♦ The resurrection of Jesus Christ ♦ The doctrine of the Trinity ♦ Satan as a fallen angel

In this chapter we will examine some essential Christian beliefs. There will be a statement of the belief followed by verses of biblical scripture that support that belief. It should be understood that the scriptural verses cited are only a portion of a multitude of scriptures that could have been selected. Since the Bible is so vast, to cite every verse of scripture that applies to every statement would constitute a book in itself. However, the verses given are concise in supporting the statements of belief preceding them. This chapter specifically focuses on basic Bible doctrinal beliefs of Orthodox Christianity. The following chapter supports, with sound historical, archaeological, and scientific evidence, what is presented in this chapter. Before we can comprehensively investigate what the Bible says about slavery, we must first understand Orthodox Christianity. Therefore the first two chapters of this book should be studied closely before reading further.

Christians believe that the Bible is the Word of God

Christians believe that the Bible is the only religious book that truly represents the word of God. The following scriptures support this belief. Let's take a look.....

All scripture is given by inspiration of God, and profitable for doctrine, for reproof, for correction, for instruction in righteousness: (2 Timothy 3:16)

²⁰Above all, you must understand that no prophecy of Scripture came about by the prophet's own interpretation. ²¹For prophecy never had its origin in the will of man, but

1

men spoke from God as they were carried along by the Holy
Spirit. (2 Peter 1:20-21 NIV)

44And he said unto them, These are the words which I
spake unto you, while I was yet with you, that all things
must be fulfilled, which were written in the law of Moses,
and in the prophets, and in the psalms, concerning me.
45Then opened he their understanding, that they might
understand the scriptures, (Luke 24:44-45. Jesus is speaking
in verse 44)

37And the Father who sent me has himself testified
concerning me. You have never heard his voice nor seen his
form, 38nor does his word dwell in you, for you do not
believe the one he sent. 39You diligently study the Scriptures
because you think that by them you possess eternal life.
These are the Scriptures that testify about me, 40yet you
refuse to come to me to have life. (John 7:37-40 NIV)

Jesus, the Messiah tells us first hand that what is contained in the
scriptures is what leads to eternal life. He went on to say that those
who have written the scriptures do so as a testimony of him. If then,
we understand who Jesus is, we understand what the Bible is. Jesus is
God incarnate (we will discuss this further in Chapter Two) who
endorses the scriptures of the Bible. Therefore, the Bible must be God
inspired and the unadulterated word of God. This is made even more
apparent in the following parable spoken by Jesus:

19There was a certain rich man, which was clothed in purple
and fine linen, and fared sumptuously every day:
20And there was a certain beggar named Lazarus, which was
laid at his gate, full of sores,
21And desiring to be fed with the crumbs which fell from the
rich man's table: moreover the dogs came and licked his
sores.
22And it came to pass, that the beggar died, and was carried
by the angels into Abraham's bosom: the rich man also died
and was buried:
23And in hell he lift up his eyes, being in torments, and seeth
Abraham afar off, and Lazarus in his bosom.

²⁴And he cried and said, Father Abraham, have mercy on me, and send Lazarus, that he may dip the tip of his finger in water and cool my tongue; for I am tormented in this flame.

²⁵But Abraham said, Son, remember that thou in thy lifetime receivedst thy good things, and likewise Lazarus evil things: But now he is comforted, and thou art tormented.

²⁶And beside all this, between us and you there is a great gulf fixed: so that they which would pass from hence to you cannot; neither can they pass to us, that would come from thence.

²⁷Then he said, I pray thee therefore, father, that thou wouldest send him to my father's house:

²⁸For I have five brethen; that he may testify unto them, lest they also come into this place of torment.

²⁹Abraham saith unto him, They have Moses and the prophets; let them hear them.

³⁰And he said, Nay, father Abraham; but if one went unto them from the dead, they will repent.

³¹And he said unto him, If they hear not Moses and the prophets, neither will they be persuaded, though one rose from the dead. (Luke 16:19-31. Jesus is speaking in this parable)

In the above scripture text the phrase, "Abraham's Bosom" is an Old Testament Jewish term that refers to heaven. The phrase, "Moses and the prophets" is referring to the Word of God (the Holy Bible), specifically the Old Testament. The text tells us that those who absolutely refuse to accept the Bible as the word of God will do so no matter what. If it is not in a person's heart to believe that the Bible is the word of God then they will not believe, despite evidence contrary to their disbelief. Abraham is referred to as "father"[1] because God promised to make him "a father of many nations" as seen in the book of Genesis chapter 17. It must also be noted that the rich man in the above parable went to hell not because he was rich nor even because he was cruel to Lazarus but because he never accepted the Word of God and therefore never worshipped the true God.

---

[1] A small *f* used for the word *father* refers to a human father whereas a capital *F* used for the word *Father* refers to God, the Father.

What do Christians Believe?

Christians believe in the absolute authority of the Bible.

Christians believe that any other religious book or document that does not agree with what the Bible says is not of God:

> Whoever transgresseth, and abideth not in the doctrine of Christ, hath not God. He that abideth in the doctrine of Christ, he hath both the Father and the Son. (2 John:9)

> [10]If anyone comes to you and does not bring this teaching, do not take him into your house or welcome him. [11]Anyone who welcomes him shares in his wicked work. (2 John:10-11 NIV)

> [6]I am astonished that you are so quickly deserting the one who called you by the grace of Christ and are turning to a different gospel-- [7]which is really no gospel at all. Evidently some people are throwing you into confusion and are trying to pervert the gospel of Christ. [8]But even if we or an angel from heaven should preach a gospel other than the one we preached to you, let him be eternally condemned! [9]As we have already said, so now I say again: if anybody is preaching to you a gospel other than what you accepted, let him be eternally condemned! (Galatians 1:6-9 NIV, Paul the apostle is speaking here)

> [17]I urge you, brothers, to watch out for those who cause divisions and put obstacles in your way that are contrary to the teaching you have learned. Keep away from them. [18]For such people are not serving our Lord Christ, but their own appetites. By smooth talk and flattery they deceive the minds of naïve people. (Romans 16:17-18 NIV)

> [11]And he gave some apostles; and some, prophets; and some, evangelists; and some, pastors and teachers;
> [12]For the perfecting of the saints, for the work of the ministry, for the edifying of the body of Christ:
> [13]Till we all come in the unity of faith, and of the knowledge of the Son of God, unto a perfect man, unto the measure of the stature of the fullness of Christ:
> [14]That we henceforth be no more children, tossed to and fro, and carried about with every wind of doctrine, by the sleight

of men, and cunning craftiness, whereby they lie in wait to deceive; (Ephesians 4:11-14)

[1]Now the Spirit speaketh expressly, that in the latter times some shall depart from the faith, giving heed to seducing spirits, and doctrines of devils;
[2]Speaking lies in hypocrisy; having their conscience seared with a hot iron; (1 Timothy 4:1-2)

[18]For I testify unto every man that heareth the words of the prophecy of this book, If any man shall add unto these things, God shall add unto him the plagues that are written in this book:
[19]And if any man shall take away from the words of the book of this prophecy, God shall take away his part out of the book of life, and out of the holy city, and from the things which are written in this book. (Revelation 22:18-19)

The above scriptures tell us that any attempt to stray away from, add to, take away from, or pervert the gospel of Jesus Christ is a serious infraction against God. Let's look at a few more scriptures:

[9]Then shall they deliver you up to be afflicted, and shall kill you: and ye shall be hated of all nations for my name sake.
[10]And then shall many be offended, and shall betray one another, and shall hate one another.
[11]And many false prophets shall rise, and shall deceive many.
[12]And because iniquity shall abound, the love of many shall wax cold.
[13] But he that shall endure unto the end, the same shall be saved.
[14] And this gospel of the kingdom shall be preached in all the world for a witness unto all nations; and then shall the end come. (Matthew 24:9-14. Jesus is speaking here.)

Study to shew thyself approved unto God, a workman that needeth not to be ashamed, rightly dividing the word of truth. (2 Timothy 2:15)

[17]Do not think that I have come to abolish the Law or the Prophets; I have not come to abolish them but to fulfill them.

[18]I tell you the truth, until heaven and earth disappear, not the smallest letter, the least stroke of a pen, will by any means disappear from the Law until everything is accomplished. [19]Anyone who breaks one of the least of these commandments and teaches others to do the same will be called least in the kingdom of heaven, but whoever practices and teaches these commands will be called great in the kingdom of heaven. [20]For I tell you that unless your righteousness surpasses that of the Pharisees and the teachers of the law, you will certainly not enter the kingdom of heaven. (Matthew 5:17-20 NIV. Jesus is speaking here)

Christians believe in Jesus Christ as Lord and Saviour

Christians believe that Jesus Christ is the only person that ever walked the face of the earth who has the power to save souls. Those who believe in Jesus Christ as Lord and Saviour will go to heaven when they die:

[9]That if thou shalt confess with thy mouth the Lord Jesus, and shalt believe in thine heart that God hath raised him from the dead, thou shalt be saved.
[10]For with the heart man believeth unto righteousness; and with the mouth confession is made unto salvation.
[11]For the scripture saith, Whosoever believeth on him shall not be ashamed.
[12]For there is no difference between the Jew and the Greek: for the same Lord over all is rich unto all that call upon him.
[13]For whosoever shall call upon the name of the Lord shall be saved. (Romans 10:9-13)

[16]For God so loved the world, that he gave his only begotten Son, that whosoever believeth in him should not perish, but have everlasting life.
[17]For God sent not his Son into the world to condemn the world; but that the world through him might be saved.
[18]He that believeth on him is not condemned: but he that believeth not is condemned already, because he hath not believed in the name of the only begotten Son of God. (John 3:16-18)

[32]Whosoever therefore shall confess me before men, him will I confess also before my Father which is in heaven.

[33]But whosoever shall deny me before men, him will I also deny before my father which is in heaven. (Matthew 10:32-33. Jesus is speaking here)

[9]If we receive the witness of men, the witness of God is greater: for this is the witness of God which he hath testified of his Son.

[10]He that believeth on the Son of God hath the witness in himself: he that believeth not God hath made him a liar; because he believeth not the record that God gave of his Son.

[11]And this is the record, that God hath given to us eternal life, and this life is in his Son. [12]He that hath the Son hath life; and he that hath not the Son of God hath not life. (1 John 5:9-12)

[8]Then Peter, filled with the Holy Spirit, said to them: "Rulers and elders of the people! [9]If we are being called to account today for an act of kindness shown to a cripple and are asked how he was healed, [10]then know this, you and all the people of Israel: It is by the name of Jesus Christ of Nazareth, whom you crucified but whom God raised from the dead, that this man stands before you healed. [11]He is

> "'the stone you builders rejected,
> which has become the capstone.'

[12]Salvation is found in no one else, for there is no other name under heaven given to men by which we must be saved." (Acts 4:8-12 NIV)

Christians believe in the Deity of Christ

Christians believe that there is one God who exists in three persons: The Father, The Son, and The Holy Ghost. This description of God is what Christians refer to as the Trinity. However, the word *Trinity* is not found in the Bible and is merely used as a semantic tool for explaining the Godhead. The second person of the Trinity, The Son, was manifest as a man (Jesus Christ). Christians believe that Jesus Christ is God incarnate. These beliefs are supported by biblical scripture.

It might also seem as if there is a contradiction here since the above scriptures refer to Jesus as the *Son of God* and not God himself. However, there is no contradiction when one considers the meaning of certain words and phrases during biblical times. *The New Treasury of Scripture Knowledge* edited by Jerome Smith states that the word "begotten", as applied to Jesus and as understood in the Greek, is biblically defined in the following way:

> [The word begotten] expresses the unique and eternal relationship of the Son to the Father. As firstborn does not mean born first (Col 1:15n), neither does only begotten imply a begetting, birth, or origin in time. In His preexistence, Jesus was always uniquely the Son of God (Ps 2:7. Is + *9:6. He 1:8). When used of Christ, only begotten speaks of 'unoriginated relationship.' Only begotten 'indicates that as the Son of God He was the sole representative of the Being and character of the One who sent Him' (Vine, Expository Dictionary, vol. 3, p.140). It is a word picture which portrays the relationship of the father (Ge 21:12, 22:2, 12, 16, He 11:17). Isaac, termed Abraham's only begotten son (He 11:17), though Abraham had a prior son Ishmael by Hagar (Ge 16:15) and later sons by Keturah (Ge 25:1-4. 1Ch 1:32, 33), sustains a unique relationship to Abraham as the son of promise (Ga 4:23). The same picture, portrayed in parable (Mt 21:37), emphasizes the unique authority of Jesus as sent by the Father (Jn 20:21. 1 J 4:9), and our responsibility to receive the truth declared by Him (Jn 1:14, 18. 3:18.Mt 17:5). [1]

Jesus was and is the literal Son of God. God is our spiritual Father, however, God is the literal Father of Jesus. With this understanding, one can see how Jesus can be the Son of God as well as God in the flesh. Now, we will look at some scriptures that support the belief that Jesus himself is God:

> And without controversy great is the mystery of godliness: God was manifest in the flesh, justified in the Spirit, seen of angels, preached unto the Gentiles, believed on in the world, received up into glory. (1 Tim 3:16)

The above scripture tells us that God was manifested in the flesh. When coupled with the following two verses of scripture below, it becomes plain that Jesus is whom the above scripture is referring to.

[1]In the beginning was the Word, and the Word was with God, and the Word was God.
[2]The same was in the beginning with God.
[3]All things were made by him; and without him was not any thing made that was made.
[4]In him was life; and the life was the light of men.
[5]And the light shineth in darkness; and the darkness comprehended it not. (John 1:1-5)

And the Word was made flesh, and dwelt among us, (and we beheld his glory, the glory as of the only begotten of the Father,) full of grace and truth. (John 1:14)

John 1:14 identifies the only begotten as the Word made flesh that dwelt among us. Jesus is identified as God's only begotten. The Word is identified as God. Therefore, if Jesus is the only begotten, and the only begotten is the Word and the Word is God, then Jesus is God.

Jesus is the Word that the above scriptures speak of. The Word was God. The Word was with God in the beginning and became flesh. Jesus is the only person spoken of in the Bible as God in the flesh. Therefore, Jesus is part of the Godhead (Father, Son, and Holy Ghost) and was with God in the beginning. Let's look further.

[10]Ye are my witnesses, saith the LORD, and my servant whom I have chosen: that ye may know and believe me, and understand that I am he: before me there was no God formed, neither shall there be after me.
[11]I, even I am the LORD and beside me there is no saviour.
[12]I have declared, and have saved, and I have shewed, when there was no strange god among you: therefore ye are my witnesses, saith the LORD, that I am God. (Isaiah 43: 10-12)

There is no saviour besides God. Jesus is identified throughout the Bible as Lord and Saviour. Therefore, Jesus must not only be God but a person of God as well, since the Saviour manifested himself as a man and sacrificed himself for the sins of the world. The following scripture reference points this out even further:

[1]God, after he spoke long ago to the fathers in the prophets in many portions and in many ways,

²in these last days has spoken to us in His Son, whom He appointed heir of all things, through whom also He made the world.
³And He is the radiance of His glory and the exact representation of His nature, and upholds all things by the word of His power. When He had made purification of sins, He sat down at the right hand of the Majesty on high;
⁴having become as much better than the angels, as He has inherited a more excellent name than they.
⁵For to which of the angels did He ever say,

"THOU ART MY SON,
TODAY I HAVE BEGOTTEN THEE"?
And again,
"I WILL BE A FATHER TO HIM,
AND HE SHALL BE A SON TO ME"?
⁶And when He again brings the first-born into
the world, He says,
"AND LET ALL THE ANGELS OF GOD
WORSHIP HIM."
⁷And of the angels He says,
"WHO MAKES HIS ANGELS WINDS,
AND HIS MINISTERS A FLAME OF FIRE."
⁸But of the Son He says,
"THY THRONE, O GOD, IS FOREVER AND
EVER,
AND THE RIGHTEOUS SCEPTER IS THE
SCEPTER OF HIS KINGDOM.
(Hebrews 1:1-8 NASB)

In the preceding verses of scripture, God refers to Jesus as God as evidenced in verse 8. The angels are even commanded to worship him (verse 6). Moreover, Jesus Christ has identified himself as God. Let's take a look:

⁶Jesus saith unto him, I am the way, the truth, and the life: no man cometh unto the Father, but by me.
⁷If ye had known me, ye should have known my Father also: and from henceforth ye know him, and have seen him.
⁸Phillip saith unto him, Lord, shew us the Father, and it sufficeth us. ⁹Jesus saith unto him, Have I been so long time with you, and yet hast thou not known me, Philip? he that

hath seen me hath seen the Father; and how sayest thou then, shew us the Father? (John 14:6-9)

Jesus does not mince words. He specifically said that those who have seen him have seen God the Father. This is so because Jesus is part of the Godhead. The three personages of the Godhead (Father, Son, Holy Spirit) are all part of one God. Jesus brings the point home even further by saying the following:

I and my Father are one. (John 10:30, Jesus is speaking here.)

Jesus, himself, says that He and The Father are one meaning that there is a special union between The Father and Jesus. Both parties make up the Godhead. This union is further established when examining the following:

10And we pray this in order that you may live a life worthy of the Lord and may please him in every way: bearing fruit in every good work, growing in the knowledge of God, 11being strengthened with all power according to his glorious might so that you may have great endurance and patience, and joyfully 12giving thanks to the Father, who has qualified you to share in the inheritance of the saints in the kingdom of light. 13For he has rescued us from the dominion of darkness and brought us into the Kingdom of the Son he loves, 14in whom we have redemption, the forgiveness of sins.
15He is the image of the invisible God, the firstborn over all creation. 16For by him all things were created: things in heaven and on earth, visible and invisible, whether thrones or powers or rulers or authorities; all things were created by him and for him. 17He is before all things, and in him all things hold together. 18And he is the head of the body, the church; he is the beginning and the firstborn from among the dead, so that in everything he might have the supremacy. 19For God was pleased to have all his fullness dwell in him, 20and through him to reconcile to himself all things, whether things on earth or things in heaven, by making peace through his blood, shed on the cross. (Colossians 1:10-20 NIV)

What do Christians Believe?

Verse 16 above says that by Jesus, all things were created. Therefore Jesus must be God because Genesis 1:1 tells us that "in the beginning God created the heavens and the earth." The fullness of God dwells in Jesus.

In the Old Testament, we see that God identified himself by name, that name being I AM THAT I AM. This is not only a name but an identity as well. God is the great I AM. He is the one who is, always was, and always will be. The scriptures below give the account of God identifying himself:

> ¹³And Moses said unto God, Behold, when I come unto the children of Israel, and shall say unto them, The God of your fathers hath sent me unto you; and they shall say to me, What is his name? What shall I say unto them?
> ¹⁴And God said unto Moses, I AM THAT I AM: and he said, Thus shalt thou say unto the children of Israel, I AM hath sent me unto you. (Exodus 3:13-14)

There is no question that God's name is I AM. The Jews accepted God's identity and name as I AM. Jesus identified himself as I AM as evidenced by the following conversation some of the Jews had with Jesus:

> ⁴⁸The Jews answered him, "Aren't we right in saying you are a Samaritan and demon possessed?"
> ⁴⁹"I am not possessed by a demon," said Jesus, "but I honor my Father and you dishonor me. ⁵⁰I am not seeking glory for myself; but there is one who seeks it, and he is the judge. ⁵¹I tell you the truth, if anyone keeps my word, he will never see death."
> ⁵²At this the Jews exclaimed, "Now we know that you are demon-possessed! Abraham died and so did the prophets, yet you say that if anyone keeps your word, he will never taste death. ⁵³Are you greater than our father Abraham? He died, and so did the prophets. Who do you think you are?"
> ⁵⁴Jesus replied, "If I glorify myself, my glory means nothing. My Father, whom you claim as your God, is the one who glorifies me. ⁵⁵Though you do not know him, I know him. If I said I did not, I would be a liar like you, but I do know him and keep his word. ⁵⁶Your father Abraham rejoiced at the thought of seeing my day; he saw it and was glad,"

⁵⁷You are not yet fifty years old," the Jews said to him, "and you have seen Abraham!"
⁵⁸"I tell you the truth," Jesus answered, "before Abraham was born, I am!" ⁵⁹At this, they picked up stones to stone him, but Jesus hid himself, slipping away from the temple grounds. (John 8:48-59 NIV)

The Jews wanted to Kill Jesus because by identifying himself as I AM, Jesus was making himself equal with God. Let's take a further look:

¹After these things there was a feast of the Jews, and Jesus went up to Jerusalem.
²Now there is in Jerusalem by the sheep gate a pool, which is called in Hebrew Bethesda, having five porticoes.
³In these lay a multitude of those who were sick, blind, lame, and withered, [waiting for the moving of the waters;
⁴for an angel of the Lord went down at certain seasons into the pool, and stirred up the water; whoever then first, after the stirring up of the water, stepped in was made well from whatever disease with which he was afflicted.]
⁵And a certain man was there, who had been thirty-eight years in his sickness.
⁶When Jesus saw him lying there, and knew that he had already been a long time in that condition, He said to him, "Do you wish to get well?"
⁷The sick man answered Him, "Sir, I have no man to put me into the pool when the water is stirred up, but while I am coming, another steps down before me."
⁸Jesus said to him, "Arise, take up your pallet, and walk."
⁹And immediately the man became well, and took up his pallet and began to walk.
Now it was the Sabbath on that day.
¹⁰Therefore the Jews were saying to him who was cured, "It is the Sabbath, and it is not permissible for you to carry your pallet."
¹¹But he answered them, 'He who made me well was the one who said to me, "Take up your pallet and walk.'"
¹²They asked him, "Who is the man who said to you, 'Take up your pallet, and walk'?"
¹³But he who was healed did not know who it was; for Jesus had slipped away while there was a crowd in that place.

¹⁴Afterward Jesus found him in the temple, and said to him, "Behold, you have become well; do not sin anymore, so that nothing worse may befall you."
¹⁵The man went away, and told the Jews that it was Jesus who had made him well.
¹⁶And for this reason the Jews were persecuting Jesus, because He was doing these things on the Sabbath.
¹⁷But He answered them, "My Father is working until now, and I Myself am working."
¹⁸For this cause therefore the Jews were seeking all the more to kill Him, because He not only was breaking the Sabbath, but also was calling God His own Father, making Himself equal with God. (John 5:1-18 NASB)

Each time Jesus equated himself with God, the Jews wanted to kill him. The Jews believed that Jesus was breaking the Sabbath day rules and that only God had the option to work on the Sabbath day. However, Jesus had already taught that he had not come to abolish the law but to fulfill it (Matthew 5:17).[2] Therefore the Sabbath day laws were fulfilled by Christ's coming and literal rest was no longer needed since believers in Christ automatically entered God's perpetual rest (Hebrews 3:7-19 through 4:1-11, see Appendix).

The fact that Jesus identifies himself as God is evidence of his deity because he is the only person in history who has ever claimed to be God who stood up to the test. Jesus walked on water, healed the lame and blind, prophesied about his own death, raised Lazarus from the dead, quieted the storm, walked through doors, resurrected from the grave exactly when he said he would, and the list goes on. There have been many men who have claimed to be God but none can match what Jesus did to prove it.

The Bible informs us that Jesus came to the earth as God in human form and gave himself as a living sacrifice for the redemption of our sins. During Old Testament times, before the coming of Christ, an unblemished lamb was one of the animals that God instructed his people to offer to him as a living sacrifice for their sins. When Jesus came, he took the place of the actual unblemished lamb and became the figurative unblemished Lamb of God. Because of this, animal sacrifice had become a shadow of things to come. After the coming of Jesus there was no more need for animal sacrifices for the redemption

---

[2] It reads, *Do not think that I have come to abolish the Law or the Prophets; I have not come to abolish them but to fulfill them.* (NIV)

of sin. Jesus became our sin offering. He became our sacrifice and is the Lamb of God. The following verses of scripture clarify this:

> [18]For you know that it was not with perishable things such as silver or gold that you were redeemed from the empty way of life handed down to you from your forefathers, [19]but with the precious blood of Christ, a lamb without blemish or defect. [20]He was chosen before the creation of the world, but was revealed in these last times for your sake. [21]Through him you believe in God, who raised him from the dead and glorified him, and so your faith and hope are in God. (1Peter 1:18-21 NIV)

The ultimate confirmation of the deity of Christ is his resurrection. The resurrection of Christ is the basis on which the Christian faith rests.

Christians believe in the Resurrection of Jesus Christ.

Christians believe that Jesus Christ is the only person ever to walk the earth who has been resurrected from the dead never to die again. His resurrection and the circumstances surrounding it proves his deity. Let's look at what the Bible tells us about the resurrection of Jesus Christ.

> [18]Then the Jews demanded of him, "What miraculous sign can you show us to prove your authority to do all this?"
> [19]Jesus answered them, "Destroy this temple, and I will raise it again in three days."
> [20]The Jews replied, "It has taken forty-six years to build this temple, and you are going to raise it in three days?" [21]But the temple he had spoken of was his body. [22]After he was raised from the dead, his disciples recalled what he had said. Then they believed the Scripture and the words that Jesus had spoken. (John 2:18-22 NIV)

As revealed in the preceding verses of scripture Jesus predicted his own death and resurrection. Let's continue....

> [1]Now upon the first day of the week, very early in the morning, they came unto the sepulchre, bringing the spices which they had prepared, and certain others with them.

15

²And they found the stone rolled away from the sepulchre.

³And they entered in, and found not the body of the Lord Jesus.

⁴And it came to pass, as they were much perplexed thereabout, behold two men stood by them in shining garments:

⁵And as they were afraid, and bowed down their faces to the earth, they said unto them, Why seek ye the living among the dead?

⁶He is not here, but is risen: remember how he spake unto you when he was yet in Galilee,

⁷Saying, The Son of man must be delivered into the hands of sinful men, and be crucified, and the third day rise again.

⁸And they remembered his words,

⁹And returned from the sepulchre, and told all these things unto the eleven, and to all the rest.(Luke 24:1-9)

The first people to witness the empty tomb of Jesus were women who had come to the tomb with prepared spices. Verse 10 of the same chapter informs us that three of the women were Mary Magdelene, Joanna, and Mary, the mother of James. The account goes on to tell us that the women went to the apostles to tell them that they had been approached by angels who told them that Jesus had risen. But the apostles did not believe the women until they themselves saw the risen Lord.

Jesus appeared to many (including the apostles) in his resurrected body. The following verses of scripture give account of this. Let's take a look:

²⁴Now Thomas (called Didymus), one of the Twelve, was not with the disciples when Jesus came. ²⁵So the other disciples told him, "We have seen the Lord!"

But he said to them, "Unless I see the nail marks in his hands and put my finger where the nails were, and put my hand into his side, I will not believe it."

²⁶A week later his disciples were in the house again, and Thomas was with them. Though the doors were locked, Jesus came and stood among them and said, "Peace be with you!" ²⁷Then he said to Thomas, "Put your finger here; see my hands. Reach out your hand and put it into my side. Stop doubting and believe."

²⁸Thomas said to him, "My Lord and my God!"

[29]Then Jesus told him, "Because you have seen me, you have believed; blessed are those who have not seen and yet have believed."

[30]Jesus did many other miraculous signs in the presence of his disciples, which are not recorded in this book. [31]But these are written that you may believe that Jesus is the Christ, the Son of God, and that by believing you may have life in his name. (John 20:24-31 NIV)

Thomas only believed after he had seen the risen Jesus for himself. However, those who believe and have not yet seen are blessed indeed because their belief is based on faith.

After his resurrection, Jesus did not die again but was instead, after a period of time, taken up into heaven to sit at the right hand of God, which was his place before the beginning of time.

[19]So then after the Lord had spoken unto them, he was received up into heaven, and sat on the right hand of God.
[20]And they went forth, and preached every where, the Lord working with them, and confirming the word with signs following. A-men. (Mark 16:19-20)

The entire Christian faith rests upon the fact that Jesus resurrected from the grave, as the following scriptures attest to:

[12]Now if Christ be preached that he rose from the dead, how say some among you that there is no resurrection of the dead?
[13] But if there be no resurrection of the dead, then Christ is not risen:
[14] And if Christ be not risen, then is our preaching vain, and your faith is also vain. (1 Corinthians 15:12-14)

The resurrection of Jesus Christ is the single historical event that justifies belief in Christ as God incarnate. Jesus predicted his own death and resurrection. He knew that he would rise from the grave exactly three days after his death. After his resurrection, he showed himself to people and eventually ascended into heaven in front of witnesses. No one else in the history of the world has done all of this.

What do Christians Believe?

Christians believe in the Doctrine of the Trinity

Christians believe that there is one God that represents himself in three persons: The Father, The Son and The Holy Ghost. They are separate in office but equal in Godliness.

> 26And God said, Let us make man in our image, after our likeness: and let them have dominion over the fish of the sea, and over the fowl of the air, and over the cattle, and over all the earth, and over every creeping thing that creepeth upon the earth.
> 27So God created man in his own image, in the image of God created he him; male and female created he them. (Genesis 1:26-27)

Verse 26 says that God said "Let *us* make man in *our* image." Verse 27 tells us that *God* created man in *his* own image." The words "us" and "our" denote plurality while the words "God" and "his" are singular. Therefore God must be a singular being who manifests and represents himself in three different persons those being the Father, the Son and the Holy Ghost.

> 18And Jesus came and spake unto them, saying, All power is given unto me in heaven and in earth.
> 19Go ye therefore, and teach all nations, baptizing them in the name of the Father, and of the Son, and of the Holy Ghost: (Matthew 28:18-19)

Jesus himself mandated that believers be baptized in the name of the Father, Son, and Holy Ghost. However, he never alluded to more than one God. Therefore, all three must be personages of the Godhead working together as one.

Christians believe that there is a spiritual being whose name is Satan who is a fallen angel

Before Satan became Satan, he was Lucifer. As we shall see, Lucifer was a beautiful angel assigned to cover the glory of God. However, there came a time when Lucifer wanted to overthrow God and become God himself. Because of this, a war was waged in Heaven between Lucifer and Michael the archangel. Lucifer then became Satan. Satan in the Greek means *adversary*. Lucifer rebelled against

God and therefore became his adversary, his enemy. Satan and his army of angels, a third of the angelic hosts, were defeated and thrown out of Heaven. When Satan was ousted from heaven he took a portion of the heavenly hosts with him who are now referred to as demons. Not only did Lucifer become God's enemy but he became man's enemy also. Before Satan was exiled from heaven his function was to cover the glory of God. However, he wanted to be like God and became rebellious. This is when God banished him from heaven. Just as Satan tricked Eve in the Garden of Eden he continues today to try to turn us against God and tempt us to sin. Satan would rather that we worship him instead of God. The Bible tells us that those of us who are not children of God (those who have not confessed a belief in the Lordship of Jesus Christ) are children of the devil (Satan). Let's look at some scriptures that support this historical view of Satan:

[12]How art thou fallen from heaven, O Lucifer, son of the morning! how art thou cut down to the ground, which didst weaken the nations!
[13]For thou hast said in thine heart, I will ascend into heaven, I will exalt my throne above the stars of God: I will sit also upon the mount of the congregation, in the sides of the North:
[14]I will ascend above the heights of the clouds; I will be like the most High.
[15]Yet thou shall be brought down to hell, to the sides of the pit. (Isaiah 14:12-15)

Satan, who was once named Lucifer by God, which in the Hebrew means "day star" or "angel of light" decided that he wanted to be God and attempted to dethrone God. Instead, Lucifer was thrown out of heaven. Let's look further.

[11]The word of the Lord came to me; [12]"Son of man, take up a lament concerning the king of Tyre and say to him: 'This is what the Sovereign Lord says:

"'You were the model of perfection,
Full of wisdom and perfect in beauty.
[13]You were in Eden,
the garden of God;
every precious stone adorned you:

19

> ruby, topaz and emerald,
> chrysolite, onyx and jasper,
> sapphire, turquoise and beryl.
> Your settings and mountings were made
> of gold;
> On the day you were created they were
> prepared.
> [14]You were anointed as a guardian cherub,
> for so I ordained you.
> You were on the holy mount of God;
> You walked among the fiery stones.
> [15]You were blameless in your ways
> from the day you were created
> till wickedness was found in you.
> [16]Through your widespread trade
> you were filled with violence,
> and you sinned.
> So I drove you in disgrace from the mount
> of God,
> And I expelled you, O guardian cherub,
> From among the fiery stones.
> [17]Your heart became proud
> on account of your beauty,
> and you corrupted your wisdom
> because of your splendor.
> So I threw you to the earth;
> I made a spectacle of you before kings,
> (Ezekiel 28:11-17 NIV)

The King of Tyre refers to the historical king of Tyre who was Ithobalus ll. Scholars agree that Lucifer is the supernatural king of Tyre. Therefore, there is a double reference. Statements that could refer to the human being are actually referring to the historical king while statements contrary to human characteristics are speaking of Lucifer. With this understanding the passage is made clearer.

The verses of scripture also talk about Lucifer's perfect beauty and how precious stones are the actual makeup of his supernatural body. Satan is a cherub which is a certain rank order (or kind) of angel. Verse 15 tells us that Lucifer's ways were perfect until sin was found in him. Satan lost his honorable title of Lucifer and was exiled from heaven. Let's look at a few more scriptures on this issue:

> [7]And there was war in heaven: Michael and his angels fought against the dragon; and the dragon fought and his angels.
> [8]And prevailed not; neither was their place found any more in heaven
> [9]And the great dragon was cast out, that old serpent, called the Devil, and Satan, which deceiveth the whole world: he was cast out into the earth, and his angels were cast out with him. (Revelation 12:7-9)

The scriptures tell us that Satan didn't leave heaven quietly. God commanded the righteous angels (Michael and his angels) to fight against the dragon (Satan). Satan and his angels (demons) were thrown out of heaven by means of war.

> [7]And the Lord said unto Satan, Whence comest thou? Then Satan answered the LORD, and said, From going to and fro in the earth, and from walking up and down in it. (Job 1:6-7)

Since Satan did not succeed in overthrowing God, he now aims to spiritually overthrow man by tempting man to sin, do evil, and turn against God.

> Be sober, be vigilant; because your adversary the devil, as a roaring lion, walketh about, seeking whom he may devour: (1 Peter 5:8)

As stated before, the word "Satan" means adversary. So whenever the Bible speaks of the devil, it is talking about Satan.

> [24]Another parable put he forth unto them, saying, The kingdom of heaven is likened unto a man which sowed good seed in his field:
> [25]But while men slept, his enemy came and sowed tares among the wheat, and went his way.
> [26] But when the blade was sprung up, and it brought forth fruit, then appeared the tares also.
> [27]So the servants of the householder came and said unto him, Sir, didst not thou sow good seed in thy field? from whence then hath it tares?

28He said unto them, an enemy hath done this. The servants said unto him, Wilt thou then that we go and gather them up?

29But he said, Nay; lest while ye gather up the tares, ye root up also the wheat with them.

30Let both grow together until the harvest: and in the time of harvest I will say to the reapers, Gather ye together first the tares, and bind them in bundles to burn them: but gather the wheat into my barn. (Matthew 13:24-30)

Tares are a particular kind of weed that grows especially in grain fields. Jesus explains the preceding parable in the following way:

36Then Jesus sent the multitude away, and went into the house: and his disciples came unto him, saying, declare unto us the parable of the tares of the field.

37He answered and said unto them, He that soweth the good seed is the Son of man;

38The field is the world; the good seed are the children of the kingdom; but the tares are the children of the wicked one;

39The enemy that sowed them is the devil; the harvest is the end of the world; and the reapers are the angels.

40As therefore the tares are gathered and burned in the fire; so shall it be in the end of this world. (St. Matthew 13:36-40)

Jesus identifies the enemy that sowed the tares as the devil, Satan himself. The good seed is described as the children of the Kingdom (children of God). However, the tares are identified as the children of the wicked one (the devil). When studying further, the Bible tells us that those who do not believe in Jesus Christ as Lord and Saviour and therefore continue to satisfy the flesh (to sin) without remorse or repentance, are children of the devil. However, those who confess a heartfelt belief in Jesus Christ as Lord and Saviour and live so accordingly are children of God.

This chapter has presented a general overview of what Christians believe. Some may find these beliefs difficult to accept. Therefore, the following chapter has been included to help the reader examine evidence that supports these beliefs.

CHAPTER TWO

♦

WHY DO CHRISTIANS BELIEVE WHAT THEY BELIEVE?

♦Evidences giving proof that the Bible is the Word of God ♦Evidences giving proof of the Deity of Christ ♦Evidences giving proof that Jesus was resurrected and sits at the right hand of the Father ♦Evidences giving proof that the Devil exists

No other religious book presents a more logical explanation for life itself other than the Bible. For many Christians, the information cited in the previous chapter simply makes sense. Then, there are those Christians who don't know why they believe, they just believe. Still, there are those Christians who have experienced such a great personal relationship with Jesus that they know all too well that the things taught in the Bible must be true. Still, there are Christians who have studied and found that there are historical, archaeological, and scientific evidences that defend and support the Bible and its contents. This defense of the Bible through such evidences is termed *Christian apologetics*. Here, we will focus on those evidences.

Evidences giving proof that The Bible is the Word of God

♦The Bible was written by more than forty authors, in three different languages (Hebrew, Aramaic, and Greek), in different years and centuries, and on three different continents (Asia, Africa, and Europe).[1] Many of the authors never met one another. Despite this, the Bible is in total agreement with itself. No author contradicts another author. This, alone, is a miracle when we think of the diversity of man. In this day and time, if we were to ask forty people, who speak different languages, to write an essay on the same subject over a period of years, without conferring with one another, it would stand to reason that not all forty would agree with one another in their writings. The Old Testament was written between 1400 B.C. and 400 B.C. (approximately a 1000 years). Following this was a period of 400 years where no biblical text was written (the silent years). The

---

[1] Some of the information cited in this chapter is a paraphrased rendition of factual information gathered form the book, *A Ready Defense*, written by Josh McDowall.

Why do Christians Believe what they Believe?

New Testament was written between 45 and 95 A.D., about 50 years. Now, just think how remarkable it is that all the authors of the Bible agreed with one another, especially since the Bible was written over a time span of roughly 1500 years. Their literary congeniality certainly could not have happened by chance. There had to have been a common factor, a person directing them in their writings. That person was God.

◆Out of all the books ever written, the Bible has been the most circulated and published worldwide. No other book has been translated into as many languages as the Bible has. This is not an accident but rather, has taken place by Divine will.

◆No other book in history has been so vehemently attacked as the Bible has. Withstanding historical attempts to destroy, ban, and outlaw the Bible, it has survived. Not only has the Bible survived attempts to destroy it but it has also prevailed in spite of the lack of technology during the eras in which it was written. Being recorded on material that perishes and having to be copied and recopied for hundreds of years before the invention of the printing press did not diminish the style, correctness, or existence of the Bible. Compared with other ancient writings, it has more manuscript evidence than any ten pieces of classical literature combined. Josh McDowell quotes Bernard Ramm regarding the accuracy and the number of biblical manuscripts:

> Jews preserved it as no other manuscript has ever been preserved. With their massora (parva, magna, and finalis) [methods of counting] they kept tabs on every letter, syllable, word and paragraph. They had special classes of men within their culture whose sole duty was to preserve and transmit these documents with practically perfect fidelity - scribes, lawyers, massoretes. Who ever counted the letters and syllables and words of Plato or Aristotle? Cicero or Seneca? [1]

◆Regardless of world scrutiny and doubt, many prophecies of the Bible have materialized. When taking the 1948 Palestinian restoration of Israel as a nation for an example, we see that the Old Testament prophet Ezekiel predicted this restoration (just one of many biblical predictions concerning Israel) when he spoke to the Jews by saying,

> After many days you will be summoned; in the latter years
> you will come into the land that is restored from the sword,
> whose inhabitants have been gathered from many nations to
> the mountains of Israel which had been a continual waste;
> but its people were brought out from the nations, and they
> are living securely, all of them. (Ezekiel 38:8 NASB)

Before 1948 there were many people, including some Christian
scholars, who shed doubt on the biblical prophecies that spoke of the
restoration of Israel as a nation in Palestine. Despite this, the biblical
prophecy prevailed as did and will many other biblical prophecies.

♦ Christ himself gave credence to the scriptures. Let's take a look:

> 44 And he said unto them, These are the words which I spake
> unto you, while I was yet with you, that all things must be
> fulfilled, which were written in the law of Moses, and in the
> prophets, and in the psalms, concerning me.
> 45 Then opened he their understanding, that they might
> understand the scriptures. (Luke 24:44-45)

The first 39 books of the Bible comprise the Old Testament, while
the remaining 27 books make up the New Testament. There are 66
books in all. The Old Testament books are the books that were
written by Moses and the prophets before the coming of Jesus Christ.
The New Testament books are the books written by the apostles and
their assistants after the advent of Christ.

Moses wrote the first five books of the Old Testament and the
prophets of God wrote the rest of the Old Testament books. The
prophets responsible for writing the Old Testament were Isaiah,
Hosea, Joel, Jeremiah, Nahum, Habakkuk, Zephaniah, Ezekiel,
Daniel, David, Samuel, Solomon, and others. Jesus was very specific
when referring to the writings of the Old Testament. His reference to
Old Testament writings also made for his endorsement of them.

Disciples were students and followers of Jesus. Jesus chose twelve
specific men from among his many disciples. These twelve were the
apostles. They had a specific calling. The word *apostle* itself comes
from the Greek word *apostolos* meaning messenger or ambassador. It
is a verb and specifically means *to be sent* on behalf of another. The
apostles were to act as personal representatives of the living Christ. It
was their job to begin to spread the gospel worldwide. They were
sent into the world on behalf of and as a personal representative of

the manifested Christ. The following verses of scripture bring light to this:

> 13And when it was day, he called unto him his disciples; and of them he chose twelve, whom also he named apostles;
> 14Simon, (whom he also named Peter) and Andrew his brother, James and John, Philip and Bartholomew,
> 15Matthew and Thomas, James the son of Alphaeus, and Simon called Zelotes.
> 16And Judas the brother of James, and Judas Iscariot, which also was the traitor. (Luke 6: 13-16)

The apostles, with some exception wrote the majority of the New Testament. Not all of the apostles wrote New Testament books. Mark who was an assistant to Peter wrote the gospel of Mark. Luke who was an assistant to Paul wrote the gospel of Luke. Paul became an apostle when during his traveling near the city of Damascus, the Lord spoke to him from heaven and he was converted. Paul's apostleship thus began and he suffered greatly for the namesake of the Lord. Paul authored more New Testament books than any other New Testament author.

The books of the New Testament were referred to as scripture just as the books of the Old Testament. Jesus endorsed the writings of the prophets and apostles as scripture. All scripture is inspired by God. Jesus is a person of the Godhead and therefore inspired the prophets and apostles to write what they wrote. The apostles may also be considered prophets because the office of a prophet had a broader meaning during New Testament times and included those who preached the gospel of Christ as well as those who correctly foretold future things. Jesus's endorsement of the scriptures is revealed in the verses of scripture below:

> Jesus answered and said unto them, Ye do err, not knowing the scriptures, nor the power of God. (Matthew 22:29)

> 25And He said to them, "O foolish men and slow of heart to believe in all that the prophets have spoken!
> 26"Was it not necessary for the Christ to suffer these things and to enter into His glory?"
> 27And beginning with Moses and with all the prophets, He explained to them the things concerning Himself in all the Scriptures. (Luke 24:25-27 NASB)

Since Jesus is God, then his support and endorsement of the biblical scriptures give evidence to the Bible as being the word of God.

♦ Not once has an archeological finding contradicted the Bible. As a matter of fact, archaeological discoveries have given more credibility to the authenticity of the Bible. For example, the existence of the nation of Hittites recorded in Genesis of the Old Testament was once doubted. The Hittites were thought to be a mythological nation of people since the Bible is the only book in history that mentions them. However, archaeological findings now give evidence that an ancient nation of Hittite people did in fact exist and had done so for more than 1200 years. This discovery not only stunned many opponents of the Bible but also astonished many archaeologists as well.

Evidences Giving Proof of the Deity of Christ

♦ The name *Jesus* is the Greek version of the Hebrew name *Joshua* which means "Yahweh delivered." *Yahweh* is the most revered Hebrew name for God.

♦ The scriptures tell us that Jesus was born of the virgin Mary by the spirit of the Holy Ghost. This in itself is a miracle. To get a better understanding of this, let's take a look at the historical account:

> [26]In the sixth month, God sent the angel Gabriel to Nazareth, a town in Galilee, [27]to a virgin pledged to be married to a man named Joseph, a descendant of David. The virgin's name was Mary. [28]The angel went to her and said, "Greetings, you who are highly favored! The Lord is with you."
> [29]Mary was greatly troubled at his words and wondered what kind of greeting this might be. [30]But the angel said to her, "Do not be afraid, Mary, you have found favor with God. [31]You will be with child and give birth to a son, and you are to give him the name Jesus. [32]He will be great and will be called the Son of the Most High. The Lord God will give him the throne of his father David, [33]and he will reign over the house of Jacob forever; his kingdom will never end."
> [34]"How will this be," Mary asked the angel, "since I am a virgin?"

³⁵The angel answered, "The Holy Spirit will come upon you, and the power of the Most High will overshadow you. So the holy one to be born will be called the Son of God." (Luke 1:26-35 NIV)

The account tells us that Jesus is the literal Son of God. Jesus is the only literal Son of God who ever was and ever will be. Those of us who are in Christ are also referred to as sons of God but on a spiritual level, not a literal physical level. Since Jesus is the literal Son of God, then he is just as much God as he was human. Isaiah 7:14 prophesied that the Messiah would be born of a virgin. It says:

Therefore the Lord himself will give you a sign: The virgin will be with child and will give birth to a son, and will call him Immanuel.

"Immanuel" means "God with us." Matthew 1:18-24 reveals that the prophecy was fulfilled. It says:

¹⁸This is how the birth of Jesus Christ came about: His mother Mary was pledged to be married to Joseph, but before they came together, she was found to be with child through the Holy Spirit. ¹⁹Because Joseph her husband was a righteous man and did not want to expose her to public disgrace, he had in mind to divorce her quietly.
²⁰But after he had considered this, an angel of the Lord appeared to him in a dream and said, "Joseph son of David, do not be afraid to take Mary home as your wife, because what is conceived in her is from the Holy Spirit. ²¹She will give birth to a son, and you are to give him the name Jesus, because he will save his people from their sins."
²²All this took place to fulfill what the Lord had said through the prophet: ²³"The virgin will be with child and will give birth to a son, and they will call him Immanuel" which means, "God with us."
²⁴When Joseph woke up, he did what the angel of the Lord had commanded him and took Mary home as his wife. But he had no union with her until she gave birth to a son. And he gave him the name Jesus. (NIV)

Many critics of the Bible have spoken against the account of Jesus' conception by arguing their view that something like this is virtually impossible. Some have even perverted the gospel by saying that the Holy Spirit had sex with Mary. However, the scriptures say no such thing. The scriptures tell us that Mary was overshadowed by the power of the Holy Ghost, not that she had sex with the Holy Ghost.

Although we can be sure that virgin-birth skeptics lived during the time of Jesus' birth, no skepticism surrounding Jesus' birth is expressed in the Bible. For that matter, no extra-biblical ancient historical book expresses any skepticism of the account of Jesus' conception. The conditions surrounding Jesus' conception were well accepted by ancient peoples despite the seeming impossibility of it all. In addition, medical technology has proven that it is no longer necessary for a woman to have sex to become pregnant. Man's process of in vitro fertilization is a medical procedure whereby a woman is impregnated without having sex. Now, if man can do it.... why can't God?

♦ The Old Testament prophets predicted (prophesied) that a Messiah would come. They gave over three hundred predictions concerning his coming. At the time of their predictions the Messiah (Jesus) had not yet come. The prophets predicted how the Messiah would come, what would happen to him when he came, his genealogy, how he would die, and so forth. There are sixty-one very distinctive Old Testament messianic prophecies which include prophecies indicating that the Messiah would be born of a virgin, come from the tribe of Judah, be born at Bethlehem, be called Lord, be called Immanuel (God with us), teach in parables, be resurrected, be betrayed by a "friend" (Judas), be sold for thirty pieces of silver, be beaten and crucified, be buried in a rich man's tomb, perform many miracles, preach the word of God and so on.

Josh McDowall explains all of this very well in the following quote:

> In the Old Testament there are sixty major messianic prophecies and approximately 270 ramifications that were fulfilled in one person, Jesus Christ. It is helpful to look at all these predictions fulfilled in Christ as His 'address.' You've probably never realized how important the details of your name and address are - and yet these details set you apart from the five billion other people who also inhabit this planet. With even greater detail, God wrote an address in history to single out His Son, the Messiah, the Savior of

mankind, from anyone who has ever lived in history - past, present, or future. The specifics of this address can be found in the Old Testament, a document written over a period of a thousand years, which contains more than three hundred references to His coming. Using the science of probability, we find the chances of just forty-eight of these prophecies being fulfilled in one person to be right at one in 10^{157} (a one followed by 157 zeros!). [2]

Now, 10 to the first power is the multiplication of one ten and equals ten. 10 to the tenth power (10^{10}) is the multiplication of ten tens and would look like this: $10 \times 10 \times 10 \times 10 \times 10 \times 10 \times 10 \times 10 \times 10 \times 10$ equaling 10, 000, 000, 000 (ten billion). Therefore, one in ten to the one hundred and fifty seventh power (10^{157}) looks like this: 1 in 10,000,000,000,000,000,000,000,000,000,000,000,000,000,000,000,000 000,000,000,000,000,000,000,000,000,000,000,000,000,000,000,000,000 000,000,000,000,000,000,000,000,000,000,000,000,000,000,000,000.

God gave the prophets their foreknowledge concerning Jesus Christ in order that they may impart to others those factors that would identify him. We will briefly take a more in-depth look at some of these messianic prophecies:

Micah 5:2 predicted that the Messiah would be born in Bethlehem. It says,

> But you, Bethlehem Ephrathah,
>   though you are small among the clans
>   of Judah,
> out of you will come for me
>   one who will be ruler over Israel,
> whose origins are from of old,
>   from ancient times. (NIV)

Matthew 2:1 reveals that the prophecy was fulfilled. It says,

> After Jesus was born in Bethlehem in Judea, during the time of King Herod, Magi from the east came to Jerusalem and asked, "Where is the one who has been born king of the Jews? We saw his star in the east and have come to worship him. (NIV)

Why do Christians Believe what they Believe?

Not only would the Messiah be God but Deuteronomy 18:18 predicted that the Messiah would be a prophet as well. It says,

> [God speaking] I will raise up for them a prophet like you from among their brothers; I will put my words in his mouth, and he will tell them everything I command him. (NIV)

Matthew 21:11 reveals that the prophecy was fulfilled. It says,

> The crowds answered, "This is Jesus, the prophet from Nazareth in Galilee." (NIV)

Isaiah 40:3 predicted that the coming of the Messiah would be preceded by a messenger who would tell of him. It says,

> The voice of him that crieth in the wilderness, Prepare ye the way of the LORD, make straight in the desert a highway for our God.

Matthew 3:1-3 reveals that this prophecy was fulfilled. It says,

> [1]In those days John the Baptist came, preaching in the Desert of Judea [2]and saying, "Repent, for the kingdom of heaven is near." [3]This is he who was spoken of through the prophet Isaiah:
>
> > "A voice of one calling in the desert,
> > 'Prepare the way for the Lord,
> > make straight paths for him.'" (NIV)

Psalm 105:1-5 teaches us that the Lord is able to bless with wonderful acts and work many miracles. It says,

> [1]Give thanks to the LORD, call on his name;
> > make known among the nations what
> > > he has done.
> [2]Sing to him, sing praise to him;
> > tell of all his wonderful acts.
> [3]Glory in his holy name;
> > let the hearts of those who seek the
> > > LORD rejoice.

> 4Look to the LORD and his strength;
> seek his face always
> 5Remember the wonders he has done,
> his miracles, and the judgments he
> pronounced, (NIV)

Matthew 9:35 reveals that Jesus worked many miracles during his earthly ministry. It says,

> Jesus went through all the towns and villages, teaching in their synagogues, preaching the good news of the kingdom and healing every disease and sickness. (NIV)

Psalm 16:9-10 predicts the resurrection of Christ. It says,

> 9Therefore my heart is glad and my tongue
> rejoices;
> my body also will rest secure,
> 10because you will not abandon me to the
> grave,
> nor will you let your Holy One see
> decay. (NIV)

In this psalm, David was speaking to God. Not only does David (the psalmist) predict the resurrection of Christ but Jesus predicted his own death and resurrection in John 2:18-22, which says:

> 18Then the Jews demanded of him, "What miraculous sign can you show us to prove your authority to do all this?"
> 19Jesus answered them, "Destroy this temple, and I will raise it again in three days."
> 20The Jews replied, "It has taken forty-six years to build this temple, and you are going to raise it in three days?" 21But the temple he had spoken of was his body. 22After he was raised from the dead, his disciples recalled what he had said. Then they believed the Scripture and the words that Jesus had spoken. (NIV)

Luke 24:1-8 speaks more on the fulfilling of the resurrection prophecy. It says:

¹On the first day of the week, very early in the morning, the women took the spices they had prepared and went to the tomb. ²They found the stone rolled away from the tomb, ³but when they entered, they did not find the body of the Lord Jesus. ⁴While they were wondering about this, suddenly two men in clothes that gleamed like lightning stood beside them. ⁵In their fright the women bowed down with their faces to the ground, but the men said to them, "Why do you look for the living among the dead? ⁶He is not here; he has risen! Remember how he told you, while he was still with you in Galilee: ⁷"The Son of Man must be delivered into the hands of sinful men, be crucified and on the third day be raised again.'" ⁸Then they remembered his words. (NIV)

Just as the psalmist predicted, the body of Jesus never saw decay.

The prophecies that have been spoken of here only scratch the surface of the number of messianic prophecies contained in the Old Testament. Some other prophecies are as follows: That the Messiah would have a ministry in Galilee, preach to many, be rejected by Jews and Gentiles alike, be betrayed by a friend (Judas Iscariot), be sold for thirty pieces of silver, endure humiliation and torture in the form of whippings, be crucified, be pierced by the sword, be buried in a rich man's tomb, and the list goes on.

No one other than Jesus Christ has fulfilled all of the messianic prophecies. This is an historical fact. As previously stated, the probability of one man fulfilling only forty-eight of the prophecies is one in ten to the one hundred and fifty seventh power. This number is so large that seemingly there are no words to describe it. Therefore when looking at the fulfillment of messianic prophecy, the only logical conclusion we can arrive at is that Jesus is God, our Messiah, our Lord and our Saviour.

♦There are many non-biblical historical accounts as to the life of Jesus. These accounts correlate with the historical accounts in the Bible. One example of this is seen in the complete works of the historian, Flavius Josephus who was born in A.D. 37. The life of Jesus is included in his writings and his writings correlate with biblical accounts.

Why do Christians Believe what they Believe?

♦ Anyone claiming to be God in the days of Jesus was risking execution. The Jews saw Jesus' claim to be God as blasphemous. Jesus continued with his claims to be God despite the fact that he knew that he would be put to death in a most painful and agonizing way because of his claims. If Jesus was not God then he was suffering from delusions. In looking at our wide source of apologetic information, common sense would tell us that the probability of Jesus being God is substantially higher than the probability of him suffering from delusions. If Jesus was suffering from delusions, then all of his disciples, all of the apostles, everyone who believed in him, everyone he healed, and everyone who saw the risen Christ would have had to be suffering from delusions as well.

♦ Many men and women were martyrs for Christ. The historical account of the horrific deaths most of the apostle's met, points at the dedication and commitment of those martyred for Christ in ancient times as the following quote attests to:

> Though the facts are cloudy, here is one suggested list of how the apostles met their deaths: Peter, crucified at Rome, head downward. James, beheaded at Jerusalem (Acts 12:2). John, plunged into a boiling cauldron during persecution under Emperor Domitian, from which he was miraculously saved, later to be banished to the Isle of Patmos (where he wrote the Book of Revelation), from which he was returned to Ephesus where he died a natural death. Andrew, crucified at Patras, Greece on an X-shaped cross that now bears his name. Philip, hanged, crucified, or stoned in Asia Minor. Bartholomew, flayed alive and beheaded in Armenia. Matthew, slain with a sword in Ethiopia. Thomas, his body run through with a lance in India. James the Less, thrown from a tower in Jerusalem, stoned, and clubbed, from which he recovered, then later sawed into pieces. Judas (Thaddaeus/Labbaeus), shot to death with arrows in Mesopotamia. Simon the Zealot, fatally attacked by a mob near the Persian Gulf. Judas Iscariot, a suicide. [3]

As we see from the above quote, Judas Iscariot (the disciple who betrayed Jesus and handed him over to the Romans for thirty pieces of silver) committed suicide. His suicide indicates that he may have been aware of the atrocity he had committed. The other apostles died dreadful deaths as well as did thousands of others in that time for the sake of Christ. Those who died for the namesake of Christ were martyrs which means they died willingly for what they believed. History shows us that most martyrs have died for factual causes.

♦Jesus claimed to be God and he backed up his claim by working profound miracles and healings. The greatest miracle of all was his resurrection and his predictions of it that preceded it. There is no other account of any other person in history who performed as many miracles as did Jesus. Reaction to this is aptly described in the following quotation from *A Ready Defense.*

> Who you decide Jesus Christ is must not be an idle, intellectual exercise. You cannot put Him on the shelf as a great moral teacher. That is not a valid option. He is either a liar, a lunatic, or Lord and God.[4]

Evidences giving proof that Jesus was resurrected and sits at the right hand of the Father

♦There is absolutely no question that a man named Jesus walked the earth some two thousand years ago, claimed to be God, was crucified for his claims, died and was buried. The most adamant critics of Christianity believe this to be so. However, their beliefs come to a grinding halt when the historical account of Jesus' resurrection comes into play. The irony of all this is that most of these critics will accept complete biographical accounts of any other historical figure but when it comes to Jesus Christ they begin to pick and choose what and what not to believe especially when looking at the issue of the resurrection. The resurrection of Jesus Christ is part of the complete account of the historicity of Jesus and no one has ever been able to disprove that it actually occurred. We must either accept the complete biblical account or reject it. There is no "in-between." It is all or nothing.

♦There have been many attempts to disclaim the resurrection of Jesus Christ. Many skeptics have said that the disciples stole the body. Others have said that Jesus never really died. Still, some have said that another man was buried in his place. Whatever the disclaimers, no one has ever successfully denied that three days after Jesus was buried his body was not found in the tomb. The body simply wasn't there. The historical account of Jesus' burial discredits any disclaimer saying that his body wasn't buried. It was. The resurrection of Jesus

Christ has never been disproved because there is no evidence against it.

When Jesus was buried, the Roman Guards were ordered to stand guard at the tomb. As another security precaution, a huge stone was rolled in to cover the tomb and a Roman seal was placed on it. The reason for the extra security centered on Jesus' own prediction that he would rise from the grave three days after his death. The chief priests and the Pharisees did not believe that Jesus would actually resurrect from the grave but instead believed that his body would be stolen in an attempt to make it look as if he had risen. The extra security was issued in support of their assumptions.

A Roman guard who fell asleep at his post would be beaten and burned. In the face of such a penalty one would think that the Roman Guard would have made certain that Jesus' body stayed buried in the tomb. However, the Roman Guard didn't because they couldn't. No man can fight the power of God.

There were at least sixteen men that comprised the Roman Guard the night they kept watch over Jesus' tomb. Despite all of these precautions, the biblical historical account tells us that an angel of God descended from heaven causing an earthquake and that this angel moved the stone from in front of the tomb and sat on it (Matthew 28:2).[2] The Scriptures go on to inform us that the soldiers who were guarding the tomb were petrified with fear and became virtually comatose. When the soldiers awoke from their stupor the body of Jesus was gone. They went into the city to explain the occurrence to the chief priests. The elders told the soldiers to say that the disciples came and stole the body. The soldiers did as they were instructed and many of the Jews believed this lie. However, It is very unlikely that all of the soldiers guarding the tomb would fall asleep at their posts knowing the punishment that awaited them if they did so. They were to guard the tomb "with their lives." What other explanation could there be for their incompetence other than the fact that Jesus was actually resurrected just as the biblical account says he was. The entire account of Jesus' execution and resurrection can be found in the gospel of Matthew 26:62-66 coupled with Matthew Chapters 27 and 28 (See Appendix).

---

[2] It reads, *There was a violent earthquake, for an angel of the Lord came down from heaven and, going to the tomb, rolled back the stone and sat on it.* (NIV)

♦There were many eyewitness accounts of the miracles that Jesus performed and of his bodily appearance after his resurrection. If the miracles and resurrection never occurred then each eyewitness had to have purposely lied or had to have been simultaneously suffering identical auditory and visual hallucinations which would lead to delusions. Two people may experience a similar hallucination but the possibility of the same two people experiencing the exact same hallucination is extremely remote and becomes even more remote when looking at the possibility of those same two people experiencing the exact same hallucination at the exact same time. However, this is inadvertently what people are saying when they deny the resurrection of Christ. The eyewitnesses had no reason to lie about what they saw. As a matter of fact, they would have had more reason to deny what they saw since, at the time, a confession of faith in Christ most often could have meant certain death. One must either believe in the resurrection of Jesus Christ or ignore all the evidences that support it.

Evidences Giving Proof That The Devil (Satan) Exists

♦1 Peter 5:8-9 says,

> Be sober, be vigilant; because your adversary the devil, as a roaring lion, walketh about, seeking whom he may devour: Whom resist stedfast in the faith, knowing that the same afflictions are accomplished in your brethren that are in the world.

The devil is someone to be resisted. The Bible states that he is a tempter and a liar. He is the enemy. Every evil deed that was ever done was done because someone did not resist the temptations of the devil. Every evil deed is evidence that the devil exists.

CHAPTER THREE

◆

SLAVERY: A BRIEF HISTORY

◆ A brief history of Arab enslavement of Africans ◆ The Koran and Slavery ◆ Islamic enslavement of people in Modern Times ◆ A brief History of the Atlantic Slave Trade: The enslavement of Blacks by Europe and the West

Slavery has existed in history from the earliest times of man. All nations, in some way or another, have a history of enslaving people and most religions, including Judaism, Islam, and Christianity have historically endorsed slavery. But since this book is an apologetic (a defense of the Christian faith) particularly addressed to an African-American reading audience, this chapter specifically focuses on the history of Arab and American enslavement of Africans. The incomplete knowledge that some blacks have when it comes to this history has a direct effect on many of the misconceptions black Americans have when it comes to the Bible and race relations. It is therefore essential to take a look at it before going into our in-depth examination of what the Bible *really* says about slavery.

A Brief History of Arab enslavement of Africans

The institution of slavery was common place during ancient times.[1] History reveals that the ancient lands of Lydia, Egypt, Greece, and Rome, all had slaves. A great portion of those persons enslaved by the Romans were from Northern Europe. However, the Egyptians most notably enslaved the Ethiopians. The Ethiopians were black. The Greeks and Romans made no distinction when it came to the color of one's skin. Interracial marriages were common and frequent. There were interracial marriages cited in the Bible. Moses was an Israelite, a Jew. Therefore, Moses' marriage to his wife is what we today would consider interracial because his wife was an Ethiopian woman.

---

[1] Some of the information under the heading, *A brief history of Arab enslavement of Africans*, is a paraphrased rendition of factual information gathered from the book, *Defending Black Faith*, written by Craig S. Keener and Glenn Usry.

Despite the fact that the Bible makes no difference between black and white, Elijah Muhammad, first successor to the founder of the Nation of Islam (see Introduction), accused Christianity of being a black-slave-making religion. However, in biblical times, there was no such thing as race. People were defined by their nationality. When considering Jesus, we know that he was a Jew born in an Asian land and that it is very possible that he was a person of color. However, the Hadith, which is the religious companion book to the Koran, describes Muhammad as being a white man who owned hundreds of black slaves. Both Orthodox Muslims and the Nation of Islam accept the Hadith as part of the teachings of their faith.

The Nation of Islam was founded by Wallace Fard in 1930 and is not considered to be a true Islamic religion by orthodox Muslims.[2] Orthodox Muslims believe that God is spirit only, whereas, members of the Nation of Islam believe that Wallace Fard was "God in person" and that Elijah Muhammad was a messiah. When Wallace Fard disappeared in 1934 without a trace, Elijah Muhammad became Wallace Fard's first successor. Elijah Muhammad wrote and in 1965 published a book entitled, *Message to the Black Man in America*. In the book he attacks Christianity by labeling it as a black-slave-making religion and claiming Islam as "the natural religion of the black man." Elijah Muhammad's accusations against Christianity had a great effect on the black community since Christianity had been associated with white people and white people had been associated with slavery.[3] The fact that Genesis 9:18-27 (see Chapter Six) had been misinterpreted to mean that blacks were cursed to be slaves only added to the misconception that Christianity was somehow for whites only and that blacks were not allowed God's free gift of salvation. This type of thinking prevailed despite the fact that many historical biblical figures were black.

The Nation of Islam has perpetuated the notion that Islam is the "natural religion" of the black man. They justify this by saying that the white man went to Africa, kidnapped Africans, enslaved them, and took away their "natural religion" of Islam by forcing Christianity upon them. But when looking more closely, history gives

---

[2] To learn more about the Nation of Islam read *The Trouble with Farrakhan and the Nation of Islam: Another Message to the Black Man in America*, a book written by this same author.

[3] In movies, America's Hollywood has mostly depicted Jesus and all other historical figures in the Bible, as white, except for a few movies, one of which, is *Jesus Christ Superstar* in which a black man portrayed Judas.

the true account. By the end of the second century, the majority of North Africans were Christian. Contrary to popular belief, much of Africa had heard and accepted the gospel of Jesus Christ long before Christian missionaries from other lands began to seek to make new converts there. East African countries including Egypt, the Sudan, and Ethiopia, were Christian. However, during the middle of the seventh century, Islamic Arab nations, invaded most parts of North Africa and occupied the land. At the onset of this overtaking, the Arabs promised the North Africans religious freedom. However, they did not keep their promise and by the eighth century many North African Christians were made to choose between becoming Islamic or being discriminated against as a result of not embracing Islam. Furthermore, Christians who converted to Islam and then converted back to Christianity were slaughtered.

Aside from the above, the most discrediting account of historical Islamic slave mastering comes about when looking at the historical enslavement of East and North Africans by Islamic Arab fundamentalists of that the time.

Despite the prevalence of slavery in the early Roman Empire, it had mostly vanished from Europe in the early Middle ages. It was the Arab's slave trade that paved the way for Western slavery of Africans. The sixth century Muhammad himself held slaves while Jesus had no physical slaves. Because Islamic Arabs enslaved more Africans in their slave trade than the Europeans did during their slave trade, some African citizens of today, according to Keener and Usry, believe in and embrace the idea that the Middle East should pay reparations to today's Africans.[4] Even after Britain, France, and the United States abolished slavery and outlawed slave trading, many nations in the Islamic Arab world continued to enslave Africans for well over a century after their neighboring slave-trading nations ceased.

Arab nations had an extensive head start when it came to the enslavement of Africans. Arab nations began enslaving Africans roughly one thousand years or so before the West began to involve itself in the viciousness of slave trading. Arab Muslims enslaved more than eleven million Christian Africans during this time all in the name of Muhammad, the Koran, the Hadith, and Islam and they continue to do so today as we will discuss later. During the time of the Arab's slave trading of Africans, the Arab's modus operandi was

---

[4] Additionally, many of today's African scholars believe that Europe and America owe Africa reparations into the hundreds of trillions of dollars.

to kidnap Africans and force them to march across the Sahara desert. Many Africans were not physically able to make it across the Sahara and were therefore slaughtered or abandoned and given up to die from exposure. It appears that prejudices against dark skin peoples began with the Arab slave trade as explained below by Craig Keener and Glenn Usry, authors of *Defending Black Faith*.

> Although some Muslims in the West have exploited the notion that Islam historically escaped the curse of racial prejudice, nineteenth-century Western thinkers created this idea merely as a foil to challenge Western racism. The notion was never more than propaganda, as scholars trained in medieval Arab literature have shown. Given the widespread respect for Africa in Greek and Roman sources, Western prejudice against Africans may itself have derived in significant measure from attitudes of Arab slave traders. Certainly early Christianity emphasized the equality of all, specifically including Africans, and, like a few other groups such as the cult of Isis, swept aside racial distinctions in its common fellowship. Islam can function and sometimes has functioned as a multicultural brotherhood as well, but the economic temptation involved in slavery led to a period with many examples of Arab prejudice.
>
> Arab prejudice did not begin with color, its slavery began as multiracial, and Arabs favored White slaves. Nevertheless, they came to associate slavery especially with Blacks. One writer concludes that, for whatever reasons, 'the Arabs had always considered Africans as especially suited to be their servants.' Although exploited later by White racists, the tradition transferring the curse of Canaan's subjugation to all Hamite, hence (on their reading) African, peoples predates its abuse by Europeans. Ninth-century Islam associated the tradition of Ham's blackness with the thesis that Ham was 'cursed' with blackness. Many Muslims used this 'curse' to justify enslaving Africans, even when they were fellow Muslims. Although Genesis speaks of Canaan's rather than Ham's enslavement, Arabs transferred the curse of slavery to all of Ham's descendants, whom they took to be Black Africans. [1]

Interestingly enough, as mentioned earlier and in the Introduction, the Nation of Islam has labeled Christianity a "black-slave-making religion." But as we have learned from the preceding quote, the myth of the black curse (see Chapter Six) was propagated by the Islamic Arabs long before pro-slavery Christian westerners began cultivating that same lie.

At this juncture it is necessary to give a brief historical account of how Islam was born. The next few paragraphs will serve as such.

The writings contained within the Koran are based on the visions of the sixth century Muhammad who was born in Mecca in the year 570 A.D. Muslims consider Muhammad a prophet. In the sixth century, Mecca was the main city in Western Arabia where merchant trading took place. The religion of Islam is mainly identified with the culture of Arabia during the seventh century and encompasses quite a bit of early Arab culture.

The word *Allah* is the Arabic translation of the word *God*. However, when Muslims refer to Allah they are not referring to the God of the Bible. They are instead referring to a god that they say is spirit only and has no son.

Muhammad was orphaned when he was six years old and was raised by his uncle. At age twenty-five he married a wealthy widow from Mecca. As a result of this marriage, coupled with good business sense, Muhammad adopted a high position of power and prestige in Mecca.

During Muhammad's time, it was common practice to go to the caves and "seek God." Muhammad would often involve himself in this type of meditation. In 610 A.D., during a meditation, Muhammad, according to himself, saw the angel Gabriel in a dream. Muhammad claimed the angel gave him revelations. Since Muhammad could not read nor write, he recited the message that he claimed to have gotten and others documented what he said. These recitations were eventually collected and put together in a book called the Koran, of which the Arabic for is *Quran*. The word *Quran* means *recitation*. The Koran speaks against the teachings of the Bible and reduces Jesus to a mere prophet and no more. Muslims also consider Ishmael[5] (the ancestor of Muhammad and the Arabs) to be a prophet, however, the Bible does not consider him as such.

The writings of the Hadith contain further teachings of Muhammad recorded by his family members. These extra teachings are not generally found in the Koran but are well respected by Muslims.

---

[5] See Chapter Five under headings: *Slavery and the Family* and *Spiritual slavery* for the biblical historical account of Ishmael.

Slavery: A Brief History

When taking the following into account: the history of the Arab Islamic enslavement of Africans, the fact that Africans who were enslaved by Arabs were Christians prior to their enslavement, and the fact that the sixth century Muhammad owned black slaves and thought of them as lowly, it is baffling as to why the Nation of Islam has labeled Christianity a black-slave-making religion and has further identified Islam as the original or true religion of the black man. It would seem that the label of black-slave-making religion would more appropriately fit Islam.

According to Keener and Usry, slaves of ancient times serving in the Middle East were captured during war. Ancient Islamic nations also had a history of recruiting slaves by kidnapping small children and selling them into bondage. Arabs themselves could also be enslaved because they owed a debt or committed a crime. Arabs could also sell themselves or their children into slavery. However, at the onset of the writing of the Koran, Middle East laws were made against enslaving free Muslims. Furthermore, the Koran urged that no slave be mistreated and that slaves be allowed the opportunity to earn or purchase their freedom. The result of this was that people could only be enslaved if they were born into slavery by virtue of their parents being slaves or if they were captured in war. The availability of slaves therefore became diminished. Consequently, Islamic Arabs began looking to enslave people from the outside. The Arabs enslaved both black and white people. However, the white slaves were acquired from Caucasoid lands whereby many volunteered the selling of their female relatives. Conversely, the Arabs forced blacks into slavery through raiding and kidnapping. Furthermore, many Africans aided in the kidnapping of their own people so that they might gain financially by turning their neighbors over to be sold in the Arab market. In order to reach Arabia and the Persian Gulf, black slaves were transported through the Sahara from West Africa and down the Nile and across the Red Sea from East Africa. White slaves came from Turkey, Greece, East and Central Europe (known as Saqaliba, Slavs[6] for short). The Arabs transported the Slavs across the Mediterranean.

During the Middle Ages (the late fifth to the late fifteenth centuries) the Arab world's desire to possess a slave society increased the occurrences of Islamic raids on African lands for the purpose of kidnapping and slave trading. Black slaves were priced lower than white slaves and white slaves were used mostly in the Arab armies.

---

[6] The word *Slav* is where the word *slave* originated.

Slave women, black or white, were used mainly for the sexual pleasure of their slave master. Islamic law allowed for such sexual abuses between a slave master and his female slave. However, the law did not afford an Arab woman who owned male slaves the same sexual abuses.

The Arabs had military slaves and domestic slaves. However, thousands of slaves worked in agriculture and in the Saharan salt mines. Arabs also began fostering the growth of cotton, sugar, and rice. Records show that the Middle East developed many rice plantations during the Middle ages. It is believed that there were cotton and sugar plantations as well.

The Koran and Slavery

The Koran supports the institution of slavery. The Koran does not do away with slavery but instead gives rules as to how slaves are to be treated. The Koran admonishes Muslims to be kind to their slaves. The Koran encourages slave masters to allow a slave to pay for his freedom and denounces cruelty to slaves. The Koran further encourages the slave master to free his slave in exchange for forgiveness of sin and as an act of goodwill. What the Koran doesn't do is abolish slavery. Neither does it label slavery in and of itself a sin.

Islamic enslavement of people in Modern Times

Sudan is one of the many countries belonging to the continent of Africa. Over the past few years Sudan has experienced intense civil unrest. An Islamic government controls Sudan. This government has no tolerance for religious freedom. Anyone who is not Islamic is seen as an enemy. Northern Sudan is comprised of Arab Islamic fundamentalists while Southern Sudan is comprised mostly of Christian black Africans. There is civil war between the two sides. The war is due to the fact that the Northern Arabs are attempting to force the Southern Africans to conform to Islam.

The reemergence of slave trading has resulted from this conflict. Northern Islamic Arabs have continuously raided Christian southern villages. They kill the men. The women and children are kidnapped and taken back to the North to be sold as slaves. Women are often repeatedly gang raped by hoards of Islamic men. Often young boys are taken to what are considered concentration camps. In these camps the Christian boys are forced to read the Koran and are trained to fight in the anti-Christian Islamic military armies. Hundreds of thousands of southern Sudanese Christians have been tortured or killed for not renouncing their Christian faith. In certain villages all boys and men aged nine and up have met death by crucifixion. So far, one million Southern Sudanese Christians have died as a result of the terrorism of the slave trade.

The Southern Sudanese are receiving little or no help from other countries. Southern Sudanese officials have expressed that they feel this lack of help may be due to the fact that those being persecuted and enslaved are black. Christian Solidarity International (CSI) has been struggling to counteract the slave trade with the only means they have currently available to them: buy the slaves and then set them free. CSI have Arab traders that are insiders working for them. The insiders visit homes of Northern slave masters and pretend to be interested in purchasing slaves for themselves or purchasing slaves to resell them in the market. After financial negotiations are made, the insider purchases the slave. The slave is taken back to his or her family and is thereby liberated. It costs about fifty dollars to buy a Christian southern Sudanese slave. CSI has freed roughly three thousand slaves this way since 1995.

A Brief History of the Atlantic Slave Trade: the enslavement of Blacks by Europe and the West

The history of the Atlantic slave trade begins with the Portuguese.[7] During the 1400s the Portuguese set out for West Africa by sailing the Atlantic Ocean. West Africa was rich with gold. Portugal, at the time, was a poor state. The Portuguese therefore wanted access to the gold. However, they wanted to avoid North Africa, which had become, as we have seen, a majority Muslim territory. Mali, a West African country was the major source of gold and provided gold to Europe for their coins. Once the Portuguese had access of the gold, their intent was to use the gold as money to aid them in traveling to India. Their plan was to take a southern route as so to avoid the trading centers along the western region of Asia. These trading centers were also controlled by the Muslims. The ultimate goal of the Portuguese was to involve themselves in India's trade of silks, spices, and other

---

[7] Much of the information under the heading: *A brief history of the Atlantic slave trade and the enslavement of blacks by Europe and the West,* is a paraphrased rendition of factual information gathered from the book, *History of Africa,* written by Kevin Shillington.

commodities after which they planned to sell to the Europeans for increased prices thereby making considerable profit for themselves.

The Portuguese reached West Africa in about 1470 near the Akan region. They began to exchange copper, brass, and European clothing materials for gold. The Portuguese had also bought slaves from Benin before reaching the West African coast. Inner continent territorial raids were prominent in Africa. The raiding army often times enslaved the people from the territory raided. Therefore, the Portuguese were able to buy slaves within Africa itself. In the 1480s the Portuguese occupied the uninhabited lands of Principe and Sao Tome. These are Islands near the equator not far from the coast of West Africa. They constructed sugar plantations on their new territory and cultivated the plantations by using African slave labor. However, administration of the plantations was handed over to the Europeans. Creating and controlling sugar plantations was not new to the Portuguese. The Portuguese, along with the southern Spaniards had developed the business of sugar plantations earlier in the century. With the earlier development of plantations, southern Russian Slavs were captured and enslaved to work the plantations. The Portuguese continued to overtake and occupy islands along the Atlantic Ocean. With every conquest, they developed sugar plantations and eventually became Europe's leading supplier of sugar.

The African slave labor used in the thriving Portuguese sugar plantations along with the European administration of those plantations became the standard by which America and the Caribbean people would base their eventual system of slavery.

During this time the Spaniards decided to extend the slave trading of Africans into North and South America and the Caribbean. Today Canada, the United States, and Mexico make up North America while Venezuela, Columbia, Brazil, Peru, and Argentina make up South America. Jamaica is part of the Caribbean Islands. After Christopher Columbus' voyage to America in 1492, European peoples began to colonize in the Caribbean Islands. They treated the native Islanders violently. A great majority of the Islanders not only died from the violence but also died from the diseases that the Europeans brought. The Europeans had brought with them convicted criminals from Europe that they had planned to use as slaves in the New World. However, most of the prisoners died from tropical diseases. Because of this, the Europeans were left without anyone to work the mines and cultivate the tobacco crops. Consequently, it wasn't long before the Europeans began to look upon the African people as a great source for unpaid slave labor. The Portuguese had already proven how well productivity could expand with the use of African slave labor and it was also well known that Africans were not as likely to succumb to unfamiliar diseases. Furthermore, the Europeans were aware that the West Coast was proliferated with African Chieftains eager to sell other Africans (who were lawbreakers or prisoners of war) into the slave trade in return for firearms or other commodities.

As a result of the aforementioned, the year 1532 marks the first time Africans were transported across the Atlantic for the purpose of enslavement. Some historians cite the date to be as early as 1502. The number of Africans forced across the Atlantic were small until the year 1630 when England, France, and Germany began to become active in the slave trade as a result of the increase of sugar plantations on the Caribbean Islands and in Brazil. Thus began the African holocaust. In the early seventeenth century, America as well, began to take part in this atrocity. The African West Coast now known as Nigeria became identified as the Slave Coast.

Before leaving Africa, African slave captives were bound together by chains and made to walk to the coast. They were then imprisoned in wooden cages while their African captors awaited the arrival of the European slaving ships. Once the European slave traders set foot on the coast, the captors, without regard to the humiliating circumstances (there was no separation of men and women), made the captives remove all of their clothing so that they could be examined for disease. The captives were literally treated no better than livestock. The majority of the captives were as young as fourteen years of age but no older than thirty-five. Once the slavers decided that the human captives were healthy enough for the strenuous voyage ahead, they paid for their human cargo and piled them into their slave ships.

Conditions on board the slave ships were heinous. All the captives were chained together and made to lie on decks in rows. There were about three decks on each slave ship and each deck had no more than about a foot and a half headspace above them. Therefore the captives were never able to sit up during the duration of the trip which lasted about six weeks or so. Captives lied in their own urine, vomit, and defecation, as well as the urine, vomit, and defecation of others for the entire trip. It has been said that the stench of slave ships could be detected miles away from the coasts of their destinations. Because of the inhumane and unsanitary conditions on the slave ships, many captives succumbed to disease. When this happened, the slave traders threw them overboard to be fed to the sharks. The food and water allotted the captives was just barely enough for their survival.

With its ever-increasing plantations of tobacco and cotton, America filled her demand for African slaves as well. 1619 was the year in which the first African slaves were brought to America. The slave trade continued to flourish because many slaves had to be replaced. During the 1600s and the 1700s most slaves did not survive life on the plantation past ten years. The food and water given the slaves were very little and fatalities due to exhaustion came quick.

During the late 1700s, the profits that the Europeans gained from slave trading began to wane when the prices for slaves increased three-fold because of the steady increase of slave traders set up along the West Coast of Africa. Britain became the biggest in the slave trading business when it came to European control. However, as the economics of the slave trade began to dissipate so did the enthusiasm of continuing the trade. Some Europeans began to argue for the rights of freedom and liberty especially after America's war against Britain came to an end in 1783. Countries began abolishing the slave trade but not slavery itself. In 1807 Britain abolished its slave trade. In Holland the trade was abolished in 1814 and in France it was abolished in 1817. In America slave trading was abolished in 1808. The abolishment of slave trading made it illegal to transport human cargo across the Atlantic. However, slaves were illegally smuggled across the Atlantic up to the late 1800s.

In 1792 Toussaint L'Ouverture led a slave revolt in Haiti involving thousands of African slaves. This revolution was successful and in 1804 the black people of Haiti created their own government. However, Haiti has always been lacking in the resources needed to adequately provide for it's people and very little help has come from the outside. Consequently they still suffer from the effects of slavery imposed upon them more than 200 years ago.

It should be noted that European and Western slave traders would probably not have been as successful in enslaving so many Africans if certain African rulers had not aided the slave traders in their plight to capture and enslave Africans. However, there were also those African rulers that desperately fought against those involved in the slave trade. Although their fight was in vain they risked their own lives in an effort to help others obtain liberty.

According to Jose Luciano Franio in his 1978 article entitled, *The Slave Trade in the Caribbean and Latin America,* the destinations of Atlantic slave ships (from Africa) from 1666 to the 1800s were the Caribbean Islands, North America, and South America. Three million

Slavery: A Brief History

African slaves were imported by the English for English, French, and Spanish Colonies. A quarter of a million Africans died during the voyage. From 1680 to 1786 America kidnapped and imported two million Africans to the English colonies for the purpose of enslavement. From 1716 to 1756 three and a half million Africans were kidnapped and taken to American colonies for the purpose of enslavement. From 1752 to 1762 Jamaica kidnapped and imported about seventy thousand Africans. Guadeloupe imported forty thousand. By 1776, England's yearly import was thirty-eight thousand, France's was twenty thousand, the Portuguese imported ten thousand and the Dutch four thousand. It is estimated that at least 28 million Africans, between the years 1650 and 1900, were kidnapped, held in bondage, and forced into slavery with 17 million being exported by Muslim traders and 12 million being exported across the Atlantic: a holocaust indeed.

PART TWO

CHAPTER FOUR
♦
SLAVERY, KIDNAPPING, AND OPPRESSION: THE BIBLICAL PERSPECTIVE

♦Slavery Defined ♦ Does God condone Kidnapping? ♦ The Historical account of Joseph: a man Kidnapped and sold into Slavery ♦God's Response to Oppression ♦ Let my people go! The miracles of God

Slavery Defined:

Before we begin our discussion it is important to realize that there is no human being alive today whose ancestors were not slave masters.

> Slavery has existed from as early time as historical records furnish any information of the social and political condition of mankind. There was no country, in the most ancient time of its history, of which the people had made any considerable advances in industry or refinement, in which slavery had not been previously and long established, and in general use. [1]

The Old Testament was written for the most part in Hebrew and the New Testament was written in Greek. Sometimes Aramaic words were also used in the original text. The Greek and Hebrew languages preserve many distinctions in vocabulary not present in the English language. In the Greek and Hebrew the word *slave* is included in the category of those who serve. There are eleven words in the Hebrew language, one word in the Aramaic language, and eleven words in the Greek language that distinguish different types or kinds of servitude. However, the very widely used King James Version of the Bible many times uses the word *servant* without making a distinction as to what kind of servant is being spoken of. This is because the King James Version was written in England in the sixteenth Century and the people of that land and era referred to slaves as servants. The sixteenth century English that was spoken then is not spoken now. The New International Version (NIV) and the Revised American Standard Bible (NASB) are more distinct in their application of the words *slave, slavery,* and *servant.* Therefore, this book uses a combination of those versions along with the 1611 King James Version.

According to Larry Pierce, author of the On-line Bible Lexicon, the Hebrew words that distinguish different kinds of servitude are:

> *Ebed*: a forced laborer, a worshipper of God, a prophet of God, a citizen under governmental rule, or a word used as a salutation denoting equality between two people. This word is used the most often in the Old Testament when speaking of servitude.
> *Shiphchah*: a slave girl, a maid,
> *Sakiyr*: a hired labourer, a hired soldier (mercenary),
> *Na'ar*: a young boy, a faithful servant usually serving someone with high rank
> *Abad:* this word is a derivative of the Greek word "ebed" and means service whereby one labors for another, serves God, has willingly placed oneself into service, has been enticed to serve, is subject under governmental rule, or has been coerced into serving,
> *Abuddah*: a household servant,
> *Sharath:* to serve in the form of ministering
> *Enowsh*: a man, men, or mankind
> *Abodah:* service under captivity, service of God, to labour or work,
> *Ben*: son, son of God, people of a nation, member of a family or group,
> *Amah*: a handmaid, concubine, or female slave. [2]

The words that distinguish different kinds of servitude in the Greek language are:

> *Oiketes:* to serve as a housekeeper either voluntarily, by force, or as an employee,
> *Eusebes*: an adjective meaning devout and dutiful service unto another,
> *Douloo*: a verb meaning to be given into bondage as a servant, to be under bondage as a servant, to be forced into bondage as a servant, or to give of oneself to another to the degree where the condition of servitude could be metaphorically defined as bondage
> *Pais*: a child, a servant, an attendant, a minister,
> *Doulos*: a bondman, a slave as we know it, a servant, can be metaphorically used to describe a servant of God. This word is

used most often in the New Testament when speaking of servitude.

Sundoulos: a fellowservant, a person who serves along with others under the rulership of a king, a servant of Christ, angels who are servants of Christ,

Therapon: a servant of God,

Diakonos: a minister, the servant of a king, a deacon, an attendant, a waiter, an errand runner

Huperetes: a rower on a ship, an officer, a minister, one who serves with his hands, a soldier or officer of a king, and attendant, an assistant, a preacher's assistant

Misthotos: a hired servant,

Soma: a body, a body of people, a slave. [3]

The Aramaic word *abad* (which should not be confused with the Hebrew word *abad*) is a noun meaning *slave* or *servant* and is used sparingly in the Old and New Testaments. It should be noted that the Greek word *doulos* is considered to be a general term for servitude despite its specific meaning cited above. It is used one hundred and twenty-two times in the New Testament.

The word *andrapodon,* which peculiarly denotes slavery, does not occur at all, though the correlative word *andrapodistes,* occurs once (1 Timothy 1:10) with the most marked disapprobation of the thing denoted by it:-'The law is made for murderers of fathers and murderers of mothers, for manslayers, for whoremongers, for men-stealers, for liars. [4]

The correlative word *andrapodistes* corresponds to the word *menstealers* cited in the King James Version, which in today's language translates to the word *kidnappers.* Barnes refers to the Greek word *andrapodon* as a peculiar denotation of slavery because the word alludes to kidnapping. In biblical times, kidnapping a man and selling him into slavery was not readily practiced. Therefore the Bible makes little reference to it, hence: it's peculiarity.

For our purposes we will define slavery as such: Slavery is the condition whereby one person has taken or been given, complete authority over, and imposes forced labor upon, another person with the latter person (the slave) being an unwilling participant in the situation and being deemed as owned by the former. This is slavery as we, in America, know it. However, slavery, in biblical times encompassed more: During Biblical times, as we shall see, the following was the case:

> A person could become a slave as a result of capture in war, default on a debt, inability to support and 'voluntary' selling oneself, being sold as a child by destitute parents, birth to slave parents, conviction of a crime, or kidnapping and piracy. Slavery cut across races and nationalities. [5]

With this understanding we can safely surmise that most slaves were so unwillingly, even if they sold themselves into servitude.

Does God condone Kidnapping?

Kidnapping a man and selling him into slavery was not readily practiced during biblical times because the Bible basically speaks against this form of slavery. Let's take a look:

> [9]Knowing this, that the law is not made for a righteous man, but for the lawless and disobedient, for the ungodly and for sinners, for unholy and profane, for murderers of fathers and murderers of mothers, for manslayers,
> [10]For whoremongers, for them that defile themselves with mankind, for menstealers, for liars, for perjured persons, and if there be any other thing that is contrary to sound doctrine;
> [11]According to the glorious gospel of the blessed God, which was committed to my trust. (1 Timothy 1:9-11)

In the above scripture reference, the apostle Paul is speaking in a letter (epistle) to Timothy who was a pastor at a church in Ephesus. The key word in the scripture cited is *menstealers*. Paul puts menstealers in the same category as murderers, liars, whoremongers, defilers of themselves with mankind (fornicators), the unholy, and so on. We can therefore logically conclude that to be a manstealer is to behave in a sinful manner (a way contrary to God). A manstealer is one who steals men, a kidnapper. This is how Africans were brought to America to be sold as slaves. They were stolen from their native land. Kidnapping virtually always leads to some form of slavery. The New International Version of the Bible substitutes the word menstealers for the phrase *slave traders*. History shows us that although slavery in general did not necessary involve kidnapping, slave trading always did. Let's see what else the word of God has to say about kidnapping.

> And he who kidnaps a man, whether he sells him or he is found in his possession, shall surely be put to death. (Exodus 21:16 NASB)

> If a man be found stealing any of his brethren of the children of Israel, and maketh merchandise of him, or selleth him; then that thief shall die; and thou shalt put evil away from among you. (Deuteronomy 24:7)

Although many of the Mosaic laws of the Old Testament were fulfilled (and therefore became obsolete) at Jesus' first coming, these laws give us a good idea as to how God feels about certain issues. Even though the New Testament does not tell us to execute those who are guilty of kidnapping, the Old Testament writings make clear the disgust God still feels for the act itself. As one can see, the doctrine of the Bible does not uphold the act of kidnapping. Therefore, the early Americans who did so were wrong in God's eyes. The above scriptures tell us that during the times of Moses, the punishment for kidnapping was death. As Barnes puts it,

> The crime referred to in this law of Moses is stated in a three-fold form: stealing, selling, and holding a man. All these are put on a level, and in each case the penalty was the same-death. This is, of course, the highest penalty that can be inflicted, and this shows that Moses ranked this among the highest crimes known to his laws. If a man was stolen, no matter whether he was sold, or whether he was retained as property, he who had been guilty of the crime was to suffer death. It is worthy of observation, also, that Moses distinguishes this in the strongest manner from all other kinds of theft. In no other instance in his laws is theft punishable with death. If property was stolen, there was to be merely a restoration. If a man had stolen an ox and killed or sold it, he was to restore five oxen; if a sheep, four sheep. If the theft was found in his hand alive, he was to restore double. Exodus 22:4. In the case of the theft of a man, however, the very first act drew down the severest penalty. By this statute, therefore, Moses made the broadest possible distinction between the theft of a man and the theft of

property, and his statutes frown upon every law, and every institution, and every view, theoretical or practical, which regards man as on a level with the brute. [6]

We must understand that the Mosaic laws (the laws handed down to the Israelites by Moses) were laws given to Moses by God who in turn gave them to the Jews (Israelites). Therefore, by God's Old Testament law, if the early Americans, who went to Africa and involved themselves in the kidnapping of the people there, had lived in the time of Moses, they all would have been put to death.

The Historical account of Joseph: a man Kidnapped and sold into Slavery.

There is a specific incident, which occurred before the time of Moses, that the Bible tells us of whereby a man was stolen. We know, however, that God was not pleased with what took place. The incident surrounds the life of Joseph but before going into the historical account surrounding Joseph's kidnapping, some background needs to be established……..

The historical account of Joseph actually begins with Abram (later referred to as Abraham). Abraham was a man whose life account is given to us in the book of Genesis. Abraham, a faithful servant of God, was a descendent of Shem who was a son of Noah. Because of his faithfulness, God promised to make Abraham's offspring a great nation for generations to come. God would multiply his offspring *as the stars of the heaven, and as the sand which is upon the sea shore;* (Genesis 22:17). Abraham and Sarah (Abraham's wife) had a son named Isaac. Isaac married Rebecca and they had twin sons: Esau and Jacob. Esau was the firstborn (whom Isaac favored) and Jacob was the second born. Esau sold his birthright to Jacob for a mere pottage of lentils. Of course Esau regretted this later.

Eventually, through the trickery of Jacob, as expounded upon in Genesis 27: 1-41 (see Appendix), Esau not only lost his birthright but also lost the blessings of his father which were supposed to be automatically given to the firstborn. However, these blessings were instead given to Jacob. God changed Jacob's name to Israel. The Israelites are the descendants of Abraham, Issac, and Jacob. They are the Jews. Because of Jacob's birthright, his descendants would be in governmental authority over Esau's descendants. Esau's descendants would be in subjection to Israel but not enslaved by them. The following biblical quote reveals to us exactly how Isaac (and ultimately God) blessed Jacob:

> [28]Therefore God give thee of the dew of heaven, and the fatness of the earth, and plenty of corn and wine:
> [29]Let people serve thee, and nations bow down to thee: be lord over thy brethren, and let thy mother's sons bow down to thee: cursed be every one that curseth thee, and blessed be he that blesseth thee. (Genesis 27:28-29)

The offspring of Jacob and Esau became separate nations which was so prophesied by the Lord as attested to in the verses of scripture below:

> And the Lord said unto her, Two nations are in thy womb, and two manner of people shall be separated from thy bowels: and the one people shall be stronger than the other people; and the elder shall serve the younger. (Genesis 25:23)

> [39]And Isaac his father answered and said unto him, Behold, thy dwelling shall be the fatness of the earth, and of the dew of heaven from above;
> [40]And by thy sword shalt thou live, and shalt serve thy brother; and it shall come to pass when thou shalt have the dominion, that thou shalt break his yoke from off thy neck. (Genesis 27:39-40).

Here the Hebrew word used for the word *serve* is *Abad* which means to serve as subjects, not as slaves. Let's continue.

Jacob consequently left his home because Esau had set out to kill him. However, The Lord continued to keep his promise to Abraham by blessing his offspring through Jacob. The following biblical quote is the account of the prophetic dream given to Jacob:

> [12]And he dreamed, and behold a ladder set up on the earth, and the top of it reached to heaven: and behold the angels of God ascending and descending on it.
> [13]And, behold, the Lord stood above it, and said, I am the LORD God of Abraham thy father, and the God of Isaac: the land whereon thou liest, to thee will I give it, and to thy seed;

¹⁴And thy seed shall be as the dust of the earth, and thou shalt spread abroad to the west, and to the east, and to the north, and to the south: and in thee and in thy seed shall all the families of the earth be blessed.
¹⁵And behold, I am with thee, and will keep thee in all places whither thou goest, and will bring thee again into this land; for I will not leave thee, until I have done that which I have spoken to thee of. (Genesis 28:12-15)

The scriptural quote just cited includes the historical account of God promising land to the Jews and the famous vision *Jacob's ladder.* God eventually changed Jacob's name to Israel as the following scripture reference attests to:

And he said, Thy name shall be called no more Jacob, but Israel: for as a prince hast thou power with God and with men, and hast prevailed. (Genesis 32:28).

Now that we have some background information we will move on to the historical account of Joseph's kidnapping......

Israel married Rachel and had a son named Joseph. Israel had other sons as well but favored Joseph. Israel's other sons became jealous of Joseph. Because of this they eventually kidnapped Joseph and sold him to the Ishmaelites. The following verses of scripture give the account.

²³So when Joseph came to his brothers, they stripped him of his robe—the richly ornamented robe he was wearing—²⁴and they took him and threw him into the cistern. Now the cistern was empty; there was no water in it.
²⁵As they sat down to eat their meal, they looked up and saw a caravan of Ishmaelites coming from Gilead. Their camels were loaded with spices, balm and myrrh, and they were on their way to take them down to Egypt.
²⁶Judah said to his brothers, "What will we gain if we kill our brother and cover up his blood? ²⁷Come, let's sell him to the Ishmaelites and not lay our hands on him; after all, he is our brother, our own flesh and blood." His brothers agreed.
²⁸So when the Midianite merchants came by, his brothers pulled Joseph up out of the cistern and sold him for twenty

shekels of silver to the Ishmaelites, who took him to Egypt. (Genesis 37: 23-28 NIV)

The scriptures go on to say that the Midianites sold Joseph to the Egyptians. It is believed that the Midianites and the Ishmaelites were interrelated since the Midianites were descendants of Abraham's son, Midian, who's mother, Keturah, was Abraham's concubine.[1]

Since Joseph was one of God's children and heir to the promise, God blessed Joseph despite the condition of slavery he was in. This is attested to in the following scriptures.

[1]Now Joseph had been taken down to Egypt, Potiphar, an Egyptian who was one of Pharaoh's officials, the captain of the guard, bought him from the Ishmaelites who had taken him there.

[2]The Lord was with Joseph and he prospered, and he lived in the house of his Egyptian master. [3]When his master saw that the Lord was with him and that the Lord gave him success in everything he did, [4]Joseph found favor in his eyes and became his attendant. Potiphar put him in charge of his household, and he entrusted to his care everything he owned. [5]From the time he put him in charge of his household and of all that he owned, the Lord blessed the household of the Egyptian because of Joseph. The blessing of the Lord was on everything Potiphar had, both in the house and in the field. [6]So he left in Joseph's care everything he had; with Joseph in charge, he did not concern himself with anything except the food he ate. (Genesis 39:1-6 NIV)

Because of his brothers' jealousy, Joseph was sold into slavery. Ironically, God continued to bless Joseph despite the fact that he was a slave. Moreover not only was Joseph favored inside of his master's

---

[1] A concubine was a secondary wife either won in battle or bought and regarded as the property of her husband. Those with concubines were usually wealthy men in leadership positions. Concubines had legal rights as attested to in Exodus 21:1-11 and Deuteronomy 21: 10-14 (see Appendix). Although God allowed men to have concubines during this time, it is clear when reading Deuteronomy 17:17 (see Appendix) that the most holiest way of living, when it came to relationships between men and women, was and still is through monogamy.

home but he became ruler over all of Egypt as the following scripture reference tells us:

> [38]And Pharoah said unto his servants, Can we find such a one as this is, a man in whom the Spirit of God is?
>
> [39]And Pharaoh said unto Joseph, Forasmuch as God hath shewed thee all this, there is none so discreet and wise as thou art:
>
> [40]Thou shalt be over my house, and according unto thy word shall all my people be ruled: only in the throne will I be greater than thou.
>
> [41]And Pharaoh said unto Joseph, See, I have set thee over all the land of Egypt.
>
> [42]And Pharaoh took off his ring from his hand, and put it upon Joseph's hand, and arrayed him in vestures of fine linen, and put a gold chain about his neck;
>
> [43]And he made him to ride in the second chariot which he had; and they cried before him, Bow the knee: and he made him ruler over all the land of Egypt. (Genesis 41:38-43).

The biblical account goes on to inform us that at some point during Joseph's reign the lands surrounding Egypt suffered drought which led to famine. However, in Egypt food was plentiful. Consequently people in other lands came to purchase food from Egypt. Joseph's brothers were among those people. It had been so long since Joseph's brothers had seen Joseph that they did not initially recognize him upon being reunited with him. At first, Joseph did not want them to recognize him, but he knew who they were:

> [7]And Joseph saw his brethren, and he knew them, but made himself strange unto them, and spake roughly unto them; and he said unto them, Whence come ye? And they said, From the land of Canaan to buy food.
>
> [8]And Joseph knew his brethren, but they knew not him. (Genesis 42:7-8).

Joseph eventually let his brothers know who he was:

> [1]Then Joseph could no longer control himself before all his attendants, and he cried out, "Have everyone leave my presence!" So there was no one with Joseph when he made himself known to his brothers. [2]And he wept so loudly that

the Egyptians heard him, and Pharaoh's household heard about it.

³Joseph said to his brothers, "I am Joseph! Is my father still living?" But his brothers were terrified at his presence.

⁴Then Joseph said to his brothers, "Come close to me." When they had done so, he said, "I am your brother Joseph, the one you sold into Egypt! ⁵And now, do not be distressed and do not be angry with yourselves for selling me here, because it was to save lives that God sent me ahead of you. ⁶For two years now there has been famine in the land, and for the next five years there will not be plowing and reaping. ⁷But God sent me ahead of you to preserve for you a remnant on earth and to save your lives by a great deliverance. ⁸So then, it was not you who sent me here, but God. He made me father to Pharaoh, lord of his entire household and ruler of all Egypt. (Genesis 45:1-8 NIV)

Apparently from what Joseph says in the above quote, God allowed certain events to take place in order that Joseph would obtain the position he did in Egypt. The scriptures below teach us that Israel and his descendants benefited from this:

And Joseph placed his father and his brethren, and gave them a possession in the land of Egypt, in the best of the land, in the land of Rameses, as Pharaoh had commanded (Genesis 47:11).

And Israel dwelt in the land of Egypt, in the country of Goshen; and they had possessions therein, and grew, and multiplied exceedingly. (Genesis 47:27).

The circumstances surrounding Joseph's plight points to the indisputable fact that God is a God of justice. Joseph was sold into slavery but God turned everything around so that Joseph became ruler over those who were master over him. Not only that, but God arranged the series of events so that Joseph was able to move his family (the nation of Israel, the Jews) into a land where there was no famine: Egypt. Therefore, the nation of Israel who at the time was despised by the Egyptians settled amongst them and they multiplied exceedingly in a land where food was plentiful.

Just as there was a reason that God allowed Joseph to be kidnapped and sold into slavery there was also a reason that God allowed Africans to be kidnapped and sold into slavery. From what we have seen so far, we know that God is a just God. One should not speculate as to why God allowed Africans to be enslaved, but let's face it, God knows what he's doing even if we don't. It is certain that Joseph wasn't very happy about being sold into slavery. He had no idea that God was going to turn his negative into a positive. He had no idea that he would eventually rule over his oppressors. He had no idea that God was orchestrating the entire chain of events and that in the end he would receive the victory for the glory of God. Not only did Joseph become ruler over his captors but he also eventually helped his brothers who sold him into slavery.

God's Response to Oppression

God does not look at slavery the same way we do. Although, the word of God (the Bible) never really says anything per se against the institution of slavery in general, it does make some profound statements against oppression. God does not necessarily see slavery and oppression as synonymous with one another. There are scriptures in the Bible that set certain rules as to how masters should treat slaves. These rules are contrary to what we would view as oppressive treatment. To oppress someone is a sin in God's eyes. Oppression is the mistreatment of a human being.

As we will see, slavery, as God regulated it, is a non-oppressive system whereby one person is either voluntarily or involuntarily under the wage free authority of another person for a limited amount of time. Biblical exception to this understanding of slavery as God regulated it is seen in times of war when nations were cursed with enslavement because of their disobedience to God.

It has been speculated that God allowed slavery in ancient times in order for the economic system of that era to maintain its equilibrium. Also, on several occasions God used slavery as a punishment for nations that had turned against him. Despite this, God always delivered His people from slavery. Although God allowed slavery, God commanded that a slave not be oppressed. Slavery was not supposed to be synonymous with oppression. For our purposes we will define the word *oppress* as such: to rule in a non-diplomatic, dehumanizing way often times coupled with unjust harshness whereby those being oppressed become high risk candidates for emotional or physical collapse. Let's look further.....

Slavery, Kidnapping, and Oppression

> [15]You shall not hand over to his master a slave who has escaped from his master to you.
> [16]He shall live with you in your midst, in the place which he shall choose in one of your towns where it pleases him; you shall not mistreat him. (Deuteronomy 23: 15-16 NASB)

The same scripture reads the following way in the New International Version:

> [15]If a slave has taken refuge with you, do not hand him over to his master. [16]Let him live among you wherever he likes and in whatever town he chooses. Do not oppress him.

God instructed the Israelites not to return a runaway slave to his master but instead to give him a place to live of his choosing and not oppress him. So, there was to be no punishment for a runaway slave. This is a far cry from the way runaway slaves were treated in early America. Runaway slaves in early America were whipped and some even killed as punishment for attempting to escape their bondage. This was done partly as a method of sending a message to other slaves who may have been contemplating an escape. This was also just another example of continued oppression that black slaves suffered during that time.

The King James Version of the Bible uses the word *servant* in place of the word *slave* and only uses the word *slave* once and its plural once. The King James Version of the Bible was the only available English version in America during the antebellum years. Therefore, many early American slave owners probably minimized the above scripture since the word *servant* was used instead of the more definitive word *slave*. However, the infamous John Brown, was fully aware of the immoral implications of returning an escaped slave to his or her master. He knew that America's practice of capturing and forcing the return of runaway slaves to their masters was against the will of God. This knowledge of America's defiance of this particular run-away-slave scripture reference in Deuteronomy is what triggered Brown's historical fight against slavery. Let's continue with our look at oppression.

> Thou shalt neither vex a stranger, nor oppress him: for ye were strangers in the land of Egypt. (Exodus 22:21)

Slavery, Kidnapping, and Oppression

God commanded the children of Israel not to vex or oppress a stranger. To vex means to embitter or to annoy. A stranger in those times would have also included a person who did not believe in the true God (a heathen by definition). However, despite the person's religious beliefs, the Israelites were to treat them kindly. In contrast to this, when we look at how the African slave was treated in America we see that he was certainly vexed and oppressed through the hands of his master. The vexation and oppression imposed upon the African slave, was, when looking at the scriptures, clearly an act against the will of God. African slaves could have very well been defined as strangers during the time of their enslavement for they were kidnapped and brought against their will to America. So, they were strangers indeed.

The following quotes have not been included to cause discomfort or bitterness. However, it is important that we explore just how vexed and oppressed the African slaves were so there will be no question as to whether or not they were mistreated. The quotes below come from actual slave accounts found in George Rawick's book, *The American Slave From Sundown to Sunup.*[2]

The slave narratives contain many stories of complicated and indeed gruesome methods of punishment. Wes Beady, born in 1849 in Texas, had this account of one particular overseer's practice: 'He'd drive four stakes in the ground and tie a nigger down and beat him till he's raw. Then he'd take a brick and grind it up in a powder and mix it with lard and put it all over him and roll him in a sheet. It'd be two days or more 'fore that nigger could work 'gain. I seed one nigger done that way for stealin' a meat bone from the meathouse.'[7]

Anne Clark, aged 112 in 1937, was a repository of horror stories, tales that unfortunately had their counterparts in the reminiscences of many other former slaves: 'When women was with child they'd dig a hole in the groun' and put their stomach in the 'ole and then beat 'em. They'd allus whop us.'[8]

---

[2] *The American Slave: From Sundown to Sunup*, George Rawick, © 1972 by Greenwood Publishing Company. Reproduced with permission of Greenwood Publishing Group, Inc., Westport , CT.

Sallie Carder of Burwin, Oklahoma, matter-of-factly describes some of the needed equipment for punishing slaves: 'Dere was a white post in front of my door with ropes to tie the slaves to whip dem. Dey used a plain strap, another one wid holes in it, and one dey call de cat wid nine tails which was a number of straps plated and de ends unplated. Dey would whip de slaves wid a wide strap wid holes in it and de holes would make blisters. Den dey would take de cat wid nine tails and burst de blisters and den rub de sores wid turpentine and red pepper.' [9]

Below, Rawick[3] describes what a patroller was and then quotes from an account of a slave who experienced the brutality of the patrollers:

The patrollers intervened in every aspect of slave life. Moreover, as they were not the owners, they often had less concern that slaves would be unable to work as a result of brutal treatment. Ida Henry of Oklahoma City described the patrollers:

De patrollers wouldn't allow de slaves to hold night services, and one night dey caught me mother out praying. Dey stripped her naked and tied her hands together and wid a rope tied to de handcuffs and threw one end of de rope over a limb and tied de other end to de pommel of a saddle on a horse. As me mother weighted 'bout 200, dey pulled her up so dat her toes could barely touch de ground and whipped her. Dat same night she ran away and stayed over a day and returned. [10]

Rawick concludes the following:

The ex-slaves' accounts of their treatment make clear that most slaves suffered beatings and whippings; that they were often poorly fed, clothed, and housed; that they were often overworked; and that slave women were regularly used as sexual objects by whites, while slave men were

---

[3] *The American Slave: From Sundown to Sunup*, George Rawick, © 1972 by Greenwood publishing Company, Reproduced with permission of Greenwood Publishing Group, Inc., Westport, CT.

often used as breeding bulls and slave children were
frequently abused. [11]

There is no question that African slaves were mistreated and
abused in America. They were oppressed and treated inhumanely.
Not only were they constantly beaten and raped but many were
forbidden to pray. Those caught praying would be beaten severely. It
was almost as if the slave masters were afraid God would hear the
prayers of the slaves and deliver them.

When studying the scriptures we learn that God did not sanction
the mistreatment of slaves. However, many slave masters, at the time,
justified their mistreatment of African slaves by falsely stating that
the Bible says that blacks are a cursed people (discussed in detail in
Chapter Six). Because of this belief, the slave masters felt they could
treat blacks anyway they pleased. From this, American racism was
born and free blacks were mistreated as well. However, as discussed
in the Introduction, God is not a racist and does not condone racism.

Not only does the Old Testament command slave masters not to
oppress their slaves, but neighbors are commanded not to oppress
their neighbors and employers are commanded not to oppress their
employees. Let's take a look.

> And if thou sell ought unto thy neighbor, or buyest ought of
> thy neighbour's hand, ye shall not oppress one another:
> (Leviticus 25:14)

> [14]Thou shalt not oppress an hired servant that is poor and
> needy, whether he be of thy brethren, or of thy strangers that
> are in thy land within thy gates:
> [15]At his day thou shalt give him his hire, neither shall the
> sun go down upon it; for he is poor, and setteth his heart
> upon it: lest he cry against thee unto the Lord, and it be sin
> unto thee. (Deuteronomy 24:14-15)

The word of God further commands that neither the poor nor the
afflicted should be oppressed. For that matter, the Word of God
instructs that no one should oppress anyone else and that all of who
are oppressed should be relieved of their oppression. The Word of
God also tells us that God will punish oppressors. The following
verses of scripture attest to these things:

22Rob not the poor, because he is poor: neither oppress the afflicted in the gate:
23For the Lord will plead their cause, and spoil the soul of those that spoiled them. (Proverbs 22: 22-23)

17Lord, thou hast heard the desire of the humble: thou wilt prepare their heart, thou wilt cause thine ear to hear:
18To judge the fatherless and the oppressed, that the man of the earth may no more oppress. (Psalms 10:17-18)

6The Lord executeth righteousness and judgement for all that are oppressed.
7He made known his ways unto Moses, his acts unto the children of Israel. (Psalms 103:6-7)

16Wash you, make you clean; put away the evil of your doings from before mine eyes; cease to do evil;
17Learn to do well; seek judgment, relieve the oppressed, judge the fatherless, plead for the widow. (Isaiah 1:16-17)

Is not this the fast that I have chosen? to loose the bands of wickedness, to undo the heavy burdens, and to let the oppressed go free, and that ye break every yoke?"
(Isaiah 58:6)

As for his father, because he cruelly oppressed, spoiled his brother by violence, and did that which is not good among his people, lo, even he shall die in his iniquity.
(Ezekiel 18:18)

In the first scripture reference cited above (Proverbs), we are instructed not to oppress the afflicted. It also says that the Lord will plead the cause of the oppressed before God and tells us that there is punishment for the oppressor. In the second reference David speaks to the Lord asking that men would no more oppress one another. The third reference assures us that God's justice will be given to those who are oppressed no matter what the conditions are. We will explore one example of God's unconditional response to oppression when we look at the historical account of the Israelites' exodus from Egypt later on in this chapter. The fourth reference associates oppression with evil and instructs us to relieve others of oppression.

Slavery, Kidnapping, and Oppression

The fifth reference defines oppression as a yoke and something to be freed from. And the sixth reference, defines acts of violence against the oppressed as cruel oppression calling it a sin (iniquity).

With all that we have discussed so far, it is quite evident that God was not pleased with the way black slaves were treated not too long ago in America. God may have allowed slavery to occur but this does not mean that he condoned the oppression and mistreatment that came with it. However, there are some of those who might be under the impression that God is condoning oppression when he tells us to turn the other cheek in the face of adversity. Let's take a look:

> 38Ye have heard that it hath been said, An eye for an eye, and a tooth for a tooth:
> 39But I say unto you, That ye resist not evil: but whosoever shall smite thee on thy right cheek, turn to him the other also. (Matthew 5:38-39)

> 43Ye have heard that it hath been said, Thou shalt love thy neighbour, and hate thine enemy.
> 44But I say unto you, Love your enemies, bless them that curse you, do good to them that hate you, and pray for them which despitefully use you, and persecute you;
> 45That ye may be the children of your Father which is in heaven: for he maketh his sun to rise on the evil and on the good, and sendeth rain on the just and on the unjust.
> 46For if ye love them which love you, what reward have ye? do not even the publicans the same?
> 47and if ye salute your brethren only, what do ye more than others? do not even the publicans so?
> 48Be ye therefore perfect, even as your Father which is in heaven is perfect. (Matthew 5:43-48)

In the Old Testament, criminals were punished by having done to them what they did to their victims. However, Jesus put this law into non-effect. The New Testament tells us that we should not retaliate against evil people. Jesus commanded us to turn the other cheek if someone should strike us. This does not mean that people are to stay in abusive situations. Nor does this give people a license to behave in an abusive manner. This also does not mean that people should not protect themselves against an attacker. The meaning is more figurative than literal and is basically admonishing us to handle persecutions as non-violently as possible. We see a prime example of "turning the other cheek" put into action when we look at the history of America's civil rights movement. The movement was spearheaded by Reverend Dr. Martin Luther King Jr. Martin Luther King was able to make the progress he made because he handled his civil rights movement nonviolently. Consequently, Dr. King did more for the American Civil rights movement than any other man in U.S. history. In instructing us to turn the other cheek, Jesus is not telling us *not* to fight, but instead *how* to fight.

God will reward Christians for loving their enemies. Jesus asks the question, "for if ye love them which love you, what reward have ye,?" By asking this Jesus is telling us that it is easy to love someone who is loveable, however, a real sign of godliness reveals itself when we love someone who is hard to love. Many early American slave owners were not very loveable. But according to the above scripture references, their slaves were to love them anyway. God knows that this wasn't an easy task but he isn't asking us to do anything he hasn't done. Jesus loved his enemies. While hanging on the cross he asked The Father to "forgive them, for they know not what they do."[4] The people that Jesus was asking The Father to forgive were the very same people who nailed him to the cross.

God has not asked the Christian to "turn the other cheek" without any recourse for enduring ill treatment. Vengeance belongs to God not man. Therefore, it is left up to God to punish a man for his evil. The following verses of scripture basically sum up God's recourse for those who have been abused and mistreated:

> [17]Do not repay anyone evil for evil. Be careful to do what is right in the eyes of everybody.
> [18]If it is possible, as far as it depends on you, live at peace with everyone. [19]Do not take revenge, my friends, but leave room for God's wrath, for it is written: "It is mine to avenge; I will repay," says the Lord. [20]On the contrary:
>
> > "If your enemy is hungry, feed him;
> > if he is thirsty, give him something to drink.
> > In doing this, you will heap burning coals
> > on his head."
>
> [21]Do not be overcome by evil, but overcome evil with good. (Romans 12: 17-21 NIV)

---

[4] Luke 23:34

As we can clearly see, God's wrath will come upon those who do others harm. God is the one who will take revenge. Although God has no problem with us protecting ourselves from harm, it is not our place to take revenge. Revenge belongs to God. When God takes revenge he is then acknowledging that some wrong has occurred for which there is a need to take revenge for. Consequently, those who oppress others will eventually suffer the wrath of God and will feel the sting of his vengeance if they do not repent, because to oppress others is wrong.

While some might want to argue that God condones oppression because he has instructed us to turn the other cheek, others might want to argue that the mistreatment of blacks during slavery time in America was sanctioned by God because the Bible tells us to obey governmental authority (Romans 13:1). The American government sanctioned the mistreatment of slaves and upheld the practice of slavery until the Thirteenth amendment was added to the Constitution. However, God's command to obey government rule does not apply when the government demands that people go against the will of God. The Bible's support of this non-application is evident when looking at certain historical biblical accounts such as Shadrach, Meschack, and Abednego's refusal to bow down to the graven image of Nebuchadnezzar (recorded in the third chapter of Daniel, see Appendix) and Daniel's refusal to stop praying and giving thanks to God (recorded in the sixth chapter of Daniel, see Appendix). In both cases God delivered the men of God from execution, the charge being that they went against the authority of the government. However, Shadrach, Meschack, Abednego, and Daniel had the right to go against governmental authority because the government was asking them to go against God. God saved these men from execution because they had obeyed God rather than man.

Let my people go! The Miracles of God

For our purposes we will define the word *miracle* as: A supernatural event or action that defies all logic and scientific explanation, has a low probability or no probability of happening, and is attributed to the divine workings of God. Such events or actions have been exemplified through the ministry of Jesus Christ.

We will now take a careful look at the historical account of the ancient Egyptian's enslavement of the Jews (Israelites). In our previous discussion concerning the life of Joseph, we learned that the

Slavery, Kidnapping, and Oppression

Israelites dwelt among the Egyptians despite the Egyptian's distaste for them. The following scriptures tell us that the Egyptians felt that it was an abomination (a disgusting act) to even eat with the Israelites:

> [30]Deeply moved at the sight of his brother, Joseph hurried out and looked for a place to weep. He went into his private room and wept there.
> [31]After he had washed his face, he came out and, controlling himself, said, "Serve the food."
> [32]They served him by himself, the brothers by themselves, and the Egyptians who ate with him by themselves, because Egyptians could not eat with Hebrews, for that is detestable to Egyptians. (Genesis 43: 30-32 NIV)

There was a caste system at the time. Certain classes of Egyptians did not commune with one another. Because of his position, Joseph was in a caste system all by himself and therefore did not eat with many others. By eating alone, Joseph was simply lending himself to the cultural mores at the time. The Egyptians did not eat with the Hebrews and would certainly not eat with foreigners. Besides adhering to social custom, one of the main reasons why the Egyptians did not eat with foreigners was because many of them ate cow, an animal that the Egyptians regarded as sacred to their false god, Isis.

So, we see here that the Israelites lived amongst a people who thought lowly of them as well as worshipped a false god. During the time of the famine in Egypt there was so much distress that the Egyptians were willing to sell their land to Pharaoh. They were also willing to sell themselves into slavery in exchange for the food that Joseph had previously stored up before the famine. The following scriptures give the account.

> [13]Now there was no food in all the land, because the famine was very severe, so that the land of Egypt and the land of Canaan languished because of the famine.
> [14]And Joseph gathered all money that was found in the land of Egypt and in the land of Canaan for the grain which they bought, and Joseph brought the money into Pharaoh's house.
> [15]And when the money was all spent in the land of Egypt and in the land of Canaan, all the Egyptians came to Joseph and said, "Give us food, for why should we die in your presence? For our money is gone."

70

[16]Then Joseph said, "Give up your livestock, and I will give you food for your livestock, since your money is gone."

[17]So they brought their livestock to Joseph, and Joseph gave them food in exchange for the horses and the flocks and the herds and the donkeys; and he fed them with food in exchange for all their livestock that year.

[18]And when that year was ended, they came to him the next year and said to him, "We will not hide from my lord that our money is all spent, and the cattle are my lord's. There is nothing left for my lord except our bodies and our lands.

[19]"Why should we die before your eyes, both we and our land? Buy us and our land for food, and we and our land will be slaves to Pharaoh. So give us seed, that we may live and not die, and that the land may not be desolate." (Genesis 47:13-19 NASB)

When we read further in chapter 47 of Genesis we see that Joseph did as the Egyptians requested. He bought the people and he bought their land to give to Pharaoh. Then, he gave them seed in which to grow food. Joseph told them that they must give twenty percent ("the fifth part") of their increase to Pharaoh and keep eighty percent ("four parts") for themselves. Let's take a look:

[23]Then Joseph said unto the people, behold, I have bought you this day and your land for Pharaoh: lo, here is seed for you, and ye shall sow the land.

[24]And it shall come to pass in the increase, that ye shall give the fifth part unto Pharaoh, and four parts shall be your own, for seed of the field, and for your food, and for them of your households, and for food for your little ones.

[25]And they said, Thou hast saved our lives: let us find grace in the sight of my lord, and we will be Pharaoh's servants (Genesis 47:23-25).

Indeed the Egyptians sold themselves into slavery. Yet, what kind of slavery was this? The Egyptians sold themselves into slavery willingly. They were not kidnapped and forced into it as were the African slaves. They did not work from sunup to sundown unable to benefit from any of their labor, as was so with the African slaves. They were allowed to keep eighty percent of the benefits of their labor so that they would have food for "their households and little ones." Household and little ones? Again, what kind of slavery was this? Surely the African American slave was not able to keep eighty percent of the fruits of his labor and he most certainly was not allowed to maintain a household. His home was the slave quarters of the plantation. On the other hand, the families of the Egyptian slaves remained in tact despite their enslavement but this was not so for the African American slave. More times than not the "little ones" of the African American slave were separated from their parents and sold to other slave masters.

God allowed slavery. However, the kind of slavery that God allowed was a non-oppressive kind. If the Egyptians would have seen their ensuing enslavement as oppressive, it stands to reason that they would not have been as willing to sell themselves. Basically, the only thing that the Egyptian slaves were forced to do was pay taxes. Although we may see the paying of taxes as oppressive, God does not, as confirmed by the verses of scripture below.

> [17]Tell us therefore, what thinkest thou? Is it lawful to give tribute unto Caesar, or not?
> [18]But Jesus perceived their wickedness, and said, why tempt ye me, ye hypocrites?
> [19]Shew me the tribute money. And they brought unto him a penny. [20]And he saith unto them, whose is this image and superscription?
> [21]They say unto him, Caesar's. Then saith he unto them, Render therefore unto Caesar the things which are Caesar's; and unto God the things that are God's (Matthew 22:17-21).

We know that the Egyptians sold themselves into slavery but there is no scriptural indication as to whether or not the Israelites who were living in Egypt at that time did the same. Genesis 47:27 tells us that the Israelites lived in Egypt in the country of Goshen with their possessions and that they grew and multiplied but it does not tell us whether or not the Israelites sold themselves. We do know however that the Israelites occupied the best parts of the land of Egypt. We can be certain that they were very pleased with this arrangement. However, their satisfaction was short lived as shown by the following:

> [1]These are the names of the sons of Israel who went to Egypt with Jacob, each with his family: [2]Rueben, Simeon, Levi and Judah; [3]Issachar, Zebulun and Benjamin; [4]Dan and Naphtali;

Gad and Asher. ⁵The descendants of Jacob numbered seventy in all; Joseph was already in Egypt.

⁶Now Joseph and all his brothers and all that generation died, ⁷but the Israelites were fruitful and multiplied greatly and became exceedingly numerous, so that the land was filled with them.

⁸Then a new king, who did not know about Joseph, came to power in Egypt. ⁹"Look," he said to his people, "the Israelites have become much too numerous for us. ¹⁰Come, we must deal shrewdly with them or they will become even more numerous and, if war breaks out, will join our enemies, fight against us and leave the country.

¹¹So they put slave masters over them to oppress them with forced labor, and they built Pithom and Rameses as store cities for Pharaoh. ¹²But the more they were oppressed, the more they multiplied and spread; so the Egyptians came to dread the Israelites ¹³and worked them ruthlessly. ¹⁴They made their lives bitter with hard labor in brick and mortar and with all kinds of work in the fields; in all their hard labor the Egyptians used them ruthlessly.
(Exodus 1:1-14 NIV)

Before their enslavement, the Israelites were still blessed of the Lord and they multiplied. The Israelites and Egyptians lived peacefully together as two nations. However, Joseph eventually died and a new king or "Pharaoh" took over who had never known Joseph. This new king felt that the Israelites would eventually rise up against the Egyptians. He became afraid of their size in numbers. He therefore enslaved them and treated them cruelly. The Egyptians imposed a rigorous slavery upon the Israelites and mistreated them. Still, the more the Israelites were afflicted, the more they multiplied and grew. Ironically, the same thing happened with the African American slaves. They also multiplied and grew despite being in a condition of oppressive slavery. There were even suggestions by American white legislators, during the American slavery era, to send the slaves back to Africa. But these suggestions eventually fell on deaf ears because to undertake such a project would have left the country in a state of economic turmoil as Thomas R. Dew so clearly stated in his 1832 published debate of which the following is an extensive excerpt:

The slaves, by the last census (1830,) amounted within a small fraction to 470,000; the average value of each one of these is, $200; consequently, the whole aggregate value of the slave population of Virginia, in 1830, was $94,000,000; and allowing for the increase since, we cannot err far in putting the present value at $100,000,000. The assessed value of all the houses and lands in the State, amounts to $206,000,000, and these constitute the material items in the wealth of the State, the whole personal property besides bearing but a very small proportion to the value of slaves, lands, and houses. Now, do not these very simple statistics speak volumes upon this subject? It is gravely recommended to the State of Virginia to give up a species of property which constitutes nearly one-third of the wealth of the whole State, and almost one-half of that of Lower Virginia and with the remaining two-thirds to encounter the additional enormous expense of transportation and colonization on the coast of Africa. But the loss of $100,000,000 of property is scarcely the half of what Virginia would lose, if the immutable laws of nature could suffer (as fortunately they cannot) this tremendous scheme of colonization to be carried into full effect...

But the favorers of this scheme say they do not contend for the sudden emancipation and deportation of the whole black population; they would send off only the increase, and thereby keep down the population to its present amount, while the whites, increasing at their usual rate, would finally become relatively so numerous as to render the presence of the blacks among us for ever afterwards entirely harmless. This scheme, which at first, to the unreflecting, seems plausible, and much less wild than the project of sending off the whole, is nevertheless impracticable and visionary, as we think a few remarks will prove. It is computed that the annual increase of the slaves and free colored population of Virginia is about six thousand. Let us first, then, make a calculation of the expense of purchase and transportation. At $200 each, the six thousand will amount in value to $1,200,000. At $30 each, for transportation, which we shall soon see is too little, we have the whole expense of purchase and transportation $1,380,000 an expense to be annually incurred by Virginia to keep down her black population to its present amount. And let us ask, is there any one who can seriously argue that Virginia can incur such an annual expense as this for the next twenty-five or fifty years, until the whites have multiplied so greatly upon the blacks, as, in the opinion of the alarmists, for ever to quiet the fears of the community? Vain and delusive hope, if any were ever wild enough to entertain it! Poor old Virginia!....[11]

Many whites, during that time, were afraid that the blacks would grow so much in number that they might eventually take over the land. Interestingly enough, this is the same thing Pharaoh was afraid of regarding the Israelites. However, blacks kept multiplying at a rate that made it economically infeasible to send even a portion of blacks back to Africa. If blacks at that time had not multiplied and grew then the majority would have been sent back or black people in America would have simply become extinct. God is the one who has control over whether or not a nation will multiply. God is the one who opens up the wombs of women so that they may bear children. Therefore, since Africans multiplied at a rate that spoiled the white man's back-to-Africa-movement, it appears that God may have wanted a remnant of African people to stay in America. Let's continue to look at the historical account of the Israelite slaves:

[15]The king of Egypt said to the Hebrew midwives, whose names were Shiphrah and Puah,
[16]When you help the Hebrew women in childbirth and observe them on the delivery stool, if it is a boy, kill him; but if it is a girl, let her live." [17]The midwives, however feared God and did not do what the king of Egypt had told them to do; they let the boys live. [18]Then the king of Egypt summoned the midwives and asked them, "Why have you done this? Why have you let the boys live?"
[19]The midwives answered Pharaoh, "Hebrew women are not like Egyptian women, they are vigorous and give birth before the midwives arrive."
[20]So God was kind to the midwives and the people increased and became even more numerous. [21]And because the midwives feared God, he gave them families of their own.
[22]Then Pharaoh gave this order to all his people: "Every boy that is born you must throw into the Nile, but let every girl live." (Exodus 1:15-22 NIV)

Slavery, Kidnapping, and Oppression

The scripture never says why Pharaoh decided to kill all of the newborn males of the Israelites. However, if Pharaoh had managed to kill all of the Israelite newborn males then there would have been a decrease in generations of Israelites to follow. It also makes sense to conclude that this was Satan's way of trying to stop the coming of the Messiah (Jesus Christ). Jesus Christ was born from the tribal line of Judah which is one of the twelve tribes of Israel. Therefore, interestingly enough, Jesus came from a lineage of people whose ancestors were slaves.

In getting back to our scriptural text, it looks as if Siphrah and Puah were the only Hebrew women who were midwives for all of Israel at that time. The two Hebrew women refused to kill the male infants as commanded. Miraculously, Pharaoh did not punish the midwives in any way when they neglected to carry out his orders. He could have had them put to death but he didn't. As a matter of fact, God blessed the midwives and increased their houses despite their oppression just as God has blessed African American people despite a long struggle with existing racism and oppression. It is a miracle from God to be blessed among one's enemies. It is evident that God is a fair God even if we can not always determine why he allows certain things to happen.

Verse 22 of the scriptural quote indicates that Pharaoh gave up the idea of having only the midwives kill the Hebrew male newborns. Instead, he gave public orders to *all the Egyptians* to kill the newborns. Let's continue to look at the account and see how Moses enters into the picture:

> ¹And there went a man of the house of Levi, and took to wife a daughter of Levi.
>
> ²And the woman conceived, and bare a son: and when she saw him that he was a goodly child, she hid him three months.
>
> ³And when she could no longer hide him, she took for him an ark of bulrushes, and daubed it with slime and with pitch, and put the child therein; and she laid it in the flags by the river's brink.
>
> ⁴And his sister stood afar off, to wit what would be done to him.
>
> ⁵And the daughter of Pharaoh came down to wash herself at the river; and her maidens walked along by the river's side; and when she saw the ark among the flags, she sent her maid to fetch it.

⁶And when she had opened it, she saw the child: and, behold, the babe wept. And she had compassion on him, and said, This is one of the Hebrews' children.

⁷Then said his sister to Pharaoh's daughter, Shall I go and call to thee a nurse of the Hebrew women, that she may nurse the child for thee?

⁸And Pharaoh's daughter said to her, Go. And the maid went and called the child's mother.

⁹And Pharaoh's daughter said unto her, Take this child away, and nurse it for me, and I will give thee thy wages. And the woman took the child, and nursed it.

¹⁰And the child grew, and she brought him unto Pharaoh's daughter, and he became her son. And she called his name Moses: and she said, Because I drew him out of the water. (Exodus 2:1-10)

As cited in verse 2, Moses was a "goodly" child. This means that he was born beautiful. "Goodly" was a term used in sixteenth century England to mean attractive. Moses' mother, a woman from the Israeli tribe of Levi, was compelled to hide her son for three months because she was overcome by his beauty. She probably risked her life in doing so. God is aware of the tendency for human beings to favor attractive people. In order for Moses to survive and eventually adhere to his calling in life he had to gain favor. So God made Moses beautiful. Moses' beauty gave him favor from infancy. The fact that Moses' mother was able to conceal him for three months was a miracle (one could be certain that the Israelite homes were investigated on a regular basis in search of male newborns). Moses' infancy trip down the Nile in a basket embraces the miraculous. The fact that Moses did not drown on his way down the river was a miracle. The fact that Pharaoh's daughter had compassion on a Hebrew child was a miracle (it appears that Moses' weeping triggered her compassion). The fact that Pharaoh's daughter went against her own father's orders and adopted Moses as her own child was also a miracle. To put it in a "nutshell," a Hebrew male child who was supposed to have been killed became the son of the daughter of the man who ordered him killed. This is certainly miraculous. It is obvious that God was with the Hebrews despite their oppression just as he was with the African slaves despite their oppression.

The historical account goes on to tell us that when Moses was an adult he killed an Egyptian because the Egyptian was beating up a Hebrew. Moses' ethnicity had not been hidden from him despite his being raised in an Egyptian home. He knew he was a Jew. When Pharaoh discovered that Moses had killed an Egyptian he set out to have him slain. Moses then fled to the land of Midian and set up residence there:

> 23During that long period, the king of Egypt died. The Israelites groaned in their slavery and cried out, and their cry for help because of their slavery went up to God. 24God heard their groaning and he remembered his covenant with Abraham, with Isaac and with Jacob. 25So God looked on the Israelites and was concerned about them. (Exodus 2:23-25 NIV)

The Israelites cried out because of their bondage and God acknowledged their cries just as God acknowledged the cries of the African slaves.

As most of us know, God chose Moses to lead his people out of oppressive slavery. In speaking with Moses concerning this matter God said,

> 6Moreover he said, I am the God of thy father, the God of Abraham, the God of Isaac, and the God of Jacob. And Moses hid his face; for he was afraid to look upon God.
> 7And the Lord said, I have surely seen the affliction of my people which are in Egypt, and have heard their cry by reason of their taskmasters; for I know their sorrows;
> 8And I am come down to deliver them out of the hand of the Egyptians, and to bring them up out of that land unto a good land and a large, unto a land flowing with milk and honey; unto the place of the Canaanites, and the Hittites, and the Amorites, and the Perizzites, and the Hivites, and the Jebusites.
> 9Now therefore, behold, the cry of the children of Israel is come unto me: and I have also seen the oppression wherewith the Egyptians oppress them.
> 10Come now therefore, and I will send thee unto Pharaoh, that thou mayest bring forth my people the children of Israel out of Egypt. (Exodus 3:6-10)

God identified the children of Israel as his people because of the covenant (promise) he had made with Abraham. This does not mean he is only the God of the Jews. He is the God of the Jews as well as the

God of the Gentiles (non-Jews). He is God to anyone who will accept him and only him as God. A Jew is not automatically saved just because he is a Jew. He must accept the Lord Jesus Christ as Lord and Saviour just like anybody else in order to be saved. The scriptures below support this:

> 28For he is not a Jew, which is one outwardly; neither is that circumcision, which is outward in the flesh:
> 29But he is a Jew which is one inwardly; and circumcision is that of the heart, in the spirit, and not in the letter; whose praise is not of men, but of God. (Romans 2:28-29)

In looking further into the historical account of God's deliverance of the Israelites, we see that God placed many plagues on Egypt when Pharaoh refused to let the people go. God was not lukewarm when it came to freeing the Jews. He meant business. Let's take a look at God's instruction to Moses regarding these matters:

> 14And the LORD said unto Moses, Pharaoh's heart is hardened, he refuseth to let the people go.
> 15Get thee unto Pharaoh in the morning; lo, he goeth out unto the water; and thou shalt stand by the river's brink against he come; and the rod which was turned to serpent shalt thou take in thine hand.
> 16And thou shalt say unto him, The LORD God of the Hebrews hath sent me unto thee, saying, Let my people go, that they may serve me in the wilderness: and behold hitherto thou wouldest not hear.
> 17Thus saith the Lord, In this thou shalt know that I am the LORD: behold, I will smite with the rod that is in mine hand upon the waters which are in the river, and they shall be turned to blood.
> 18And the fish that is in the river shall die, and the river shall stink; and the Egyptians shall loathe to drink of the water of the river.
> 19And the Lord spake unto Moses, Say unto Aaron, Take thy rod, and stretch out thine hand upon the waters of Egypt, upon their streams, upon their rivers, and upon their ponds, and upon all their pools of water, that they may become blood; and that there may be blood throughout all the land of Egypt, both in vessels of wood, and in vessels of stone.

[20]And Moses and Aaron did so, as the Lord commanded; and he lifted up the rod, and smote the waters that were in the river, in the sight of Pharaoh, and in the sight of his servants; and all the waters that were in the river were turned to blood. (Exodus 7:14-20)

When Pharaoh refused to let the Jews go, God turned all of the water in the rivers of the land into blood. This was the first plague. With each succeeding refusal God plagued the people. Before Pharaoh finally submitted, the people were plagued with frogs, gnats, flies, death of livestock, skin ulcers, hail, locusts, and darkness. However, the Israelites were spared from these plagues, as the following scripture suggests:

[25]And the hail smote throughout all the land of Egypt all that was in the field, both man and beast; and the hail smote every herb of the field, and brake every tree of the field.
[26]Only in the land of Goshen, where the children of Israel were, was there no hail (Exodus 9:25-26).

After the ninth plague of darkness, Pharaoh still refused to let God's people go. Finally God brought one more plague against Egypt: all of the firstborn children of every Egyptian and the firstborn offspring of every animal owned by an Egyptian would die.

In order that the destroyer (an angel of God) not strike the firstborn children of Israel dead, God commanded each Israelite home to kill an unblemished lamb. After the lamb was killed they were to take its blood and "strike it on the two side posts and on the upper door post of the houses, wherein they shall eat it."[5] In speaking to the Israelites concerning this, Moses said the following,

For the LORD will pass through to smite the Egyptians; and when he seeth the blood upon the lintel, and on the two side posts, the LORD will pass over the door, and will not suffer the destroyer to come in unto your houses to smite you (Exodus 12:23).

It is interesting to note that Jesus is also called the Lamb of God. He is the unblemished lamb (void of sin) that shed his blood in order

---

[5] Exodus 12:7

that we may be saved. This is just one example of how many New Testament writings reflect writings of the Old Testament.

The writings in the book of Exodus go on to tell us that Pharaoh's firstborn son was one of the many killed by God's destroying angel during this last plague. Because of his son's death, Pharaoh finally submitted and let the Israelites go. However, as the Israelites fled from the land of Egypt Pharaoh changed his mind and went after them in an attempt to enslave them once again. The Egyptians caught up with the Israelites at the sea, which sat beside the land of Pihahiroth and before the land of Baalzephon. The account goes on to tell us what occurred as the Jews made their exodus out of Egypt:

> [19]And the angel of God, which went before the camp of Israel, removed and went behind them; and the pillar of the cloud went from before their face, and stood behind them:
> [20]And it came between the camp of the Egyptians and the camp of Israel; and it was a cloud and darkness to them, but it gave light by night to these: so that the one came not near the other all the night.
> [21]And Moses stretched out his hand over the sea; and the LORD caused the sea to go back by a strong east wind all that night, and made the sea dry land, and the waters were divided.
> [22]And the children of Israel went into the midst of the sea upon the dry ground: and the waters were a wall unto them on their right hand, and on their left (Exodus 14:19-22).

The account continues to tell us that the Egyptian army pursued the Israelites into the sea but the Lord caused the chariot wheels of the Egyptians to dismount. After that, God caused the waters to fall upon the Egyptians and they drowned. Israel was delivered.

In looking at the entire miraculous account of the Israelites' exodus from Egypt it is very obvious that God was angered by the way the Israelites were being treated otherwise he would not have gone through all the trouble he did to have them released. This does not sound like a God who is in favor of slavery, as we know it.

A Scriptural Analysis......

CHAPTER FIVE

♦

SCRIPTURE BY SCRIPTURE: A COMPLETE BIBLICAL INVESTIGATION

♦Slavery as a Negative Condition♦Slavery and the Family♦Slavery and the Superiority Syndrome♦Slavery as a system which Mandated Honor♦Slavery and Brotherhood♦Christians enslaved by Non-Christians♦Non-Christians enslaved by Christians♦Slavery and Authority Figures♦Slavery and Humility♦Slavery and Brutality♦Jesus as a Slave♦Spiritual Slavery

In this chapter we will concentrate on specific scriptures that relate to our subject. However, before going into our discussion, a briefing on Old and New Testament scripture is necessary.

When Jesus began his ministry he told the Jews that he did not come to destroy the law but to fulfill it (Matthew 5:17). During Old Testament times, one had to recognize and worship God as well as follow the laws of God in order to be assured eternal life. The book of Leviticus cites most of the Old Testament law that the Jews were under. There were laws governing sin offerings, peace offerings, the priesthood, what one should eat and not eat, sex, civil order, how one should treat their parents, swearing, profanity, slavery and much more. God commanded that those who cursed their parents (Leviticus 20:9), committed adultery (Leviticus 20:10), had sex with their in-laws (Leviticus 20:11-12), engaged in homosexual relations (Leviticus 20:13), just to name a few, be put to death.

When Jesus began his earthly ministry, he fulfilled the Old Testament law (for a list of Old Testament books, see Appendix). In other words, priests are no longer needed to mediate between the sinner and God because Jesus is now our high priest. The following verses of scripture support this:

> 23Now there have been many of those priests, since death prevented them from continuing in office; 24 but because Jesus lives forever, he has a permanent priesthood. 25Therefore he is able to save completely those who come to God through him, because he always lives to intercede for them.

26Such a high priest meets our need--one who is holy, blameless, pure, set apart from sinners, exalted above the heavens. 27Unlike the other high priests, he does not need to offer sacrifices day after day, first for his own sins, and then for the sins of the people. He sacrificed for their sins once for all when he offered himself. 28For the law appoints as high priests men who are weak; but the oath, which came after the law, appointed the Son, who has been made perfect forever. (Hebrews 7:23-28 NIV)

With Jesus' fulfilling of the Old Testament law, sin offerings were no longer necessary because Jesus bore the sins of the world and became the ultimate sacrifice for sin. The death penalty was no longer exercised because vengeance no longer belonged to man but instead to God (Romans 12:19). There are many more examples that can be given as to how Jesus fulfilled the law. However, even though many of the Old Testament laws do not apply to us today, many of them do. Those that do are repeated again in the New Testament (for a list of New Testament books, see Appendix), just in a different way, as we see below in Matthew 5:27-28, where Jesus says:

27Ye have heard that it was said by them of old time, Thou shalt not commit adultery
28 But I say unto you, That whosoever looketh on a woman to lust after her hath committed adultery with her already in his heart.....

Although the New Testament writings abolish the death penalty for adultery, the sin of adultery (as well as any other sin) is still an abomination to God.

There are also many times the New Testament directly supports certain laws of the Old Testament as attested to in the following verses of scripture:

9Do you not know that the wicked will not inherit the kingdom of God? Do not be deceived: Neither the sexually immoral nor idolaters nor adulterers nor male prostitutes nor homosexual offenders 10nor thieves nor the greedy nor drunkards nor slanderers nor swindlers will inherit the kingdom of God. 11And that is what some of you were. But you were washed, you were sanctified, you were justified in the name of the Lord Jesus Christ and by the Spirit of our God. (1 Corinthians 6:9-11 NIV)

With a clearer understanding of the Old and New Testaments, we can now proceed into an in depth scripture by scripture discussion on what the Bible says about slavery.

Slavery as a Negative Condition

Does God define slavery as a negative condition or is he neutral on this issue? Let's see what the scriptures have to say:

For ye suffer, if a man bring you into bondage, if a man devour you, if a man take of you, if a man exalt himself, if a man smite you on the face. (2nd Corinthians 11:20)

In the preceding scripture the words "if a man bring you into bondage" actually reads "if anyone enslave you" in the Greek. Therefore, we see that enslavement is referred to as a condition of suffering and is also compared to the likes of being devoured (destroyed, robbed) and beaten in the face (not simply slapped but beaten as the original Greek has it). Clearly then, God sees slavery as a negative condition.

It is for freedom that Christ has set us free. Stand firm, then, and do not let yourselves be burdened again by a yoke of slavery. (Galatians 5:1 NIV)

When Jesus began his ministry, there were still some who wanted to continue to follow the laws of the Old Testament instead of believing in God and living by grace. This is not to say that sin was lawful, but that God would forgive sin by accepting the offering of a repentant heart and changed ways instead of by the offering of an animal. God saw the keeping of the Mosaic law as the enslaving of oneself and told the people not to be burdened by such a yoke. Although enslavement refers to spiritual bondage in the above scripture, we should note that God uses the word *slavery* to denote a negative spiritual condition just as he used it to denote a negative physical condition.

[20]Each one should remain in the situation which he was in when God called him. [21]Were you a slave when you were

called? Don't let it trouble you—although if you can gain your freedom, do so. [22]For he who was a slave when he was called by the Lord is the Lord's freedman; similarly, he who was a free man when he was called is Christ's slave. [23]You were bought with a price; do not become slaves of men. (1 Corinthians 7:20-23 NIV)

The preceding verses of scripture are taken from the first book of Corinthians. The book of Corinthians is actually a letter that the apostle Paul wrote to the Corinthian church. In these verses he is addressing himself to Christian slaves. If Paul was telling slaves not to let the condition of their slavery bother them then apparently there must have been something to be bothered about. Paul goes on to say that a slave should by all means seek liberty, if possible. With this, the Bible is teaching that it is better to be free than to be in slavery.

As we will see later on in the chapter, the Jews were able to sell themselves into slavery. All Jewish slaves were to be released after six years of servitude and every slave, Jew or Gentile was to be released every 50 years (year of Jubilee[1]). Therefore, often times, the Jews willingly sold themselves into slavery. However, they would sell themselves only to other Jews, knowing that the fear of God was within them. But in verse 23 above, Paul is admonishing Jews not to become slaves of men but instead to become slaves of Christ. When Paul tells the Jews that they have been bought with a price he is telling them that the blood of Jesus has already paid the price of salvation for them. Therefore, instead of physically enslaving one's self to pay the price of a debt, Paul admonishes the Jews to focus first upon the price that was already paid by Jesus and to concentrate on becoming spiritual slaves of Christ rather than becoming physical slaves of men. We should accept the price that Jesus has paid for us and do all we can to serve him thus becoming his spiritual slave. Our debt to Christ should come before any other debt.

Some might say that Paul is contradicting himself in the preceding verses of scripture. In verse 20 he tells the Christian to remain in the situation in which he was called and then in verse 23 he tells Christians not to become the slaves of men. However, verse 20 was speaking to those Jews who may have been forced into slavery and verse 23 was speaking to those Jews who may have been seeking to become enslaved in order to repay a debt. The latter Jews were not to

---

[1] The word *Jubilee* is spelled with only one letter *e* and a small case letter *J* in the King James Version of the Bible.

seek to be enslaved by men but rather to spend the time and effort instead following Christ. Those who were forced into slavery were to follow Christ in the condition they were in, try not to let it bother them, and serve God while trying to obtain their freedom. We should remain faithful to God, no matter what state we are in, whether we are enslaved or free.

The scripture text also tells us that God did not consider enslaved Christians to be inferior to free Christians but rather, equal. We see this in verse 21 which tells us that a slave who is a Christian is free in Christ and a free man who is a Christian is a slave to Christ. In other words, if both the slave and the master are Christians then God sees no difference in them. Once again we can see why it was important for the early American slave owners to rationalize reasons for often times refusing to teach the entire word of God (the Bible) to their slaves. Upon conversion God would consider both the slave and the free man as his children and therefore entitled to the same rights and privileges as one another. The early American whites were not able to accept this since the type of slavery imposed upon blacks at the time was a breeding ground for racism. If God looked at the slave and the slave master as equal then the slave master could not be justified in mistreating his slave. In order for the early American slave master to defend his brutality towards the black slave he labeled the slave as an inferior brute. This is attested to in the following quote from early American author William Jay, who stated:

> A slave having no rights, cannot appear in a court of justice to ask for redress of injuries. So far as he is the subject of injury, the law regards him only as a brute, and redress can only be demanded and received by the owner. The slave may be beaten, (robbed he cannot be,) his wife and children may be insulted and abused in his presence, and he can no more institute an action for damages, than his master's horse. [1]

The term *brute* appears in early nineteenth century literature and was many times used as an adjective when defining a slave. Additionally, slaves were considered brutes by law. "Brutes" were considered inferior and not worthy of the privilege of being able to take legal action against those who mistreated them or their families.

Slavery and the Family

God has rules as to how the family of a slave should have been treated by their masters. As we shall see, God was not in favor of separation of the family.

> ¹"Now these are the ordinances which you are to set before them.
> ²"If you buy a Hebrew slave, he shall serve for six years; but on the seventh he shall go out as a free man without payment.
> ³"If he comes alone, he shall go out alone; if he is the husband of a wife, then his wife shall go out with him. (Exodus 21:1-3 NASB)

The words *Hebrew, Israelite,* and *Jew* are interchangeable in the Old Testament. The above law applied to a Hebrew buying another Hebrew. However, a Hebrew could not be sold unless he was in dept and could not pay what he owed. If sold, after six years he'd have to be released. The only other time a Hebrew could be sold into slavery was as punishment for theft.

In the preceding scriptural quote we see that God supplied a way out of unwilling servitude. In the seventh year of servitude the slave had to be set free. Although verse 2 above says that the slave was to be set free without payment, this did not mean that the slave was to leave empty-handed. The slave master was still commanded to make ample provisions for those of his slaves which were being set free. Let's take a look:

> ¹²If a fellow Hebrew, a man, or a woman, sells himself to you and serves you six years, in the seventh year you must let him go free. ¹³And when you release him, do no send him away empty-handed. ¹⁴Supply him liberally from your flock, your threshing floor and your winepress. Give to him as the LORD your God redeemed you. ¹⁵Remember that you were slaves in Egypt and the LORD your God redeemed you. That is why I give you this command today. (Deuteronomy 15: 12-15 NIV)

The departing slave was to be liberally provided for in order that he or she may have the opportunity to live comfortably as a free person. This is certainly a far cry from the broken promise of forty acres and a mule. Furthermore, if members of a family became slaves together then they would have to be set free together. The reverse is also true. God mandated that slave families be kept together. With this, we see how important family cohesiveness was and is to God. Did the white slave owners of American history adhere to God's laws concerning the non-separation of black slave families? The answer, of course, is no. We know from the annals of history that all too often African American slaves were separated from their family members many times never to see them again. Although slaves were allowed to marry, the law did not honor the marriage. In his writings of 1853, William Jay points to the following:

> A necessary consequence of slavery, is the absence of the marriage relation. No slave can commit bigamy, because the law knows no more of the marriage of slaves, than it does of the marriage of brutes. A slave may, indeed, be formally married, but so far as legal rights and obligations are concerned, it is an idle ceremony. His wife may, at any moment, be legally taken from him, and sold in the market. The slave laws utterly nullify the injunction of the Supreme Lawgiver, 'What God hath joined, let not man put asunder.' Of course, these laws do not recognize the parental relation as belonging to slaves. A slave has no more legal authority over his child, than a cow has over her calf. [2]

To "put asunder" means to separate. " The verses of scripture that Jay was referring to are cited below:

> [3]Some Pharisees came to him to test him. They asked, "Is it lawful for a man to divorce his wife for any and every reason?"
> [4]"Haven't you read," he replied, "that at the beginning the Creator 'made them male and female,' [5]and said, 'For this reason a man will leave his father and mother and be united to his wife, and the two will become one flesh'? [6]So they are no longer two, but one. Therefore what God has joined together, let man not separate."[2]
> (Matthew 19: 5-6 NIV)

---

[2] It reads, *Let not man put asunder*, in the 1611 King James Version

Slave masters and antebellum American government legislation ignored the above scriptures when it came to slave families. Clearly, they sinned in doing so. The separation of the slave family was justified by the labeling of the slave as a brute.

The ideals of the American slave owners, during that time, as to how slaves were to be treated, without argument, went against God's commands regarding the same. It was not God's will that a slave remain a slave for the rest of his or her life and it most certainly was not God's will that the slave family be torn apart. God most definitely didn't look upon the slave as a brute devoid of human rights. Furthermore, New Testament passages regarding the sanctity of marriage uphold the Old Testament passages. Matthew 19:5-6 records Jesus himself as saying that a husband and his wife are one flesh and that what God has put together, no man should separate.

In order to continue our discussion we need to lead into the next verse of scripture with a couple of scriptures already cited:

> 2If you buy a Hebrew slave, he shall serve for six years; but on the seventh he shall go out as a free man without payment.
> 3If he comes alone, he shall go out alone; if he is the husband of a wife, then his wife shall go out with him.
> 4If his master gives him a wife, and she bears him sons or daughters, the wife and her children shall belong to her master, and he shall go out alone
> 5But if the slave plainly says 'I love my master, my wife and my children; I will not go out as a free man,'
> 6then his master shall bring him to God, then he shall bring him to the door or the doorpost. And his master shall pierce his ear with an awl; and he shall serve him permanently. (Exodus 21:2-6 NASB)

It should first be understood that if a man wanted to marry a woman who was already a slave he had the option to wait until the seventh year of the woman's servitude if he did not want to be in bondage with her forever. In the seventh year she would have been set free and he would have been free to marry her without her being obligated to her master. However, if he chose to marry her during her enslavement then, married or not, she belonged to her master first before she belonged to her husband. Therefore, if he chose to marry her before she was set free then it can be safely assumed that both he and the woman loved the master to the point where they would opt to stay. Furthermore, as we have seen previously, a slave during those times had the option of running away without fear of retribution.

A slave master was only allowed to keep his slave's wife if the master was the initial slaveholder of the wife before the marriage took place. In this instance, the slave had the option to stay with his wife and children but in order to do so he would have had to remain a slave forever. He would have to give up his freedom for the love of his master and his wife. We can surely see how a slave could love his wife so endearingly but it may be difficult for us to comprehend how a slave could love his master. However, we can logically deduct that it would have been easier for a slave to love a kind master as opposed to a cruel one especially if he had the same love for his master (as the scripture implies) as he did for his biological family.

A man who would have agreed to be a slave for the rest of his life would have had to be a man who was well treated by his slave master. It must also be stressed that a slave who decided to continue to serve his master and not go free would have done so willingly. Surely, a slave would be hard pressed to sincerely love a cruel master and would not opt to stay with him. The above verses of scripture imply that masters were to be kind to their servants, for why would a slave want to stay with a master who treats him savagely? If this were not the case then the given option to stay with the master would not make any sense especially in view of God's abhorrence toward oppression. As we shall see under the forthcoming heading: *Slavery as a System which Mandated Honor,* there are scriptures in the New Testament that confirm God's command for slave masters to be kind to their slaves.

> 7"And if a man sells his daughter as a female slave, she is not to go free as the male slaves do.
>
> 8"If she is displeasing in the eyes of her master who designated her for himself, then he shall let her be redeemed. He does not have authority to sell her to a foreign people because of his unfairness to her.
>
> 9"And if he designates her for his son, he shall deal with her according to the custom of daughters.
>
> 10"if he takes to himself another woman, he may not reduce her food, her clothing, or her conjugal rights.
>
> 11"And if he will not do these three things for her, then she shall go out for nothing, without payment of money. (Exodus 21: 7-9 NASB)

In the event of extreme poverty, Jews were allowed to sell their daughters into slavery at a very young age in the hope that the slave master would marry the daughter when she became of age. The slave master understood that he was obligated to marry the daughter when she became a woman. However, if the slave master found the daughter displeasing as a woman and refused to marry her then he was not at liberty to sell her to foreign persons and he was obligated to let her go free. However, he had the option of designating his son to marry her. But if the son married her and then took in another woman besides her, the son was still responsible for supplying her needs and could not reduce her food, clothing, or conjugal rights (God allowed polygamy before the coming of Christ but disallowed it after Jesus began his ministry). If the son failed to supply her needs then he was to set the slave woman free without receiving any payment for her freedom.

God allowed the Jews to keep their custom but not without setting certain laws to protect slave women from perverse men. A perverse man might think twice about buying a female slave if he is obligated to marry her and care for her. Furthermore, the book of Ephesians teaches on how husbands should treat their wives. It says:

> 25Husbands, love your wives, even as Christ also loved the church, and gave himself for it;
> 26That he might sanctify and cleanse it with the washing of water by the word,
> 27That he might present it to himself a glorious church, not having spot, or wrinkle, or any such thing; but that it should be holy and without blemish.
> 28So ought men to love their wives as their own bodies. He that loveth his wife loveth himself.
> 29For no man ever yet hated his own flesh; but nourisheth and cherisheth it, even as the Lord the church:
> 30For we are members of his body, of his flesh, and of his bones." (Ephesians 5:25-30)

A slave woman who was married to her master was to be honored no less by her husband than if she were not his slave. Slave masters were obligated to eventually marry the slave girls they bought. If they did not marry them they had to set them free or arrange for their sons to marry them. This is definitely a far cry from how black female slaves were treated by most white male slave owners during the

American slavery era. Even though the verses cited from the book of Exodus are Old Testament law, they give us a good idea of how God wanted female slaves to be treated. The white slave master certainly did not abide by God's Old Testament law to marry the black female slave that he bought. Instead he often raped her. God was certainly not in favor of the constant sexual assaults imposed upon the black female slave by white slave owners. Let's take a brief look at the Old Testament penalty for rape:

> [23]If a man happens to meet in a town a virgin pledged to be married and he sleeps with her [24]you shall take both of them to the gate of that town and stone them to death—the girl because she was in a town and did not scream for help, and the man because he violated another man's wife. You must purge the evil from among you.
> [25]But if out in the country a man happens to meet a girl pledged to be married and rapes her, only the man who has done this shall die. [26]Do nothing to the girl; she has committed no sin deserving death. This case is like that of someone who attacks and murders his neighbor, [27]for the man found the girl out in the country, and though the betrothed girl screamed, there was no one to rescue her.
> [28]If a man happens to meet a virgin who is not pledged to be married and rapes her and they are discovered, [29]he shall pay the girl's father fifty shekels of silver. He must marry the girl, for he has violated her. He can never divorce her as long as he lives. (Deuteronomy 22: 23-29 NIV)

According to God's Old Testament law and during Old Testament times, a man was to be put to death if he raped a woman who was engaged to be married. And if a man raped a woman who was not engaged to be married then he had to marry her himself in order to restore her honor. If the early American slave masters had been living in Old Testament times, they would have been put to death for the rape of black slave women or they would have had to marry the women they raped in order to make up for the dishonor they imposed upon them. White slave owners slept with and raped black slave women, but they did not marry them to make up for dishonoring them and they certainly weren't put to death for raping them. Let's continue….

> If a man sleeps with a woman who is a slave girl promised to another man but who has not been ransomed or given her freedom, there must be due punishment. Yet they are not to be put to death, because she had not been freed. (Leviticus 19:20 NIV)

The preceding scripture is not referring to a slave woman who was raped but instead refers to two consenting adults who went against God's laws. An engaged woman was to remain a virgin until her wedding day and she was not to have sex with any man, including her fiancée, before that. However, if a man had sex with a slave woman engaged to be married, then both would be punished but neither of them would be put to death because she was not free. When looking further into the area of freedom we find the following:

> [10]And ye shall hallow the fiftieth year, and proclaim liberty throughout all the land unto all the inhabitants thereof: it shall be a jubile unto you; and ye shall return every man unto his possession, and ye shall return every man unto his family. (Leviticus 25:10)

The scripture makes reference to the year of Jubilee. All Hebrew slaves were to be freed every fifty years. So, if a man or a woman became a slave six months before the year of Jubilee, then he or she would only be a slave for six months. One might be uncomfortable with the fact that it was therefore possible for some to be slaves for the entire fifty years. However, we must remember that some men in those days lived to be hundreds and hundreds of years old (i.e. Methuselah lived to be nine hundred and sixty-nine years old, Genesis 5:27) and therefore fifty years would have been a small portion of their lives. God's desire for preservation of the family is seen again in the above scripture. At Jubilee, all slaves were to be returned to their families. Let's continue:

> [38]I am the LORD your God, who brought you out of the land of Egypt to give you the land of Canaan and to be your God.
> [39]And if a countryman of yours becomes so poor with regard to you that he sells himself to you, you shall not subject him to a slave's service.
> [40]He shall be with you as a hired man, as if he were a sojourner; he shall serve with you until the year of jubilee.

⁴¹'He shall then go out from you, he and his sons with him, and shall go back to his family, that he may return to the property of his forefathers.

⁴²'For they are My servants whom I brought out from the land of Egypt; they are not to be sold in a slave sale.

⁴³'You shall not rule over him with severity, but are to revere your God. (Leviticus 25:38-43 NASB)

Here, God is speaking to the Jews. He commands them not to enslave those countrymen who might come to them in an attempt to sell themselves into slavery, but to instead pay them for their services and eventually send them back to their families so that they will not miss the inheritance of their fathers. Again, preservation of the family is no less important to God when it comes to those who are slaves than when it comes to those who are free.

There were seven situations that could have brought about enslavement for the Hebrew. A Hebrew may have been born into slavery. If a Hebrew man was poor, he could sell himself into slavery. A man was also at liberty to sell his daughter into slavery if he was poor and believed that by selling her she would eventually have a better life. A thief could be sold to make up for his theft against whom he had robbed. Prisoners of war were often times sold into slavery. A Hebrew could buy a Hebrew slave from a gentile with the aim of selling that same man to another Hebrew. Finally, one who was in debt could be enslaved by his creditor for payment of that same debt. Either situation would have a strong impact on familial cohesiveness. The latter situation is seen in the following citation of scripture:

¹Now a certain woman of the wives of the sons of the prophets cried out to Elisha, "Your servant my husband is dead, and you know that your servant feared the LORD: and the creditor has come to take my two children to be his slaves."

²And Elisha said to her, "What shall I do for you? Tell me, what do you have in the house?" And she said, "Your maidservant has nothing in the house except a jar of oil."

³Then he said, "Go, borrow vessels at large for yourself from all your neighbors, even empty vessels; do not get a few.

⁴"And you shall go in and shut the door behind you and your sons, and pour out into all these vessels; and you shall set aside what is full."

⁵So she went from him and shut the door behind her and her sons; they were bringing the vessels to her and she poured.
⁶And it came about when the vessels were full, that she said to her son, "Bring me another vessel." And he said to her, "There is not one vessel more." And the oil stopped.
⁷Then she came and told the man of God. And he said, "Go, sell the oil and pay your debt, and you and your sons can live on the rest." (2 Kings 4:1-7 NASB)

Elisha, son of Shaphat, was one of God's prophets during the kingly reign of Jehoram and Jehoshaphat. The woman who was in distress was an Israelite. Her husband who had served Elisha was dead. However, her husband was in debt when he died. His creditors wanted to enslave her two sons as payment. According to the custom of the times, the creditors were well within their rights to do so. From the tone of the scriptures we can safely assume that the woman did not want this to happen. She became desperate and went to Elisha for help. When Elisha asked what she had in the house to use as payment she told him that all she had was a little oil. Oil was a commodity at that time and could be sold. Elisha instructed her to gather all the empty vessels she could. She did so. A little oil was poured into each vessel and then God filled each vessel to its capacity. Through Elisha, God miraculously supplied the woman with an abundance of oil. She was able to sell some of it to pay off the creditors and keep the rest for herself. She and her sons would live comfortably without the threat of her sons being forced into slavery. The debtor's sons were delivered from possible enslavement and God was the one who delivered them. In doing so, God kept the family together and rewarded the woman for her husband's faithful service to Elisha.

The historical account of Sarah's childbearing at an old age gives us another example of God's desire to keep families together. Let's take a look:

¹And the Lord visited Sarah as he had said, and the Lord did unto Sarah as he had spoken.
²For Sarah conceived, and bare Abraham a son in his old age, at the set time of which God had spoken to him.
³And Abraham called the name of his son that was born unto him, whom Sarah bare to him, Isaac.
⁴And Abraham circumcised his son Isaac being eight days old, as God had commanded him.

⁵And Abraham was an hundred years old, when his son Isaac was born unto him.

⁶And Sarah said, God hath made me laugh, so that all that hear will laugh with me.

⁷And she said, Who would have said unto Abraham, that Sarah should have given children suck? for I have born him a son in his old age.

⁸And the child grew, and was weaned: and Abraham made a great feast the same day that Isaac was weaned.

⁹And Sarah saw the son of Hagar the Egyptian, which she had born unto Abraham, mocking.

¹⁰Wherefore she said unto Abraham, Cast out this bondwoman and her son: for the son of this bondwoman shall not be heir with my son, even with Isaac.

¹¹And the thing was very grievous in Abraham's sight because of his son.

¹²And God said unto Abraham, Let it not be grievous in thy sight because of the lad, and because of thy bondwoman; in all that Sarah hath said unto thee, hearken unto her voice, for in Isaac shall thy seed be called.

¹³And also of the son of the bondwoman will I make a nation, because he is thy seed.

¹⁴And Abraham rose up early in the morning, and took bread, and a bottle of water, and gave it unto Hagar, putting it on her shoulder, and the child, and sent her away: and she departed, and wandered in the wilderness of Beersheba.

¹⁵And the water was spent in the bottle, and she cast the child under one of the shrubs.

¹⁶And she went, and sat her down over against him a good way off, as it were a bowshot: for she said, Let me not see the death of the child. And she sat over against him, and lift up her voice and wept.

¹⁷And God heard the voice of the lad; and the angel of God called to Hagar out of heaven, and said unto her, What aileth thee, Hagar? fear not; for God hath heard the voice of the lad where he is.

¹⁸Arise, lift up the lad, and hold him in thine hand; for I will make him a great nation." (Genesis 21:1-18)

Hagar was the servant of Abraham and Sarah. Sarah was not able to bear children and laughed when the Lord told Abraham that she would bear a son in her old age. In her impatience she eventually instructed her handmaid (Hagar) to sleep with Abraham and bear his children thus making Hagar a surrogate mother. Once Hagar was pregnant with Abraham's son, Sarah became jealous. Sarah began to mistreat Hagar and Hagar eventually fled from her (this account is found in Genesis 16:1-11, see Appendix). An angel of the Lord spoke to Hagar telling her to go back to Sarah. The angel told her that God would make of her son a great nation. The angel also told her that God had recognized her afflictions. Once again we see God's desire for preservation of the family in the fact that God commanded Hagar to go back to Abram because she was pregnant with his son.

Hagar was not punished in any way for running away from her masters. God understood why she ran away and knew that she had been mistreated. As the account tells us, Hagar returned to her masters and eventually bore her son whom she named Ishmael. Sarah treated the child as her own. Later on Sarah became pregnant just as God had promised. She bore a son and named him Isaac. On the day that Isaac was weaned Abraham made a great feast for him and Ishmael mocked Isaac. Sarah became angry and dismissed Hagar and Ishmael from her house. This troubled Abraham but he did not go against his wife's wishes and allowed Hagar to leave. This was the second time Hagar was forced to leave the house because of Sarah's wrath. But God was with Hagar regardless of Sarah's cruel treatment of her. God kept his promise to Hagar and made her a great nation from the seed of her son. The familial ties between Ishmael and his mother remained in tact as so did the familial ties between Abraham, Sarah, and Isaac.

God was also with the black slaves of the early American era despite the slave master's mistreatment of them. Contrary to the desire to send blacks back to Africa and the incessant separation of black slave families during the antebellum years, the black family unit remained a strong one at least into the beginning of the twentieth century. Let's continue:

[34]Now Sheshan had no sons, but daughters. And Sheshan had a servant, an Egyptian, whose name was Jarha.
[35]And Sheshan gave his daughter to Jarha his servant to wife; and she bare him Attai." (1 Chronicles 2:34-35)

Sheshan was an Israelite who had servants. Since he had no son, he gave his daughter to be a wife to his servant named Jarha. Sheshan did not look upon his servant as someone who was beneath him. Instead he looked upon his servant as someone who was good enough to marry his daughter, the point being, that slaves were not thought of as inferior beings during those times. If they had been, then Sheshan certainly would have not given his daughter over to marry one. However, things were quite different when it came to African slaves. They were thought of as inferior and the very thought of a black man having any kind of relations with a white woman brought on the fury of white men. Interracial marriages were forbidden during the nineteenth century and were not readily accepted during the twentieth century. However, God never made marriage into a racial issue.

> A son honoureth his father, and a servant his master: if then I be a father, where is mine honour? and if I be a master, where is my fear? saith the LORD of hosts unto you, O priests, that despise my name. And ye say, Wherein have we despised thy name? (Malachi 1:6)

A slave was to honor his master just as a son honors his father. With this being the case then the reverse must have also been true, that being, that a master was to treat his slave just as he would have treated his own son. If the early American slaveholders had followed this principle then floggings, beatings, rapes, separation of family, hard labor an the like would never have been inflicted upon the African slaves and the 'cat-o-nine tails' (a whipping devise that tore at the flesh) would have never been invented.

Slavery and the Superiority Syndrome

Here we will investigate whether or not the Bible indicates that some people are superior to others. We will see what God says about equal rights and tie this into our subject matter. Let's start by looking at the following verses.

> 13If I have despised the claim of my male or female slaves when they filed a complaint against me,
> 14What then could I do when God arises, And when he calls me to account, what will I answer him?
> 15Did not He who made me in the womb make him, And the same one fashion us in the womb? (Job 31:13-15 NASB)

Job is speaking here. Job was a man who was persecuted by Satan. The historical account of his ordeal with Satan is found in the book of

Scripture by Scripture

Job located in the Old Testament. Job is described as blameless and upright (Job 1:1 NIV). Satan attacked Job because Job was living righteously before God. In defense of himself, Job lists certain things he is not guilty of including lust, adultery, and the like (Job chapter 31, see Appendix). Included among the list is the fact, as we have seen, that Job is not guilty of mistreating his slaves. If one of Job's slaves came to him with a complaint, he listened. Job knew he had to answer to God if he should mistreat his slaves and that God would call him to account for his actions (verse 14, previous page). Furthermore, if righteousness includes being just towards one's slave, which it does, then unrighteousness would include being unjust towards one's slave.

When Job asks the question, "Did not He who made me in the womb make him?" he is really asking a rhetorical question and by asking it he is saying that he and his slave are equal since God made them both in the same fashion in the womb. Let's look further:

¹And all the people gathered themselves together as one man into the street that was before the water gate; and they spake unto Ezra the scribe to bring the book of the law of Moses, which their Lord had commanded to Israel.

²And Ezra the priest brought the law before the congregation both of men and women, and all that could hear with understanding, upon the first day of the seventh month.

³And he read therein before the street that was before the water gate from the morning until midday, before the men and the women, and those that could understand; and the ears of all the people were attentive unto the book of the law.

⁴And Ezra the scribe stood upon a pulpit of wood, which they had made for the purpose; and beside him stood Mattithiah, and Shema, and Anaiah, and Urijah, and Hilkiah, and Maaseiah, on his right hand; and on his left hand, Pedaiah, and Mishael, and Malchiah, and Hashum, and Hashbadana, Zechariah, and Meshullam.

⁵And Ezra opened the book in the sight of all the people; (for he was above all the people;) and when he opened it, all the people stood up:

⁶And Ezra blessed the LORD, the great God. And all the people answered, A-men, A-men, with lifting up their hands: and they bowed their heads, and worshipped the Lord with their faces to the ground.

7Also Jeshua, and Bani, and Sherebiah, Jamin, Akkub, Shabbethai, Hodijah, Maaseiah, Kelita, Azariah, Jozabad, Hanan, Pelaiah, and the Levites, caused the people to understand the law: and the people stood in their place. 8So they read in the book in the law of God distinctly, and gave the sense, and caused them to understand the reading. (Nehemiah 8:1-8)

The phrase, "all the people," included slaves, since slaves are people too and there is no doubt that slaves were in the congregation of people spoken of in the preceding verses of scripture. There was no separation of church service for the slave and master. They both went to the same service. They both heard the same gospel. The word of God was not kept from anyone. They worshipped God together on equal ground. This is the way God wanted it. God never instructed slave masters to keep any portion of the gospel from their slaves. However, during slavery times in early America, many scriptures that have been given thus far in this book were withheld from slaves.

Let nothing be done through strife or vainglory; but in lowliness of mind let each esteem other better than themselves. (Philippians 2:3)

The Bible teaches us not to think of ourselves better than others. However, the early American slave masters certainly did not abide by this teaching. It would be safe to say that most of them felt superior to their slaves. This feeling of superiority did not stem from any teaching of the Bible (as we clearly see from reading the above scripture) although the slave masters of that time attempted, and with great success, to convince others that it did.

8But now you must rid yourselves of all such things as these: anger, rage, malice, slander, and filthy language from your lips. 9Do not lie to each other, since you have taken off your old self with its practices 10and have put on the new self, which is being renewed in knowledge in the image of its Creator. 11Here there is no Greek or Jew, circumcised or uncircumcised, barbarian, Scythian, slave or free, but Christ is all, and is in all. (Colossians 3:8-11 NIV)

God looks at all who are in Christ in the same way whether they are slaves or slave owners, kings or vagabonds, black or white. In

God's eyes there are only two kinds of people: those who are saved and those who are not.

>[8]If ye fulfill the royal law according to the scripture, Thou shalt love thy neighbour as thyself, ye do well:
>[9]But if ye have respect to persons, ye commit sin, and are convinced of the law as transgressors. (James 2:8-9)

Respect of persons is putting one person above another and is a sin in God's eyes. God never condoned prejudice and racism. Verse 9 teaches that to have respect of persons is a sin. With this, it is clear that God never put one race of people above another. How could he have when he made all people from one blood? How could he when his Word teaches against favoritism and respect of persons? The following scripture attests to man being made from one blood:

>[24]God that made the world and all things therein, seeing that he is Lord of heaven and earth, dwelleth not in temples made with hands;
>[25]Neither is worshipped with men's hands, as though he needed any thing, seeing he giveth to all life, and breath, and all things;
>[26]And hath made of one blood all nations of men for to dwell on all the face of the earth, and hath determined the times before appointed, and the bounds of their habitation. (Acts 17:24-26)

Verse 26 teaches us that God has made all human beings from one blood. Adam was the first man and from Adam God made every nation of man. With this being the case, there is no man that is superior to another. We are all cut from the same fabric.

Slavery as a System which Mandated Honor

We have heard many times that the Bible says that slaves were to obey and honor their masters. However, we hear very little about whether or not slave masters were to reciprocate that honor. Let's see what the word of God has to say.

>[1]Masters, provide your slaves with what is right and fair, because you know that you also have a Master in heaven.
>[2]Devote yourselves to prayer, being watchful and thankful.

³And pray for us, too, that God may open a door for our message, so that we may proclaim the mystery of Christ, for which I am in chains. ⁴Pray that I may proclaim it clearly, as I should. ⁵Be wise in the way you act toward outsiders; make the most of every opportunity. ⁶Let your conversation be always full of grace, seasoned with salt, so that you may know how to answer everyone. (Colossians 4: 1-6 NIV)

Masters were to provide for their slaves the way they would want God to provide for them. They were to give their slaves what was right and fair. They were to speak to every man (which included slaves) with respect and grace. They were to be careful in their language towards every man. They were to remember that they have a Master in heaven and that they should give to their slaves what is just and equal if they want God to give them what is just and equal. Of course, we know that the majority of the early American slave masters did not follow these commands. Not only that, but many of them hid these scriptures from their slaves.

The following verses of scripture are taken from the book of Philemon. The book of Philemon is described best as a letter written to Philemon from Paul the apostle. It is only one chapter in length. History tells us that Philemon was a slave owner. One of his slaves, whose name was Onesimus, robbed him and ran away to Rome. While in Rome Onesimus was converted to Christianity. The apostle Paul was the human tool God used to convert Onesimus. Paul sends Onesimus back to Philemon. Let's take a look:

¹²I am sending him—who is my very heart—back to you. ¹³I would have liked to keep him with me so that he could take your place in helping me while I am in chains for the gospel. ¹⁴But I did not want to do anything without your consent, so that any favor you do will be spontaneous and not forced. ¹⁵Perhaps the reason he was separated from you for a little while was that you might have him back for good—¹⁶no longer as a slave, but better than a slave, as a dear brother. He is very dear to me but even dearer to you, both as a man and as a brother in the Lord.

¹⁷So if you consider me a partner, welcome him as you would welcome me. ¹⁸If he has done you any wrong or owes you anything, charge it to me. (Philemon 12-17 NIV)

When reading the entire letter (See Appendix) it is easy to conclude that Onesimus must have told Paul what he did. Paul in turn, wrote a letter to Philemon, gave it to Onesimus, and sent him back to Philemon with the letter. In the letter Paul expresses his love for Onesimus. Paul asks that Philemon give Onesimus his freedom and look upon him as his brother. Paul and Onesimus had become close and Paul considered Onesimus his brother. What Paul was essentially doing was asking Philemon to forgive Onesimus, accept him back as he would a member of his family and give him his freedom. Paul asked that Philemon would treat Onesimus no different than he would treat Paul himself.

Remember, by law Onesimus had the option whether or not to return to Philemon. Paul did not force his hand. It would seem from the text that Onesimus desired to return to his master but realized that Philemon had the option to punish him. It is interesting to note how Paul admonishes Philemon to be kind to Onesimus, to honor him as Paul honored him.

In his biblical writings, Paul never condemned the institution of slavery itself but he did emphatically instruct slave owners time and time again to be kind to their slaves. The letter (epistle) to Philemon is just another example of this. Let's move further.

²And a certain centurion's slave, who was highly regarded by him, was sick and about to die.

³And when he heard about Jesus, he sent some Jewish elders asking Him to come and save the life of his slave.

⁴And when they had come to Jesus, they earnestly entreated Him, saying, "He is worthy for You to grant this to him;

⁵For he loves our nation, and it was he who built our synagogue."

⁶Now Jesus started on His way with them; and when He was already not far from the house, the centurion sent friends, saying to Him, "Lord, do not trouble Yourself further, for I am not worthy for You to come under my roof;

⁷for this reason I did not even consider myself worthy to come to You, but just say the word, and my servant will be healed.

⁸"For I, too, am a man under authority, with soldiers under me; and I say to this one, 'Go!' and he goes' and to another, 'Come!' and he comes; and to my slave, 'Do this!' and he does it."

9Now when Jesus heard this, He marveled at him, and turned and said to the multitude that was following Him, "I say to you, not even in Israel have I found such great faith." 10And when those who had been sent returned to the house, they found the slave in good health. (Luke 7:2-10 NASB)

A centurion was an officer in the Roman army. He had great authority. These verses of scripture have been included in order to illustrate the great love this particular master had for his slave. The centurion wanted his slave to be healed. The centurion had such great faith in Jesus that he realized that Jesus' words alone could heal his slave. Jesus healed the slave. However, for our purposes, the emphasis here is more on how much the centurion honored and loved his slave.

When we look at biblical writings we see that the system of slavery was designed to be a humanitarian one. God did not sanction the kind of brutal slavery that existed in America. Let's continue.

23"For this reason the kingdom of heaven may be compared to a certain king who wished to settle accounts with his slaves.

24"And when he had begun to settle them, there was brought to him one who owed him ten thousand talents.

25"But since he did not have the means to repay, his lord commanded him to be sold, along with his wife and children and all that he had, and repayment to be made.

26"The slave therefore falling down, prostrated himself before him, saying "Have patience with me, and I will repay you everything.'

27"And the lord of that slave felt compassion and released him and forgave him the debt.

28"But that slave went out and found one of his fellow slaves who owed him a hundred denarii, and he seized him and began to choke him, saying, 'Pay back what you owe.'

29"So his fellow slave fell down and began to entreat him, saying, 'Have patience with me and I will repay you.'

30"He was unwilling however, but went and threw him in prison until he should pay back what was owed.

31"So when his fellow slaves saw what had happened, they were deeply grieved and came and reported to their lord all that had happened.

³²"Then summoning him, his lord said to him, 'You wicked slave, I forgave you all that debt because you entreated me. ³³'Should you not also have had mercy on your fellow slave, even as I had mercy on you?' ³⁴And his lord, moved with anger, handed him over to the torturers until he should repay all that was owed him. ³⁵So shall My heavenly Father also do to you, if each of you does not forgive his brother from your heart. (Matthew 18:23-35 NASB)

A talent denotes several million dollars while a denarii is a day's wages. The slave in question owed millions to his master, the king. However, after the slave appealed to the king for mercy regarding the debt, the king honored his slave's request, released him, and forgave the debt. Unfortunately, when it came time to show the same mercy and honor toward his fellow slave who owed him considerably less than what he had owed the king, the slave did not return the mercy and honor that had been given to him. Two lessons are learned here: one is that we should strive to be forgiving towards one another no matter the infraction, if we want God to be forgiving towards us. The second, and the lesson most appropriate for this discussion, is that the parable that Jesus gives here, teaches us that those in authority over slaves were to be merciful and forgiving towards their slaves. They were to honor their slaves' requests. The majority of early American slave owners did not abide by the teachings of this parable.

⁵Slaves, obey your earthly masters with respect and fear, and with sincerity of heart, just as you would obey Christ. ⁶Obey them not only to win their favor when their eye is on you, but like slaves of Christ, doing the will of God from your heart. ⁷Serve wholeheartedly as if you were serving the Lord, not men, ⁸because you know that the Lord will reward everyone for whatever good he does, whether he is slave or free.

⁹And masters, treat your slaves in the same way. Do not threaten them, since you know that he who is both their Master and yours is in heaven, and there is no favoritism with him. (Ephesians 6:5-9 NIV)

These are the verses of scripture Oprah Winfrey had unknowingly referred to (see Introduction). The scriptures say that slaves are to obey their masters with respect and fear. However, it also says that slave masters are not to threaten their slaves and are to treat them as they themselves would want to be treated. The King James Version and New American Standard versions of the Bible translate the phrase *respect and fear* as *fear and trembling*. To serve with fear and trembling is a figurative phrase and means to serve with respect of the one in authority. Christians are commanded to serve God with fear and trembling. The scripture says that slaves are to obey their masters as unto Christ. This in no way says that the master is equal to God but instead says that slaves are to respond to their masters with the same respect they would give in responding to Christ. God will consequently repay the slave for every good deed done towards his or her slave master.

The scriptures emphasize that God does not favor one person over another. God is not a respecter of persons. It is a sin for a slave master to threaten his slave in any way. There is a biblical command against it. Slave masters are not above God's chastisement. God does not think better of the slave master than he does of the slave. Verse 9 points out that both the slave and the slave master have the same Master in heaven. This makes them equal as human beings. God is not a racist and does not condone the ill treatment of slaves. It is certain that the scriptures regarding how slave masters are to treat slaves were kept from many a black slave during the American slavery era. As a matter of fact, the slave master may have been at a spiritual disadvantage when compared to the slave as exemplified when looking at Mark 10:31 which says that "many who are first will be last and the last first" (NIV).

> [45]"Who then is the faithful and sensible slave whom his master put in charge of his household to give them their food at the proper time?
> [46]"Blessed is that slave whom his master finds so doing when he comes.
> [47]"Truly I say to you, that he will put him in charge of all his possessions.
> [48]"But if that evil slave says in his heart, 'My master is not coming for a long time,'
> [49]and shall begin to beat his fellow slaves and eat and drink with drunkards;
> [50]the master of that slave will come on a day when he does not expect him and at an hour which he does not know.

[51]and shall cut him in pieces and assign him a place with the hypocrites; weeping shall be there and the gnashing of teeth. (Matthew 24: 45-51 NASB)

Here, Jesus is speaking a parable using an analogy involving the relationship between slave and master to emphasize his point about spiritual faithfulness. Aside from the main point, the analogy tells us quite a bit about how God feels slave masters should treat their slaves. In this parable a slave has become the ruler of other slaves. This ruler became puffed up and began to beat his fellow slaves. The scripture goes on to say that God would eventually punish this wicked servant for his dastardly deeds. Once again the Bible has emphasized that a slave should never be treated inhumanely by those in authority over him or her. The atrocities committed during the American slave era were against God and what he stands for.

Slavery and Brotherhood

The reference to brotherhood here applies to spiritual brotherhood not biological siblings. According to the Bible, those who believe in Jesus Christ as Lord and Saviour are God's children and those who are God's children are brothers and sisters (in Christ) to one another. As we shall see, God preferred that man should not enslave his brother. Let's first take a more detailed look at the following verses of scripture previously cited under *Slavery and the Family:*

[39]'And if a countryman of yours becomes so poor with regard to you that he sells himself to you, you shall not subject him to a slave's service.
[40]'He shall be with you as a hired man, as if he were a sojourner; he shall serve with you until the year of jubilee.
[41]'he shall then go out from you, he and his sons with him, and shall go back to his family, that he may return to the property of his forefathers.
[42]'For they are My servants whom I brought out from the land of Egypt; they are not to be sold in a slave sale.
[43]'You shall not rule over him with severity, but are to revere your God. (Leviticus 25: 39-43 NASB)

God made special allowances for Hebrew slaves. At that time the Israelites were worshippers of the one and only true God, Yahweh. A person was considered a heathen if he did not worship the one and only God. If a Hebrew did not worship God then he too would be considered a heathen. One of the things that really grieves God is the act of worshipping other gods (false gods, small case "g") instead of him. The first commandment among the *Ten Commandments* that God gave Israel through Moses was the following:

> ³Thou shalt have no other gods before me.
> ⁴Thou shalt not make unto thee any graven image, or any likeness of any thing that is in heaven above, or that is in the earth beneath, or that is in the water under the earth:
> ⁵Thou shalt not bow down thyself to them, nor serve them: for I the LORD thy God am a jealous God, visiting the iniquity of the fathers upon the children unto the third and fourth generation of them that hate me;
> ⁶And shewing mercy unto thousands of them that love me, and keep my commandments. (Exodus 20:3-6)

We see that God gave favor to those who worshipped him. He therefore gave more consideration to the Hebrew slave as opposed to the heathen slave. At this point in history, a Hebrew slave had to be financially compensated for his labor, he absolutely had to be freed at the year of Jubilee if not before, and he was to be treated kindly by his slave master.

> ⁸And the sons of Israel carried away captive of their brethren 200,000 women, sons, and daughters; and took also a great deal of spoil from them, and they brought the spoil to Samaria.
> ⁹But a prophet of the Lord was there, whose name was Oded; and he went out to meet the army which came to Samaria and said to them, "Behold, because the LORD, the God of your fathers, was angry with Judah, He has delivered them into your hand, and you have slain them in a rage which has even reached heaven.
> ¹⁰"And now you are proposing to subjugate for yourselves the people of Judah and Jerusalem for male and female slaves. Surely, do you not have transgressions of your own against the Lord your God?
> ¹¹"Now therefore, listen to me and return the captives whom you captured from your brothers, for the burning anger of the Lord is against you" (2 Chronicles 28:8-11 NASB)

Scripture by Scripture

According to the Old Testament scriptures there are twelve tribes of Israel. There are many accounts in the Old Testament that tell us of times where many of the tribes would turn against God and begin to worship false gods. The tribes also fought against one another. In the preceding scripture reference, two-hundred thousand people of the tribe of Judah were taken as slaves by Israel, their own brothers. As we can clearly see, God was not pleased. Israel (the tribe itself) had to be reminded that there were some among them who were sinning against God and they were therefore wrong to judge their brethren (Judah). God wanted Israel to show Judah the mercy that God had shown them. God was angry with Israel's enslavement of Judah. Verses 10 and 11 allude to God's distaste for the enslavement of one man over another with verse 10 suggesting that slavery can be a punishment for transgressions and with verse 11's notation of God's anger at Israel for enslaving Judah.

Here is but another historical example which reveals to us that God sees the physical bondage of a man as grievous. This is not to say that slavery in and of itself is a sin but rather a condition displeasing to God. However, it is a condition that he has time and again regulated and allowed for reasons often unbeknownst to us. Let's continue.

⁸This is the word that came unto Jeremiah from the LORD, after that the king Zedekiah had made a covenant with all the people which were at Jerusalem, to proclaim liberty unto them;

⁹That every man should let his manservant, and every man his maidservant, being an Hebrew or an Hebrewess, go free; that none should serve himself of them, to wit, of a Jew his brother.

¹⁰Now when all the princes, and all the people, which had entered into the covenant, heard that every one should let his manservant, and every one his maidservant, go free, that none should serve themselves of them any more, then they obeyed, and let them go.

¹¹But afterward they turned, and caused the servants and the handmaids, whom they had let go free, to return, and brought them into subjection for servants and for handmaids.

¹²Therefore the word of the Lord came to Jeremiah from the LORD, saying,

¹³Thus saith the Lord, the God of Israel; I made a covenant with your fathers in the day that I brought them forth out of the land of Egypt, out of the house of bondmen, saying,

¹⁴At the end of seven years let ye go every man his brother an Hebrew, which hath been sold unto thee; and when he hath served thee six years thou shalt let him go free from thee: but your fathers hearkened not unto me, neither inclined their ear.

¹⁵And ye were now turned, and had done right in my sight, in proclaiming liberty every man to his neighbour; and ye had made a covenant before me in the house which is called by my name:

¹⁶But ye turned and polluted my name, and caused every man his servant, and every man his handmaid, whom he had set at liberty at their pleasure, to return, and brought them into subjection, to be unto you for servants and for handmaids.

¹⁷Therefore thus saith the Lord; Ye have not hearkened unto me, in proclaiming liberty, every one to his brother, and every man to his neighbour: behold, I proclaim a liberty for you, saith the Lord, to the sword, to the pestilence, and to the famine; and I will make you to be removed into all the kingdoms of the earth. (Jeremiah 34:8-17)

God had commanded that the nation of Israel set free all Israelite slaves. Once again we see here that God is not in favor of his children enslaving one another. Jeremiah tells us that the slave masters did as God said and freed the slaves but after a while they forced the ex-slaves back into slavery. By doing this they were rebelling against God. God therefore punished the Israelites with pestilence and famine for their disobedience. God also promised to scatter them over all the earth. Apparently, God would rather that men be free. God kept true to his promise to scatter the Jews. They are scattered to this day. During the American antebellum years there were many Christian black slaves. Most of them were enslaved by Christian whites. In God's eyes, one's brother is more so one who is a brother spiritually as opposed to a brother biologically. In other words, Christians are brothers and sisters with one another in Christ. Therefore, it was wrong for a believer to enslave another believer during Old Testament times. If white American slave owners had abided by this then they would have at least had to release all the black slaves who were Christians. But of course, this rarely happened. Let's continue.

> And Laban said unto Jacob, Because thou art my brother, shouldest thou therefore serve me for nought? tell me, what shall thy wages be?(Genesis 29:15)

Laban was actually Jacob's uncle biologically, but brother in spirit. Jacob served Laban free of charge for fourteen years in order to marry Laban's daughter, Rachel. During this dispensation[3], cousin to cousin marriages were not sinful.

Although Jacob served for free he was not a slave, as we know it. Jacob willingly went into servitude in order to win the hand of Rachel and his service to Laban was more of a barter between two men than anything else. God allowed this.

Christians enslaved by Non-Christians

We have seen thus far that God considered slavery a negative condition and was not pleased when brother enslaved brother. The word Christian does not appear in the Bible until the New Testament book of Acts. It is a term used to identify those who follow Jesus Christ, and believe in him. However, it is used generically in this work to identify the Old Testament followers of, and believers in, God as well. Although the Jews were often times reprimanded by God for turning away from him, they, as a nation, make up God's children of the promise. However, because of their historic disobedience to God, the Bible informs us that God has only spared a remnant of them and only a remnant of them will be saved (Isaiah 10: 22-23, Ezekiel 12:8-16, Romans 9:27-28, see Appendix). With this in mind, let's take a look at how God felt about believers being enslaved by non-believers.

> [13]And God said to Abram, "Know for certain that your descendants will be strangers in a land that is not theirs, where they will be enslaved and oppressed four hundred years.

---

[3] The period of the Abrahamic covenant before the onset of the period of the Jewish Law.

[14]"But I will also judge the nation whom they will serve; and afterward they will come out with many possessions. (Genesis 15: 13-14 NASB)

God informed Abram that the nation of Israel would suffer oppressive slavery for four hundred years. God also told Abram that He would deliver Israel from their oppression and judge the nation (chastise Egypt) that put them in bondage. God judged Egypt by sending plagues against them (see Chapter Four).

[47]And if a sojourner or stranger wax rich by thee, and thy brother that dwelleth by him wax poor, and sell himself unto the stranger or sojourner by thee, or to the stock of the stranger's family:
[48]After that he is sold he may be redeemed again; one of his brethren may redeem him:
[49]Either his uncle, or his uncle's son, may redeem him, or any that is nigh of kin unto him of his family may redeem him; or if he be able, he may redeem himself.
[50]And he shall reckon with him that bought him from the year that he was sold to him unto the year of jubile: and the price of his sale shall be according unto the number of years, according to the time of an hired servant shall it be with him.
[51]If there be yet many years behind, according unto them he shall give again the price of this redemption out of the money that he was bought for.
[52]And if there remain but few years unto the year of jubile, then he shall count with him, and according unto his years shall he give him again the price of his redemption.
[53]And as a yearly hired servant shall he be with him: and the other shall not rule with rigour over him in thy sight.
[54]And if he be not redeemed in these years, then he shall go out in the year of jubile, both he, and his children with him.
[55]For unto me the children of Israel are servants; they are my servants whom I brought forth out of the land of Egypt: I am the LORD your God." (Leviticus 25:47-55)

Here we learn that a poor Hebrew who sold himself to a stranger (i.e. heathen) could be redeemed at any time by a member of his family (he did not have to serve the entire six years). The price for his freedom would have been equal to the annual salary of a hired servant multiplied by the years he (the Hebrew who sold himself into slavery) would have served until Jubilee. If these were to be several years then the family member (or the slave himself) would have to pay over the calculated amount for the redemption fee. However, if there were just a few years before Jubilee then the family member or slave himself was only accountable for the exact redemptive amount. In addition to this, the stranger had to treat the Hebrew slave as a hired servant. This means that the slave master would have to pay his slave thereby providing the possibility that the slave could eventually redeem himself. The slave master also had to treat the slave with respect and kindness. This law specifically applied to Hebrews who were slaves of heathens. We can see from this that God ultimately protects his people whether bond or free. It is no wonder that the early American slave masters were so apprehensive about teaching black slaves the gospel of Jesus Christ!

> [12]The Zidonians also, and the Amalekites, and the Maonites, did oppress you; and ye cried to me, and I delivered you out of their hand.
> [13]Yet ye have forsaken me, and served other gods: wherefore I will deliver you no more.
> [14]Go and cry unto the gods which ye have chosen; let them deliver you in the time of your tribulation. (Judges 10:12-14)

God reminded the Israelites how he delivered them from their enemies but would deliver them no more if they turned away from worshipping him. One of the punishments that God inflicted upon those who did not recognize him as the true God was to hand them over to their enemies into slavery. As we will see, because the Jews (Israelites) often turned away from God, God therefore, often allowed the Jews to be enslaved by their enemies as punishment. The Jews had a pattern of turning away from God. Despite this, every time they came back to God he would deliver them from their captivity. The majority of Africans who were kidnapped and brought to America as slaves were Muslims. They had been Christians before the Islamic peoples invaded the land and forced them to convert to Islam. Islam is a religion that does not recognize the God of the Bible. Some would say, therefore that God allowed Africans to be kidnapped and enslaved in America because they had turned away from him just as the Israelites had turned from him on several occasions. However, such conclusions are merely speculation and don't take away the sins that accompanied the enslavement of Africans. Americans were still wrong for enslaving the Africans. We must remember that Africans were kidnapped and sold into slavery. We have already seen that kidnapping is a sin in the eyes of God. No sin can be justified. Therefore, regardless of the fact that the majority of Africans were pagans at the time of their captivity in America, there is absolutely no justification for the enslavement of them. Let's look further:

> 15Lo I will bring a nation upon you from far, O house of Israel, saith the LORD: it is a mighty nation, it is an ancient nation, a nation whose language thou knowest not, neither understandest what they say.
> 16Their quiver is as an open sepulchre, they are all mighty men.
> 17And they shall eat up thine harvest, and thy bread, which thy sons and thy daughters should eat: they shall eat up thy flocks and thine herds: they shall eat up thy vines and thy fig trees: they shall impoverish thy fenced cities, wherein thou trustedst, with the sword.
> 18Nevertheless in those days saith the Lord, I will not make a full end with you.
> 19And it shall come to pass, when ye shall say, Wherefore doeth the LORD our God all these things unto us? then shalt thou answer them, Like as ye have forsaken me, and served strange gods in your land, so shall ye serve strangers in a land that is not yours." (Jeremiah 5:15-19)

Once again, Israel was not exempt from the punishment of slavery. Here is but another example where Israel turned away from God as they had done in past times. Babylon was the nation that was brought upon them to subject them, which is recorded in the books of 2 Kings chapter twenty-five, Jeremiah chapter twenty-six and Jeremiah chapter 27 (see Appendix). This judgement was not brought against all of Israel (there were twelve tribes) but was specifically brought against the tribe of Judah. Despite God's anger toward Israel, he did not annihilate them as a nation. Instead, he subjected them to Babylon as punishment.

> 6And Samuel said unto the people, It is the LORD that advanced Moses and Aaron, and that brought your fathers up out of the land of Egypt.
> 7Now therefore stand still, that I may reason with you before the LORD of all the righteous acts of the LORD, which he did to you and to your fathers.

⁸When Jacob was come into Egypt, and your fathers cried unto the LORD, then the LORD sent Moses and Aaron, which brought forth your fathers out of Egypt, and made them dwell in this place.

⁹And when they forgot the LORD their God, he sold them into the hand of Sisera, captain of the host of Hazor, and into the hand of the Philistines, and into the hand of the king of Moab, and they fought against them.

¹⁰And they cried unto the LORD, and said, We have sinned, because we have forsaken the LORD, and have served Baalim and Ashtaroth: but now deliver us out of the hand of our enemies, and we will serve thee. (1 Samuel 12:6-10)

Again we read that when the Israelites turned against God, he allowed them to be sold into slavery. Their enemies ruled over them until they (the Israelites) repented and decided to serve the Lord. Each time the Israelites repented of their sins, the Lord delivered them from their enemies. He delivered them from slavery. Each time he forgave them. God is very merciful.

⁶And God spake on this wise, That his seed should sojourn in a strange land; and that they should bring them into bondage, and entreat them evil four hundred years.

⁷And the nation to whom they shall be in bondage will I judge, said God: and after that shall they come forth, and serve me in this place. (Acts 7:6-7)

The seed spoken of here is Abraham's seed: the Israelites. The strange land is Egypt. The Egyptians enslaved the Jews and did "entreat them evil four hundred years". The evil deed was not necessarily the enslavement of the Jews but instead the oppressive treatment of the Jews by their slave masters. However, since the evil treatment was a direct result of the enslavement then the enslavement itself was evil. God would eventually judge the Egyptians for their evil deed. After their deliverance, the Jews would serve God "in this place" (i.e. the land of Canaan). If God considered the enslavement of the Jews evil because of the Egyptians mistreatment of them, it would follow that he would also feel the same way about the past enslavement of blacks in America.

Non-Christians enslaved by Christians

Under this heading we will investigate God's regulations as to how non-Christian slaves were to be treated by Christian slave masters. We will discuss whether or not God made a difference between Hebrew and heathen slaves, and if so, why? Let's look at our first scripture reference on this issue.

> 44'As for your male and female slaves whom you may have—you may acquire male and female slaves from the pagan nations that are around you.
> 45'Then, too, it is out of the sons of the sojourners who live as aliens among you that you may gain acquisition, and out of their families who are with you, whom they will have produced in your land; they also may become your possession.
> 46'You may even bequeath them to your sons after you, to receive as a possession; you can use them as permanent slaves. But in respect to your countrymen, the sons of Israel, you shall not rule with severity over one another. (Leviticus 25: 44-46)

God made a distinction between Hebrew slaves and heathen slaves. Heathen slaves would not be freed after six years as the Hebrew slaves would. They would have to serve as slaves permanently, meaning life-long. We know this because certain passages of scripture tell us that the Hebrew slaves were freed at Jubilee while other passages tell us that the heathen slaves would have to serve permanently. The above scriptural quote also implies that the heathen slaves could be treated more severely than the Hebrew slaves, which were not to be treated severely. However, this does not mean that the heathen slaves were to be abused.

We can safely assume that a heathen slave who converted to Judaism (the Old Testament counterpart to Christianity) would then have all rights and privileges as a Hebrew slave because Esther 8:17[4] teaches that any heathen that converted was considered an ethnic

---

[4] It reads, *And in each and every province, and in each and every city, wherever the king's commandment and his decree arrived, there was gladness and joy for the Jews, a feast and a holiday, And many among the peoples of the land became Jews, for the dread of the Jews had fallen on them. (NASB)*

Jew.[5] Once a heathen slave converted, he too would have to be freed after six years of servitude or freed at the year of Jubilee, whichever came first.

If the laws of the Old Testament had been in operation in early America, then any black slave who became a Christian would have had to be treated kindly by their masters and released after six years of servitude. Although many of the Old Testament laws do not apply today, the early American slave masters would have been hard pressed to come up with a biblical defense for their mistreatment of black slaves and especially the mistreatment of converted slaves. Slave masters knew that God was not pleased at their brutality towards slaves and that God was even more displeased at their brutality towards their brotherly slaves in Christ. According to Dale Taylor, author of *Everyday Life in Colonial America*, the enslavement of Christians, during the colonial period, was unlawful on an international level and therefore it was forbidden to convert Africans to Christianity. Consequently, Colonial Americans outlawed anything that might have facilitated in the teaching of the true gospel to the slaves. Slaves were not allowed to worship together without a white overseer present and were not allowed to read and write.

James Essig gives us further insight into the problem during that time with his writings about evangelist George Whitefield which says,

> In seeking to reassure masters that Christianity would make blacks better slaves, Whitefield employed a strategy that had been in use for quite some time before he set foot on American shores. His abrasive criticism of the slaveholding class, however, and his prophecy of divine judgement on the offending provinces pointed in a direction which led away from accommodation to a rejection of slavery. Long before Whitefield gave any thought to the problem, Anglican ministers and missionaries sent by the Society for the Propagation of the Gospel in Foreign Parts had learned how uncooperative southern planters could be when it came to teaching slaves the religion of Jesus. The Anglican missionaries discovered that planter resistance to slave evangelism grew out of a reluctance to apply the New

---

[5] Also Romans 2: 28-29 which reads, *A man is not a Jew if he is only one outwardly, nor is circumcision merely outward and physical. No, a man is a Jew if he is one inwardly; and circumcision is circumcision of the heart, by the Spirit, not by the written code. Such a man's praise is not from men, but from God. (NIV)*

Testament ideal of spiritual equality to blacks, and partly out of a fear about the effects that Christianity would have on the slave system. Deeply chagrined by the suggestion that she should look after the spiritual welfare of her servants, one eminent South Carolinian woman responded, 'Is it possible that any of my slaves could go to heaven, and must I see them there?' A young gentleman found the idea of fellowship with slaves so distasteful that he refused to take communion with them. As a result of an older association between slavery and heathenism, some planters thought that a slave would be entitled to freedom after he was baptized into Christianity. Other masters blamed Christianity for what they saw as an increased haughtiness on the part of their slaves. And then there was the enduring fear that religious gatherings would furnish slaves with an opportunity to hatch conspiracies against their masters. [3]

It is evident that early American slave masters were fearful of teaching their slaves the gospel of Jesus Christ because they knew what the scriptures said about the treatment of Christian slaves. For that matter, they knew what the scriptures said about the treatment of slaves as a whole. They were aware that abuse and mistreatment of a slave was a sin. Let's move further:

[10]When you march up to attack a city, make its people an offer of peace. [11]If they accept and open their gates, all the people in it shall be subject to forced labor and shall work for you. [12]If they refuse to make peace and they engage you in battle, lay siege to that city. (Deuteronomy 20:10-12 NIV)

The city that God is talking about is not just any city. It is referring to a city occupied by the enemies of Israel. God gave the Israelites the power to defeat all of their enemies. Their enemies were people who worshipped other gods. Israel was instructed not to make war with a city who accepted an offer of peace but instead to subject the people of that city to forced labor (see Appendix for all of Deuteronomy 20). God had his people to rule over those who worshipped false gods. Slavery was never an issue of color with God. In God's eyes, those who did not worship him deserved to be punished. To be made slaves or subjects and serve under others as the result of war was one of God's punishments for those who refused to worship him. God chastised those who turned against him as cited in detail in the book of Deuteronomy chapter 28 (see Appendix). The chapter informs us that Israel (not only the heathens) was also in jeopardy of being enslaved by their enemies if they turned against God. So, as we can see, although God allowed slavery, he knew that it was not a pleasant condition for men to be in which is why he imposed rules to govern the system itself and used it to punish those who turned against him.

> 43Thou hast delivered me from the strivings of the people; and thou hast made me the head of the heathen: a people whom I have not known shall serve me.
> 44As soon as they hear of me, they shall obey me: the strangers shall submit themselves unto me.
> 45The strangers shall fade away, and be afraid out of their close places.
> 46The Lord liveth; and blessed be my rock; and let the God of my salvation be exalted. (Psalms 18:43-46)

David, King of Israel, is speaking above. Again we see that those who did not serve God were enslaved. David had all heathen nations surrounding Israel in subjection to him. During their enslavement, God showed the heathens the power of the Lord through miracles and healing so that they might realize that their gods were not able to deliver them. Hopefully then they would turn around and begin to serve the only true God.

> 20As for all the people who were left of the Amorites, the Hittites, the Perizzites, the Hivites, and the Jebusites, who were not of the sons of Israel,
> 21their descendants who were let after them in the land whom the sons of Israel were unable to destroy utterly, from them Solomon levied forced laborers, even to this day.
> 22But Solomon did not make slaves of the sons of Israel; for they were men of war, his servants, his princes, his captains, his chariot commanders, and his horsemen. (1 Kings 9:20-22 NASB)

Solomon was the king of Israel after the reign of David, his father. The Amorites, Hittites, Perizzites, Hivites, and Jebusites were pagan nations that dwelt among the Israelites. In past times the Israelites had conquered, but not destroyed, each of these nations. The children of the survivors of these nations dwelt in Jerusalem and Lebanon where Solomon had jurisdiction. Solomon made slaves of the people of the pagan nations. He also had the power to enslave the Israelites but he did not. Instead the Israelites became his public servants and held positions of power.

Slavery and Authority Figures

What does God have to say about authority figures? Do those in authority have the right to oppress those who are under their leadership? Masters were in authority over their slaves, but where did "the buck" stop? Let's take a look at this issue.

> [13]Submit yourselves to every ordinance of man for the Lord's sake: whether it be to the king, as supreme;
> [14]Or unto governors, as unto them that are sent by him for the punishment of evildoers and for the praise of them that do well.
> [15]For so is the will of God, that with well doing ye may put to silence the ignorance of foolish men:
> [16]As free, and not using your liberty for a cloak of maliciousness, but as the servants of God.
> [17]Honour all men. Love the brotherhood. Fear God. Honour the king. (1 Peter 2:13-17)

Christians are to submit to authority. Christians should not be insubordinate. It is better for a Christian to submit to authority and do well under that authority than not to. A Christian is a representative of God. Therefore, if a Christian rebels against authority then those in authority will scorn God. Despite this, God's command for Christians to submit to authority is not a license from God for oppression. A free person is not to use their liberty for cruel behavior towards others.

God tells us (through Peter) to honor all men. This applied to the slave master as well as the slave. The slave was to honor his master but at the same time the master was to honor his slave. When God said that all men are to be honored he did not exclude slaves. A slave master who mistreated his slave was not treating him with honor and therefore was guilty of sin as were many early American slave holders who did not honor their slaves.

> Luxury is not fitting for a fool;
> Much less for a slave to rule over princes.
> (Proverbs 19:10 NASB)

This is not to say that a slave would not have the mental ability to rule or that God would not allow a slave to rule (i.e. Moses was born a slave and ruled regardless), but rather that people who are in authority should not allow their servants to rule them nor should a slave attempt to rule his master. In order to achieve a better understanding of this, the same can be said for the relationship between employees and their employers. It is not seemly for an employee to rule over his employer. In the same respect it was not seemly for a slave to rule over his master. The scripture reference is in no way saying that slaves are fools but rather that it is foolish for someone in authority to allow someone under his authority to rule him.

> 21Under three things the earth quakes,
> And under four, it cannot bear up;
> 22Under a slave when he becomes king,
> And a fool when he is satisfied with food,
> 23Under an unloved woman when she gets a husband,
> And a maidservant when she supplants her mistress. (Proverbs 30:21-23 NASB)

The above verses of scripture are more figurative than literal. The phrases "the earth quakes" and "cannot bear up" are figures of speech. The reference is not saying that slaves do not have the ability to become adequate Kings. This is made evident in the fact that there are biblical accounts of men born into slavery or sold into slavery who have become rulers or kings (i.e. Moses, Joseph). The passage warns us about desperate people. The scripture reference also indirectly teaches that those in power should not allow their subjects to rule them. God wants there to be a certain respect for the chain of command. The above verses of scripture support the authority of a non-oppressive governmental system.

> 7But which of you, having a slave plowing or tending sheep, will say to him when he has come in from the field, 'Come immediately and sit down to eat'?
> 8"But will he not say to him, 'Prepare something for me to eat, and properly clothe yourself and serve me until I have eaten and drunk; and afterward you will eat and drink'?
> 9"He does not thank the slave because he did the things which were commanded, does he?

¹⁰"So you too, when you do all the things which are commanded you, say, 'We are unworthy slaves; we have done only that which we ought to have done.' " (Luke 17:7-10 NASB)

In no way do the scriptures just cited encourage the mistreatment of slaves. The text is not saying that the master was at liberty to treat his slave in a disrespectful manner but is saying instead that the slave was to adhere to those duties imposed upon him or her. We are likewise servants unto the Lord. Those who are in Christ and serve him will receive rewards for their stewardship. However, God does not give us any extra credit for serving him because when we serve him we have done only that which we ought to have done. In this respect, those of us who are Christians are unworthy slaves of Christ. Since slavery was customary at the time of Jesus' ministry, Jesus used an example of the duties of a slave to make a point about serving God. A slave would get no special thanks for doing what was expected of him and neither will those who follow the commandments of God. We are supposed to follow the commandments of God just as a slave was supposed to follow the commands of his master. However, when we *do* follow God's commands, God blesses us with earthly rewards and eventually with heavenly rewards. Likewise a just master also had a duty to bless his slave by providing for him just as God provides for his servants.

Slavery and Humility

In his word, God encouraged slaves to be humble. What was God's reasoning for this? Wasn't God aware of the difficult nature of such a command? The following scriptures will shed some light on these questions and will also lead us into our next subheading: *Slavery and Brutality.*

¹⁸Servants be subject to your masters with all fear; not only to the good and gentle, but also to the froward.
¹⁹For this is thankworthy, if a man for conscience toward God endure grief, suffering wrongfully.
²⁰For what glory is it, if, when ye be buffeted for your faults, ye shall take it patiently? but if, when ye do well, and suffer for it, ye take it patiently, that is acceptable with God.

21For even hereunto were ye called: because Christ also suffered for us, leaving us an example, that ye should follow his steps:

22Who did no sin, neither was guile found in his mouth:

23Who, when he was reviled, reviled not again; when he suffered, he threatened not; but committed himself to him that judgeth righteously:

24Who his own self bare our sins in his own body on the tree, that we, being dead to sins, should live unto righteousness: by whose stripes ye were healed.

25For ye were as sheep going astray; but are now returned unto the Shepherd and Bishop of your souls.

(1 Peter 2: 18-25)

The word for *servant* in verse 18 translates into *house servant* in the Greek. Therefore, these verses were referring to a particular type of slave.

Notice that verse 19 says that a house servant suffering wrongfully at the hands of a perverse master should for conscience towards God endure grief. It was wrong for masters to treat their slaves in a harsh or perverse manner. Today this would apply to anyone in an authoritative position including employers. Verse 20 continues in telling us that a person who is treated harshly and deserves it has not really done anything noteworthy. However, it is a noteworthy deed for a person to be treated harshly, not deserve it, and endure it. The verse is not sanctioning the beating or harsh treatment of slaves but is instead saying that slaves being treated harshly by their masters were not to return evil for evil by disrespecting the master, but instead to endure.

It should also be emphasized that the verses we are discussing are basically telling the slave to forbear ill-tempered masters. However, the verses are not condoning oppression. There was a limit to what slaves had to tolerate from their slave masters. The slave being treated harshly always had the option to run away from his or her master without fear of retribution.

Verses 21 through 25 shows us that God isn't asking us to do what he hasn't done. The Son (the second person of the Godhead) manifested himself as a man (Jesus Christ) so that we may reap the gift of salvation. He was reviled, threatened, and cruelly treated. However, he did not return the same injustices but instead remained longsuffering. He is now seated at the right hand side of God.

Again, the word for *servant* in verse 18 translates more specifically as *house servant*. When we look at how important the affairs of one's household were in ancient society, we achieve an even clearer understanding as to why God felt such a command was necessary. This is exemplified in the following quote:

> Next to the state, the household was the most important unit in the Greco-Roman world, largely because of this role as a guarantor of stability in society. If order prevailed in the household, so it would in the state. Just as the household was basic to society, so it was to Christianity. The life of the early church centered in houses or households (e.g. Acts 2:2,46; 12:12; Rom. 16:5,23; 1 Cor. 16:19). Household groups were the basic units that made up the church in any given location.
>
> Household ideals also impacted the early church in significant ways. Household terms were used by the New Testament writers to express theological ideas. The church was referred to as the "household" of faith or of God (Gal. 6:10; Eph. 2:19). Household roles were appropriated by the Christian community: Christians were 'servants' of God, and their leaders were 'stewards' (1 Cor. 4:1; Titus 1:7; 1 Pet. 4:10). Because the household was so central to ancient society, much attention was given to delineating and clarifying the roles of the members of a household, be they family or servant. Standardized rules for behavior or domestic codes were developed in society, and these were adapted for use in the early church. Examples of lists of house rules or codes may be found in Colossians 3:18 ---4:11; Ephesians 5:21---6:9; 1 Peter 2: 13---3:7 [4]

Since the household was very important in early church culture, those who served in the household were not to cause confusion or disrupt the household. This entailed being obedient to the master of the household. Being obedient takes a certain amount of humility. Slaves and anyone under the authority of another person were expected to exhibit a certain amount of humility. Let's continue.

> [6]But he giveth more grace. Wherefore he saith, God resisteth the proud, but giveth grace unto the humble.
> [7]Submit yourselves therefore to God. Resist the devil, and he will flee from you.

⁸Draw nigh to God, and he will draw nigh to you. Cleanse your hands, ye sinners; and purify your hearts, ye double minded.

⁹Be afflicted, and mourn, and weep: let your laughter be turned to mourning, and your joy to heaviness. Humble yourselves in the sight of the Lord, and he shall lift you up. (James 4:6-10)

God is telling us that he will reward those who are humble. God will promote humble Christians who are in lowly positions. It is very important for those in authority to treat those under their authority the way God wants them to, otherwise, God could very well arrange things so that those under authority rise up over those in authority.

¹⁷Recompense to no man evil for evil. Provide things honest in the sight of all men.

¹⁸If it be possible, as much as lieth in you, live peaceably with all men.

¹⁹Dearly beloved, avenge not yourselves, but rather give place unto wrath: for it is written, Vengeance is mine; I will repay, saith the Lord.

²⁰Therefore if thine enemy hunger, feed him; if he thirst, give him drink: for in so doing thou shalt heap coals of fire on his head.

²¹Be not overcome of evil, but overcome evil with good. (Romans 12:17-21)

God's way is that we live peacefully with everyone no matter what they've done to us. This does not mean that we are to let people treat us "any old kind of way" but rather we are to yield to God in order that he may fight our battles for us. Again, the reason why Reverend Doctor Martin Luther King Jr. was one the most influential black Americans in facilitating positive change for blacks is largely due to the fact that he did it God's way: non-violently.

¹All who are under the yoke of slavery should consider their masters worthy of full respect, so that God's name and our teaching may not be slandered. ²Those who have believing masters are not to show less respect for them because they are brothers. Instead, they are to serve them even better, because those who benefit from their service are believers,

and dear to them. These are the things you are to teach and urge on them. (1 Timothy 6:1-2 NIV)

The passage refers to slavery as a yoke. A synonym for the word yoke is *harness*. A harness is something that when applied, limits the freedom of whomever or whatever it is applied to. Slavery is bondage. It is a type of harness that is unpleasant to wear. As we have seen previously, the word of God tells us that it is best not to be under this harness. However, if one should find himself under the yoke of slavery, then there are certain rules of behavior for the slave as well as for the slave master. Verse 1 teaches that slaves should respect their masters so that God's name will not be slandered. This command particularly applies to Christian slaves. The word of God commands Christians to abide by and respect authority. Therefore, Christian slaves who behaved contrary to their master's authority were not being good representatives of Christ thereby giving leeway to the slandering of God's name.

Christian slaves were also commanded not to show less respect for their Christian masters. Christians are spiritual brothers and sisters to one another. Therefore, Christians are in the same spiritual family. Even when looking at biological families, often times family members will treat a guest or a stranger better than they will treat their own family members. Unfortunately, this is often times the case as well with members of God's spiritual family. But God wants a functional respectful family unit just as any head of a family would. Therefore, he commands that Christian slaves not only be careful not to disrespect their Christian masters but strive to give even more respect to a Christian master than they would a non-Christian master. This way, the Christian master is guaranteed his due respect.

Slavery and Brutality

Here we will examine whether or not God intended for slavery to be brutal or whether the brutality of slavery was a direct result of human impulse contrary to the word of God.

> [4]If his master have given him a wife, and she have born him sons or daughters; the wife and her children shall be her master's, and he shall go out by himself.
> [5]And if the servant shall plainly say, I love my master, my wife and my children; I will not go out free:

⁶Then his master shall bring him unto the judges; he shall also bring him to the door, or unto the door post; and his master shall bore his ear through with an awl; and he shall serve him for ever. (Exodus 21:4-5)

When looking previously at the above scripture reference under the heading *Slavery and the Family*, we only dealt with the first half of the quote. We will now discuss the part of scripture whereby the master had permission to drive an awl through the ear of his servant. Apparently, this mark represented permanent servitude. This however does not condone the brutal brandings that were endured by the black slaves. Today an awl would be defined as a small pointed instrument used mainly for piercing holes in leather. Archaeological excavations give evidence that a tool of similar description was used during 1600 B.C (the time period of the preceding scripture reference) and was made of bone or metal. Our definition indicates that the point was probably very fine and Bible dictionaries assert that perhaps some sort of ring was placed through the slave's ear after the awl was bore through. All of this implies that the hole was not a big one and was similar to an ear piercing. Also, if the lobe was the part of the ear that the awl penetrated then the servant experienced very little pain during the process in view of the fact that the earlobe has few nerve endings. To test this, pinch your earlobe as hard as you can. Did it hurt? Quite a difference from being branded with a hot iron. Let's continue.

And when Abram heard that his brother was taken captive he armed his trained servants, born in his own house, three hundred and eighteen, and pursued them unto Dan. (Genesis 14:14)

Abram[6] had many servants. He had 318 trained soldiers and their families, which umbrellaed into several thousand people. Abram's servants were from the land of Haran. It is interesting to note that Abram armed over three hundred of his servants to help him fight against his enemies. Before the advent of the Civil War, early white American slave owners were definitely not willing to put arms into the hands of three hundred black slaves. As a matter of fact, there were laws at that time against slaves bearing arms.

---

[6] Also *Abraham*

Scripture by Scripture

Let's face it, with such widespread mistreatment of slaves during the American antebellum years the probability for an uprising would have soared if blacks had been given guns at that time. On the other hand, when we look at Abraham, we can clearly see that he was not concerned about an uprising and did not hesitate when it came to giving his servants weapons.

People are less likely to rise up against someone who has not mistreated them. Since Abraham was not worried about an uprising it stands to reason that he had not mistreated his servants. Abraham was noted in the Bible as a righteous man (Hebrews 11:17).[7] Therefore, if in being a righteous man, he did not mistreat his servants then we can conclude that the non-mistreatment of servants is a righteous act. Logically then, the mistreatment of slaves had to have been an unrighteous act. God does not condone any act of unrighteousness.

> Woe unto him that buildeth his house by unrighteousness, and his chambers by wrong; that useth his neighbour's service without wages, and giveth him not for his work; (Jeremiah 22:13)

The early American slave masters were certainly guilty of building their homes by unrighteousness. They benefited economically from their unrighteous enslavement of blacks.

> [1]And he began to speak to them in parables: "A man planted a vineyard, and put a wall around it, and dug a vat under the wine press, and built a tower, and rented it out to vine-growers and went on a journey.
> [2]"And at the harvest time he sent a slave to the vine-growers, in order to receive some of the produce of the vineyard from the vine-growers.
> [3]"And they took him, and beat him, and sent him away empty handed.
> [4]"And again he sent them another slave, and they wounded him in the head, and treated him shamefully.
> [5]"And he sent another, and that one they killed; and so with many others, beating some, and killing others.

---

[7] It reads, *By faith, Abraham when he was tried, offered up Isaac: and he that had received the promises offered up his only begotten son,*

⁶"He had one more to send, a beloved son; he sent him last
of all to them, saying, 'They will respect my son.'
⁷"But those vine-growers said to one another, 'This is the
heir; come, let us kill him, and the inheritance will be ours!'
⁸"And they took him, and killed him, and threw him out of
the vineyard.
⁹"What will the owner of the vineyard do? He will come and
destroy the vine-growers, and will give the vineyard to
others. (Mark 12:1-9 NASB)

In the parable above, Jesus is really speaking of himself when he
talks of the beloved son that the certain man sent. The intention of the
parable is to teach us the importance of accepting Christ as our Lord
and Saviour. However, there is also a secondary message to the
parable. It teaches us how a slave was not to be treated. A slave was
not to be beaten, stoned, or killed. In his parable (verse 4), Jesus
described the way the slaves were treated as shameful. Although the
preceding scriptures give indication that mistreatment of a slave by
beating, striking, or killing is shameful in God's eyes and not to be
done, the following verses of scripture, if not looked at carefully
appears to give the opposite impression. Let's take a look:

²⁰And if a man strikes his male or female slave with a rod
and he dies at his hand, he shall be punished.
²¹If, however, he survives a day or two, no vengeance shall
be taken; for he is his property. (Exodus 21:20-21 NASB)

The preceding scripture reference is not giving the slave master the
right to beat his slave. Instead, it tells us what was to happen if a
beating had occurred and the repercussions thereafter. The scripture
says that if a slave was beaten by his master and died immediately as
a result, then the master would be punished. Scripture never
indicates what kind of punishment would have been given. However,
it appears that the death penalty for killing a man found in Exodus
21:12[8], does not seem to apply to the slave master who killed his
slave. The slave master would have been "surely punished" had the
slave died immediately under his hand. However, verse 21 indicates
that the slave master would not have received any punishment if the
slave had lived a couple of days before dying.

---

[8] It reads, *He that smiteth a man, so that he die shall be surely put to death.*

It looks as if God made a distinction between malicious intent and non-malicious intent. If the slave continued to live for a day or two after the assault then this would be an indicator that it may not have been the intent of the slave master to kill the slave. However, if the slave died immediately at the hands of the slave master then there was probably malicious intent. This would be analogous to first-degree murder verses manslaughter. Someone convicted of manslaughter has killed someone without intending to. The deed was an accident and murderous intent was not in the person's heart.

We must try to understand that the preceding verses of scripture in no way indicate that God was in favor of brutality against slaves. Our previous discussions have shown this to be so. The following scripture should shed more light on the subject:

> 24Eye for eye, tooth for tooth, hand for hand, foot for foot,
> 25Burning for burning, wound for wound, stripe for stripe.
> 26And if a man smite the eye of his servant, or the eye of his maid, that it perish; he shall let him go free for his eye's sake.
> 27And if he smite out his manservant's tooth, or his maidservant's tooth; he shall let him go free for his tooth's sake. (Exodus 21:24-27)

During Old Testament times *an eye for an eye* and *a tooth for a tooth* applied. The scriptures are not clear as to whether punishment for the slave master would include an *eye for an eye*. The only punishment the slave master may have had to endure for physically abusing his slave was the mandate to set his slave free in such an instance. However, it does appear that the slave master would have had to endure the same *eye for an eye* punishment as any other man would have had to endure if he physically harmed any other person.

The word *stripe* in the preceding scripture stands for *whipping*. It is therefore quite apparent that God was opposed to whippings, bodily dismemberment, burnings, woundings, and killings.

Although the slave master may not have been put to death for killing his slave, killing the slave was a sin because it was punishable. It is also noteworthy to keep in mind that many Old Testament laws regarding slaves and slave masters became overshadowed by New Testament scriptures. This is apparent when we look at how God has dealt with man from the beginning of God's creation of man. Theologians agree that there are seven different ways God has dealt with and is administratively dealing with man. Theologians have coined these seven different administrations of God as *dispensations.*

Scripture by Scripture

According to theologians and as listed in the Holman Bible Dictionary, the seven dispensations are *Innocency* (Garden of Eden), *Conscience* (man's conscious awakening), *Human government* (God's covenant with Noah), *Promise* (God's covenant with Abraham), *Law* (the Jewish Law), *Grace* (the ministry of Jesus, his death and resurrection), and *Kingdom* (the future reign of Christ).

Old Testament laws regarding physical abuse of slaves fell into the fifth dispensation of *Law*. However, with the sixth dispensation of *Grace* (the dispensation which we are currently in) any speculated biblical allusion of slave-abuse dissipates when we look at the New Testament/Grace dispensation scripture cited in Matthew 7:12 (NIV version) which says:

> So in everything, do to others what you would have them do to you, for this sums up the Law and the Prophets.

Here, Jesus commanded that we treat others as we want to be treated. If then, one does not want to be disrespected then one should not disrespect others. To do so would be a sin. If one does not want to be physically abused then one should not physically abuse others. To do so would be a sin. If one does not want to be whipped, burned, beaten, raped, and the like, then one should not commit such atrocities against others. To do so would be a sin. If one does not want to be enslaved then one should not enslave others. To do so would be a sin. We can rest assured, especially during the present dispensation, that most people do not want to be enslaved. And for those who would not want to be enslaved, it would be a sin for them to enslave others because they would be violating God's commandment that says we are to treat others as we want to be treated.

Apparently the early American slaveholders overlooked these scriptures when they insisted that Christianity supported brutal slavery. If God's Old Testament laws had been put into effect during the American slave era then many a slave master may have been put to death, whipped, wounded, burned, or have been forced to set their slaves free as a result of their mistreatment towards them. God intended for slaves to be treated in a humane manner. The early American slave masters did not abide by God's intent. Let's look at one more scripture regarding the issue:

> A servant will not be corrected by words: for though he understand he will not answer. (Proverbs 29:19)

This verse of scripture does not promote abusive physical treatment towards the slave because in it, there is no mention of sanctioning the physical punishment of a slave. As a matter of fact, as just noted, the New Testament emphasizes and re-emphasizes the importance of the slave master treating his slave with dignity. Again, the New Testament tells us that we should treat others in the manner we want to be treated.

Jesus as a Slave

Here, we will gain more insight into the purpose and need for humility during servitude as well as investigate Jesus as a servant. As we shall see, Jesus was the most humble servant that ever lived. Through Jesus, God has experienced humility as a servant and therefore has not asked man to do anything he wouldn't do. Surely there is no double standard here.

> 44and whoever wants to be first must be slave of all.
> 45For even the Son of Man did not come to be served, but to serve, and to give his life as a ransom for many. (Jesus is speaking here, Mark 10: 44-45 NIV)

Here again is another biblical scripture that gives testimony to God's displeasure with high mindedness. Verse 45 tells us that Jesus came as a servant. He came to give his life as a ransom for those who would accept him. Those, including slaves, who humble themselves to serve others will be exalted by God.

> 5Let this mind be in you, which was also in Christ Jesus:
> 6Who, being in the form of God, thought it not robbery to be equal with God:
> 7But made himself of no reputation, and took upon him the form of a servant, and was made in the likeness of men:
> 7And being found in fashion as a man, he humbled himself, and became obedient unto death, even the death of the cross. (Philippians 2:5-8)

Jesus was not only a servant but he came as a slave. The word *servant* in the above scriptural text translates to *bond-servant* in the Greek. Jesus came upon this earth in the most humble of forms....as a slave. Who did he come to serve? He served The Father by serving us. He died on the cross for us. His dying on the cross was a service rendered to us in order that, upon confessing a belief in him and in his resurrection, we would live with him in the afterlife thereby being saved from hell. His gift was free. Salvation costs us nothing.

God gives honor to whom he will despite their position in life. God promises to exalt those who are abased (Matthew 23:12).[9] To be a slave would be the lowest abasement in life. We know that God exalted Jesus and he now sits at the right hand of the Father. Jesus went from the position of an enslaved King to the position of an enthroned King. God keeps good all his promises and we see that the American black has also been exalted above slavery against the crushing jaws of a racist system.

Although lowliness of position is not desirable, lowliness of character is. A person who has a character of lowliness is a humble person. This does not mean they are inferior. In fact, God wants us to be humble. Lowliness of position and lowliness of character are not necessarily interchangeable. There are many people in high positions who are lowly in character and many people in low positions with haughty attitudes. Furthermore, a person who has a lowly position in life is not inferior. Jesus came as God in the flesh (John 1: 1-5 and v. 14, see Chapter One) which is certainly not an inferior state of being despite his lowly position as a slave. Through the Son, God came to earth as a slave in the person of Jesus. Are we to disrespect God because of this? Of course not. We can therefore surmise that being a slave was not supposed to have been a disrespected position in life no matter how many times the position was actually disrespected.

> [24]And there was also a strife among them, which of them should be accounted the greatest.
> [25]And he said unto them, The kings of the Gentiles exercise lordship over them; and they that exercise authority upon them are called benefactors.
> [26]But ye shall not be so: but he that is greatest among you, let him be as the younger; and he that is chief, as he that doth serve.
> [27]For whether is greater, he that sitteth at meat, or he that serveth? is not he that sitteth at meat? but I am among you as he that serveth. (Luke 22:24-27)

---

[9] It reads, *And whoever shall exalt himself shall be abased; and he that shall humble himself shall be exalted.*

Scripture by Scripture

This conversation took place between Jesus and his disciples during the Passover supper. Even the disciples were frivolously concerned about which one of them was the greatest among them. Jesus basically told them that those who are in authority should learn how to serve. Jesus used himself as an example. In the eyes of the world, a great man is one who has servants at his feet. However, in the eyes of God, a great man is one who serves and does it well. Jesus was a servant. Therefore, greatness comes in many forms, for Jesus was great and was yet a servant.

Spiritual Slavery

There are two kinds of spiritual slavery: One in which the person is a slave of Christ and the other in which the person is a slave to sin. With the former, one's spirit is blessed but with the latter one's spirit is oppressed. As discussed earlier, being the spiritual slave of Christ is a good thing because by doing so one becomes a slave of righteousness and does his best to serve God. However being the spiritual slave of sin is much worse than being a physical slave. The following scriptures attest to this.

> [31]To the Jews who had believed him, Jesus said, "If you hold to my teaching, you are really my disciples. [32]Then you will know the truth, and the truth will set you free."
> [33]They answered him, "We are Abraham's descendants and have never been slaves of anyone. How can you say that we shall be set free."
> [34]Jesus replied, "I tell you the truth, everyone who sins is a slave to sin. [35]Now a slave has no permanent place in the family, but a son belongs to it forever. [36]So if the Son sets you free, you will be free indeed. [37]I know you are Abraham's descendants. Yet you are ready to kill me, because you have no room for my word. (John 8: 31-37 NIV)

In the above verses of scripture Jesus was talking to both those Jews who did not believe in him and those who did. Jesus' teachings not only applied to the Jews but also to the Gentiles.

Those who believe in the Lordship of Jesus Christ are spiritually free. They are not destined to be in the bondage of hell and they are not enslaved with a sinful life. Hence, they are saved. However, it is the reverse for those who do not believe. Jesus was telling us that it is better to be a literal slave and believe, than to be a free man and not believe, because the former is really the one who is free and the latter is actually enslaved. Paul, by using the historical account of Sarah and Hagar[10] emphasizes this point by applying a figurative analogy in his letter to the Galatians:

> [21]Tell me, you who want to be under the law, are you not aware of what the law says?
> [22]For it is written that Abraham had two sons, one by the slave woman and the other by the free woman. [23]His son by the slave woman was born in the ordinary way; but his son by the free woman was born as the result of a promise.
> [24]These things may be taken figuratively, for the women represent two covenants. One covenant is from Mount Sinai and bears children who are to be slaves: This is Hagar.
> [25]Now Hagar stands for Mount Sinai in Arabia and corresponds to the present city of Jerusalem, because she is in slavery with her children. [26]But the Jerusalem that is above is free, and she is our mother. [27]For it is written:

> > "Be glad, O barren woman,
> >   who bears no children;
> > break forth and cry aloud,
> >   you who have no labor pains;
> > because more are the children of the
> >   desolate woman
> > than of her who has a husband."

> [28]Now you, brothers, like Isaac, are children of promise. [29]At that time the son born in the ordinary persecuted the son born by the power of the Spirit. It is the same now. [30]But what does the Scripture say? "Get rid of the slave woman and her son, for the slave woman's son will never share in the inheritance with the free woman's son." [31]Therefore, brothers, we are not children of the slave woman, but of the free woman. (Galatians 4: 21-31)

As we saw earlier, Hagar was in bondage to Sarah and Abraham. Sarah could not conceive so she sent Hagar to have intercourse with her husband in order that she would have a child through Hagar.

---

[10] Read the entire account in this chapter under the heading: *Slavery and the Family.*

From this union Ishmael was born. However, he was not the child of the promise. God had promised Sarah that she would conceive. But she did not believe God and laughed. However, God made good on his promise and blessed Sarah and Abraham with a son that they were to name Isaac. Isaac was born after Ishmael was born. Eventually Sarah despised Hagar and Ishmael and asked Abraham to send Hagar and Ishmael away. Abraham was distressed at his wife's request but God instructed Abraham to do as his wife asked. God also told Abraham that he would bless Ishmael by allowing Ishmael to father a nation. Theologians indicate that Hagar settled in the desert of Arabia. It was in this land that Ishmael's seed developed into a nation. However, Israel is the nation that came from Isaac's seed because Isaac was the child of the promise.

Paul uses the historical account of Sarah and Hagar in his analogy to the Galatians concerning spiritual things because many of the Jews at the time wanted to continue to hold on to the Law instead of accepting the grace of Jesus Christ. The holding on to the Law kept them in spiritual bondage. He compares Ishmael's birth to the Law, saying that Ishmael was born in the ordinary way just like the Jews were used to the ordinary way of the law. So although Ishmael was born in the ordinary way he was still bound because he was not the child of the promise and he and his mother were persecuted by their banishment to Arabia. However, Isaac was not born in the ordinary way but instead born of a free woman and heir to the promise. Paul therefore compares the birth of Isaac to the grace of Jesus Christ. Grace is liberating and does not bring persecution as does the Law. Isaac was free and non-persecuted while Ishmael was persecuted and bound. The analogy is figurative, not literal. It is Paul's way of encouraging the Jews to tear away from the bondage of the Law and come into the saving grace of Jesus Christ. Let's continue:

> For I reckon that the sufferings of this present time are not worthy to be compared with the glory which shall be revealed in us. (Romans 8:18)

A Christian, whether slave or free, can gladly look forward to spending eternity in God's kingdom and can therefore rest assured that when he reaches heaven he will put aside the memory of any suffering endured in this present day because heaven will be so glorious.

15What then? Shall we sin because we are not under law but under grace? By no means! 16Don't you know that when you offer yourselves to someone to obey him as slaves, you are slaves to the one whom you obey—whether you are slaves to sin, which leads to death, or to obedience, which leads to righteousness? 17But thanks be to God that, though you used to be slaves to sin, you wholeheartedly obeyed the form of teaching to which you were entrusted. 18You have been set free from sin and have become slaves to righteousness. (Romans 6:15-18 NIV)

The book of Romans speaks of our deliverance from the Old Testament law. We are instead under grace. This does not mean that there is no right and wrong. It simply means that the act of following God's Old Testament law is no longer a prerequisite for entering God's kingdom. Instead, the prerequisite is a true belief and confession in Jesus Christ and then all else (i.e. fruits of the spirit and good works) will follow. In Christ we should no more be slaves to sin but instead slaves to righteousness.

For what is a man profited, if he shall gain the whole world, and lose his own soul? Or what shall a man give in exchange for his soul? (Matthew 16:26)

Nothing is as important as believing in and serving God, not fame, nor riches, nor material possession, nor passions, nothing. There are those who give up righteousness in order to obtain things that the world can give them. They don't know or serve the Lord and many of them don't want to know the Lord and they don't want to serve him. They are in the spiritual bondage of sin because they have lost their souls for the sake of the world instead of giving up worldly things for the sake of righteousness in Jesus' name.

God does not want us to be a slave to sin and unrighteousness. It is God's desire that we be made free from sin and become "slaves" of righteousness. By doing this we are friends of God, for Jesus said that we are his friends if we do what he commands us to do (John 15:14).[10] If we truly believe in the Lordship and resurrection of Jesus Christ and confess that belief then we should not become slaves to fear by questioning whether or not we have the gift of salvation. We *do* have the gift of salvation if we truly believe and therefore there is *no*

---

[10] It reads, *Ye are my friends, if ye do whatsoever I command you.*

137

question about whether or not we have the gift of salvation if we truly believe. The following verses of scripture attest to this:

> [15]For you did not receive a spirit that makes you a slave again to fear, but you received the Spirit of adoption. And by him we cry "Abba, Father." [16]The Spirit himself testifies with our spirit that we are God's children. [17]Now if we are children, then we are heirs—heirs of God and co-heirs with Christ, if indeed we share in his sufferings in order that we may also share in his glory. (Romans 8:15-17 NIV)

Verse 16 teaches that those who are saved know they are saved because the spirit of God testifies to their spirit that they are saved. They indeed have the free gift of salvation. If we are saved then we are God's children and heirs of God and co-heirs with Christ. If we are heirs then we must share in his suffering as well as his glory. Not that we will be glorified ourselves, but rather that we will bask in the glory that He shall emanate at the time of his earthly return and reign. For the Bible says we as Christians will reign with Christ forever.

Slavery is actually associated with the law while the "spirit of adoption" is associated with freedom. Jesus has adopted non-Jewish people who believe in him (i.e. gentiles). They too can enter the kingdom of heaven just as they could in the Old Testament if they turn towards the true God. Those who turn to God are no more slaves to sin.

CHAPTER SIX
◆
MORE CONCERNS

Are Blacks cursed by God? ◆ *The Miracles of the Civil War*

Are Blacks Cursed By God?

For many years a substantial number of whites in America justified the enslavement of blacks by saying that blacks were cursed by God. There are people who still believe this today and many of them feel that the Bible supports this belief. There are even some Bible commentaries that uphold the doctrine of "the cursed Black." However, this is a false doctrine.

The myth of the cursed black begins with a particular historical biblical account of Noah and his three sons. The sons of Noah were Ham, Shem, and Japheth. There is some discrepancy, when looking at different commentaries, as to the Hebrew meanings of their names. In his book, *Beyond Roots*, William McKissic gives his definition of the names. He says,

> The name Ham means 'dark or black,' Shem means 'dusky or olive colored,' and Japheth means 'bright or fair. [1]

On the other hand, Strong's Greek and Hebrew Lexicon gives the Hebrew meaning of the name Ham as "hot or warm," the Hebrew meaning of the name Shem as "reputation or fame," and the meaning of the name Japheth as "opened." We are most concerned with the meaning of the name "Ham." Most theologians would agree that if the definition of "hot" were used then the word "hot" itself is referring to the climate in which Ham lived. Strong's Lexicon also informs us that the word *Ham* was later used as a collective name for the Egyptians. Historians agree that the majority of ancient Egyptians were people of color. For many African Americans this means, to them, that Ham was black. And despite the discrepancy in the definition of the name when exploring commentaries, it appears that the majority of theologians believe that Ham was black and therefore so were the Canaanites. However, the writers of the New International Version

More Concerns

Study Bible contend that the Canaanites were Caucasian.[1] If this is indeed so then the entire *blacks are cursed* myth is even more conspiratorial than initially documented.

The Bible tells us that Canaan (Ham's son) was cursed. The problem has been that some have rendered this to mean that the entire black race is cursed since it is believed by many theologians that Ham was black. Genesis 9:18-27 contain the verses of scripture that have been misinterpreted through the years by some American whites to mean that the black race is cursed, thus the enslavement of blacks and discrimination against them justified. Let's take a look at what Genesis 9:18-27 (NIV) says:

> [18]The sons of Noah who came out of the ark were Shem, Ham and Japheth. (Ham was the father of Canaan.) [19]These were the three sons of Noah, and from them came the people who were scattered over the earth.
> [20]Noah, a man of the soil, proceeded to plant a vineyard. [21]When he drank some of its wine, he became drunk and lay uncovered inside his tent. [22]Ham, the father of Canaan, saw his father's nakedness and told his two brothers outside. [23]But Shem and Japheth took a garment and laid it across their shoulders; then they walked in backward and covered their father's nakedness. Their faces were turned the other way so that they would not see their father's nakedness.
> [24]When Noah awoke from his wine and found out what his youngest son had done to him, [25]he said,
>
> "Cursed be Canaan!
> The lowest of slaves
> will he be to his brothers."
>
> [26]He also said,
>
> "Blessed be the LORD, the God of Shem! May Canaan be the slave of Shem.
> [27]May God extend the territory of
>   Japheth;
> may Japheth live in the tents of Shem,
> and may Canaan be his slave."

---

[1] New International Version Study Bible, 10th Anniversary Edition, p. 20.

More Concerns

McKissic refutes the false doctrine of *the black curse* with the following words:

Canaan, Ham's youngest son, is perhaps associated with Ham in most Bible students' minds (more so than his older brothers) because of the curse of Canaan recorded in Genesis 9:20-26. There is no doubt about it; the Canaanites were Black.

The descendants of Ham led very advanced civilizations that predate Semitic and Japhethic civilizations by at least two thousand years, which may explain the reluctance of some scholars to identify the ancient Egyptians, Canaanites, Libyans and sometimes even the Ethiopians with the modern day Negro. Some scholars label these groups as white with dark skin. Today's Dictionary of the Bible, compiled by T.A. Bryant, states, 'The race of Ham was the most energetic of all descendants of Noah in early times of the postdiluvian world.' However, the only biblical heritage that some Blacks have been taught is the so-called 'curse of Ham.'

"A careful study of Genesis 9:25-27 reveals that it was Canaan who was cursed, not Ham. Had Ham been cursed, all Blacks would have been cursed; however in the sovereignty of God, Noah cursed Canaan for Ham's sin. Ham had four sons; only one was cursed. Like Ham, I have four children and when I spank one, the other three are not physically affected. The Bible teaches that children will suffer because of the iniquities of their parents. Canaan was cursed because of Ham's sin. The curse was a pronouncement of a particular sentence, on a particular sin, toward a particular son.

Biblically speaking, a curse lasted three or four generations (Exodus 20:5). What was the curse? Canaan was assigned servitude to Ham's brothers, Japheth and Shem. Why was Ham not cursed? According to Dr. Custance, in Hebrew thought, Noah could not have cursed Ham without cursing himself. When and how was the curse fulfilled? Most scholars believe that the curse was fulfilled when the Canaanites were conquered by Israel and became subservient to the Israelites. It is interesting to note that of Ham's four sons (Ethiopia, Egypt, Libya and Canaan), Canaan is the only one that does not exist today as a nation. [2]

Ham had four sons. They were: Cush, the father of the nation of Ethiopia, Mizraim, the father of the nation of Egypt, Phut, the father of the nation of Libya, and Canaan. At one time the Canaanites inhabited what is now called Palestine. Ethiopia, Egypt, and Libya are African countries. Native Africans who have African ancestry are usually considered to be black or to be people of color. Therefore, it stands to reason that if all blacks had been cursed then Cush, Mizraim and Phut would have had to be cursed also. However, they were not.

Although there is no real concrete evidence to prove it, many theologians believe that Noah fathered the different races through Ham, Shem, and Japheth. However, we must remember that the Bible never focuses on the color of a man's skin and therefore race is a man-made concept. In spite of this, the Bible does distinguish nations. Therefore Ham's grand-fathering of Ethiopia and other black nations is yet but another historical fact that gives credence to the viewpoint that Ham was a person of color with some degree of black blood in him.

Respectively, if Ham was black then Noah and/or his wife must have also had some black blood in him or her. During the slave era in this country, a person was considered black if there was only an eighth of black blood in he or she. Therefore, according to the standards back then, Shem and Japheth would have been defined as black no matter how fair they actually appeared. Canaan was cursed to serve Shem and Japheth. Therefore, when closely examining early American standards of defining African racial identity, one black brother was cursed to serve another black brother. If one contends that a person who possesses only an eighth of black blood should be defined as black then that same person must contend that Shem and Japheth were black. Consequently if one contends that Shem and Japheth were black then the whole theory of the black race being cursed is blown apart by the mere fact that one brother could not serve the other if all were cursed to serve. How can the entire black race be cursed if the slave as well as the one to be served were both black?

A curse lasted three or four generations. In the following quote, the Holman Bible Dictionary gives us a good understanding of what the Bible says the length of a generation is:

A generation did not necessarily have a specific number of years. Genesis 15:13-16 apparently equates 400 years with four generations, thus 100 years per generation. Numbers

32:11-13 may reckon a generation as 60 years, it including people twenty and above and giving them forty more years to die. Or one may interpret this to mean a generation is the forty years of adulthood between ages 20 and 60. God promised Jehu his sons would rule to the fourth generation, apparently meaning four sons (2 Kings 10:30; 15:12). Jehu began ruling about 841 B.C., his first son Jehoahaz about 814 B.C. and the fourth generation Zechariah died about 752 B.C. The five generations ruled less than 90 years, while the four sons' generations ruled about 60 years. This is reducing a generation to quite a small number. After his tragedies Job lived 140 years and saw four generations (Job 42:16). This would make a generation about 35 years. Basically, generation is not a specific number of years but a more or less specific period of time. (Compare Job 8:8; Isa. 51:9.) The literal Hebrew expression "generation and generation" thus means through all generations or forever (ps. 49:11). Similarly, 'to you (his, their) generations' means forever (Num. 10:). [3]

The curse of Canaan was never described in scripture to have been implemented to last through generation and generation. Therefore this curse was not to last forever. The Canaanites became slaves to Israel and they no longer exist as a nation today. They are among a nation of five other nations that were overthrown by Israel during antiquity. This is spoken of in the following scriptural text in which God is speaking to the Israelites:

[20]Behold, I send an Angel before thee, to keep thee in the way, and to bring thee into the place which I have prepared. [21]Beware of him, and obey his voice, provoke him not; for he will not pardon your transgressions: for my name is in him. [22]But if thou shalt indeed obey his voice, and do all that I speak; then I will be an enemy unto thine enemies, and an adversary unto thine adversaries. [23]For mine Angel shall go before thee, and bring thee in unto the Amorites, and the Hittites, and the Perizzites, and the Canaanites, the Hivites, and the Jebusites: and I will cut them off. (Exodus 23:20-23)

If the Canaanites, along with the other aforementioned nations, do not exist today then it would stand to reason that Noah's curse upon

Canaan ceased when the nation itself ceased to exist. In the preceding scriptures we see that the Canaanites were grouped with nations that were to be cut off. Even if Ham's sin did result in a curse that was to effect his own generations after him, because of God's mercy, the curse would have had no effect after about the third or fourth generation. It could certainly have had no effect if the generation was non-existent.

Although the Canaanites no longer exist, blacks do. Therefore the question becomes: how can a race of people, said to be the generation of a cursed people, live under a curse whereby the original nation of people cursed are non-existent and have been for some time? The Canaanites were cut off. There were never any more generations of Canaanites. When we look at all of the information we can clearly see that blacks are not living under a curse.

The Miracles of the Civil War

In looking at the historical account of Job (Job 2: 1-6, see Appendix) we see that God is sovereign over all things that happen. Nothing takes place that God doesn't allow. Sometimes we may be able to decipher the reasons why God allows certain things to happen and sometimes we may not. Many blacks tend to remember that God allowed slavery in America but tend to forget that the same God also allowed it to be abolished. When examining the historical accounts of the Civil War, we see that God not only allowed slavery to be abolished but that he also set the stage for its demise.

It was God, not Abraham Lincoln who delivered blacks from slavery. President Lincoln was simply one of the human tools God used to accomplish his work. In this section we will take a look at the annals of the Civil War so we can see first hand how God performed anti-slavery miracles during the unfolding of the abolition of slavery.

The state of Virginia was the first American colonial state to buy black slaves from the slave trade in 1619. There were twenty slaves sold. At this time settlers were still colonizing. On July 4, 1776 the Declaration of Independence was signed and put into effect. Its main purpose was to declare the American colonies independent from Britain. However, it also declared the following:

> All men are created equal, that they are endowed by their Creator with certain unalienable Rights, that among these are Life, Liberty and the pursuit of Happiness. That to secure these rights, Governments are instituted among Men,

deriving their just powers from the consent of the governed, That whenever any Form of Government becomes destructive of these ends, it is the Right of the People to alter or to abolish it, and to institute new Government, laying its foundation on such principles and organizing its powers in such form, as to them shall seem most likely to effect their Safety and Happiness. [4]

God allowed the colonies to have trouble with the British thereby resulting in the Declaration of Independence. If all men are created equal then "all men" must include slaves. So we see that by 1776 the institution of slavery actually went against American governmental law. According to the Declaration of Independence, a man had a right to fight for his freedom and people had a right to fight for the freedom of others. This refutes any argument that says the Civil War, because it generated unrest against the government, was wrong in the eyes of God. We see from the Declaration that the government actually sanctioned the war.

In 1831 an anti-slavery newspaper published by William Lloyd Garrison called *The Liberator* began circulation and became one of the most influential weapons against slavery. Twenty years later Harriet Beecher Stowe's novel *Uncle Tom's Cabin* was published and generated much support for the anti-slavery movement. In a country where there was such controversy over the issue of slavery, it was a miracle that any anti-slavery propaganda survived at all. *Uncle Tom's Cabin* sold over one million copies in little over a year. In between these times California was voted in as a free state making the free states outnumber the slave states thirteen to twelve. Because of this, many pro-slavery southern states began threatening to withdraw themselves from the United States (the Union).

As tensions mounted, the Kansas Nebraska Act came into play allowing settlers to decide for themselves whether or not to allow slavery. Many southern states withdrew from the Union after President Lincoln was elected in November of 1860. They withdrew because of Lincoln's plans to stop the further expansion of slavery (but not to abolish the system altogether). Romans 13:1[2] tells us that those who are in governmental authority are in authority because God has put them in that position. The fact that Lincoln, an anti-

---

[2] It reads, *Let every person be in subjection to the governing authorities. For there is no authority except from God, and those which exist are established by God.*

slavery protagonist, was voted in as president of the United States at the height of political unrest surrounding the issue of slavery, was no accident. It was God who placed Lincoln into power at just the right time.

When Lincoln took office he rescinded the right of any state to withdraw from the Union. The pro-slavery states (the Confederates) and the anti-slavery states (the Union) began building protective army forts in case of war. Most of the Confederate states were southern states, since that is where the cotton grew and therefore the slaves were needed. In April of 1861, Lincoln decided to re-supply the men at Fort Sumpter (a Union fort) with guns and ammunition. Charleston (a Confederate city), took Lincoln's action as a declaration of war and on April 12, 1861 Confederate guerillas attacked Fort Sumpter thus beginning the Civil War.

In April through June of 1861 slaves began escaping from the Confederate states in an effort to get to what they called the *Promised Land* (the Union states). Lincoln ordered refugee slaves returned to their masters. Lincoln was not so much a slave sympathizer as he was a Union organizer. However, God still used him to abolish slavery.

On August 6, 1861 Lincoln implemented the First Confiscation Act which gave the Union the right to use refugee slaves for battle against the Confederates. In August of 1861 General Freeman of the Confederate army declared a martial law which guaranteed any slave freedom who helped fight the Union army. Lincoln rescinded Freeman's law. Without the rescission of Freeman's law, slaves would have fought against the very people trying to insure their freedom giving the Confederates an enhanced possibility of winning the war.

On November 8, 1861 Federal forces defeated part of the South Carolina Coast and the sea Islands. Slave and plantation owners became refugees leaving ten thousand liberated slaves behind. Such a defeat was allowed by God. It should be noted that Lincoln wanted all ten thousand of these liberated slaves sent back to Africa. However, for some reason God did not allow it.

Robert E. Lee became the leading General for the Confederate army and Ullyses S. Grant became the leading General for the Union army. On July 17, 1862 Lincoln signed the Second Confiscation Act which was put into writing once again in an attempt to send freed slaves back to Africa. Apparently Lincoln did not want any free blacks in the country and wanted them sent back to Africa. Whether this was a humanitarian move or a racist one we will never know. However, if by chance it was the latter, then it is evident once again that God had to be writing the script to the Civil War chain of events since it's unlikely for a man with prejudice towards a people to liberate that same people from their oppressors.

The summer of 1862 brought more victories for the Confederate states. Because of their many victories, Great Britain began increasing its recognition of them. This was a threat to the Union. Matters would have become further complicated if foreign countries had begun treating the Confederate states as a nation and becoming their allies. The Battle of Antietam put an end to this potential threat for the Union.

The Battle of Antietam was the Battle whereby both the Confederates and the Union lost the most soldiers. Despite this, the Union still won a major victory over the Confederates because during this battle the Confederate army was forced to cease its invasion of the Union due to an extreme loss of manpower. The irony of this is that prior to this battle, the Union had lost its chance to totally annihilate Lee's Confederate army when it chanced upon General Lee's battle plans but failed to utilize the information quick enough. Despite this horrific blunder, God gave the Union army victory in the Battle of Antietam anyway.

Due to the immense bloodshed at the Battle of Antietam, Abraham Lincoln submitted his preliminary Emancipation Proclamation which was to go into full effect in January of 1863. The proclamation abolished slavery in the Confederate states.

In September of 1862, the state of Louisiana was the first Union State to incorporate black army troops. It is no mistake that the blacks at that time were given the opportunity to fight for their freedom. Only God could have manipulated events whereby blacks were legally allowed to take up arms against their oppressors.

England did not intervene in the war due to the knowledge of what was contained in the Emancipation Proclamation, realizing that the battle between the North and the South was in actuality a struggle surrounding the moral issues of slavery. President Lincoln had anticipated England's decision. Not long after the Anti-War movement began, Lincoln issued the Emancipation Proclamation as a strategic, timely ploy to preserve the Union. It was time to put an end to the war. Slavery had been basically abolished, and consequently, there was no more reason to fight. Without God's involvement this would never have been so.

Despite the issuance of the Proclamation, the fighting continued and in March of 1864 the Confederates were loosing the war. In an act of desperation, the Confederates voted to include black soldiers in their army. In order to obtain the smallest possibility of defeating the

More Concerns

Union the Confederates were forced into making a decision to give guns to the very people that they wanted kept enslaved. Alas, they were too late. Their army had become so weakened that they had to withdraw.

Lincoln insured the Confederate states that they would be welcomed back into the Union if they would simply put down their arms. Finally, on April 9 1865, General Lee signed an agreement with General Grant to surrender the Confederate army. The war was over and the states re-unified.

On April 14 1865, Lincoln was assassinated. His purpose in life had apparently been fulfilled. It took until May of that year for scattered fighting to stop. On May 30th of the same year, black school children recognized the neglected graves of Union soldiers by placing flowers on the graves. This day has become the national holiday *Memorial Day* which is celebrated annually. When we celebrate Memorial Day we are actually honoring those Union soldiers, black and white alike, who fought and died for the freedom of blacks and the re-union of the country.

On December 18, 1865 the Thirteenth Amendment was added to the Constitution forever abolishing both slavery and involuntary servitude in all of America. The Amendment was unconditional and gave Congress the power to uphold it. Literal slavery in America was dead. Praise the Lord!

EPILOGUE

♦

IN SPEAKING TO BLACKS

When looking at all of the material presented, it appears that God's way of how the system of slavery should have been conducted is a far cry from the way it was instituted in early America. We can not justifiably say that slavery in and of itself is a sin. However, we can say that through the ages there have been times when slavery has become a sinful practice as a direct result of man's inability or lack of responsibility to follow God's rules governing the system.

It has been said that the economic stresses of ancient times made slavery a necessary function of those societies. It is speculated that this is why God allowed slavery in general. However, it is best not to speculate as to the reasons why God would allow slavery but to instead focus upon what he allowed and disallowed within the system itself.

As we have seen, God did not approve of one man kidnapping another man. To steal a man and sell him into slavery was a sin. Therefore, from its very beginning, slavery was a sin in America because the entire system was established on the foundation of a broken command: Thou shalt not steal. So, although slavery in and of itself is not necessarily a sin, slavery in America was.

We can understand this concept better when we look at the following analogy: Marriage is not a sin. However, if a person who is already married marries someone else then the latter marriage is bigamous and therefore a sin. It would be presumptuous of us to draw a conclusion that all marriage is sin based on the bigamous sins of one person who misused the system of marriage just as it would be presumptuous of us to conclude that all slavery was sin based on the brutal sins of a group of people who misused the system of slavery. To add to this, it would be deceitful of us to declare that the latter marriage was not a sin since marriage in and of itself is not a sin just as it would be deceitful to declare that slavery in America was not a sin since slavery in and of itself is not a sin. Please understand that I am not making the brutality of slavery comparable to the bliss of marriage but instead I am simply comparing the functioning of two systems to emphasize a point.

Not only did Westerners sin when they helped to kidnap Africans and bring them to America but they sinned when they separated slave family members from one another. They sinned when they

149

forced runaway slaves to return to their masters. They sinned when they beat slaves and raped slave women. They sinned when they disallowed slaves their freedom. They sinned when they kept the complete teachings of God from slaves. They sinned when they twisted biblical doctrine in an attempt to support their system of slavery. They sinned when they did not treat their slaves with honor and respect. The American system of slavery was of an oppressive kind and was therefore against the will of God. God was opposed to the kidnapping and oppression, not necessarily slavery itself.

We may ask, how does one separate the two? Isn't slavery synonymous with oppression? Well, during the American slave era it certainly was. The atrocities committed against black people during that time were deplorable. Therefore, it may be difficult for us to see how God's idea of slavery has nothing to do with oppression when man's idea of oppression often times has much to do with slavery.

We have seen that God is well aware of the fact that being a slave was not the best position to be in. It was a negative condition. However, God may often times allow people to experience the adverse for reasons unbeknownst to us. The negative condition of the African American slave was in part produced by the tyrannical behavior of the slave master, the inhumane working environment, and American racist ideology overtly prevalent at the time.

God frequently used the enslavement of a nation or people as punishment when they turned against him. This is not to say that God condoned oppressive slavery for he did not. However, God has been known to use the evils of one man to punish another. The Jews were not exempt from this as seen in the book of Jeremiah chapters twenty-six and twenty-seven (see Appendix). There we read about the house of Judah (Israel) becoming captive and being made slaves of Nebuchadnezzar (the King of Babylon at the time) as punishment for turning away from God. This is certainly not being said to infer that Africans were enslaved because God was punishing them for embracing Islam. Again, one can not speculate as to why God allowed Africans to be kidnapped and brought to America as slaves. The bottom line is that stealing Africans was a sin whether or not those Africans were Christian or non-Christian. Again slavery in America was therefore, a sin.

Many black people in America have bitter feelings surrounding the injustices imposed upon Africans during the slave trade and beyond. This is understandably so. There still exists an institution of racism in America, it just isn't as blatant as it once was. However, there are those blacks, who feel that, because of our mistreatment in

America, we are somehow spiritually favored of God and that the white man as a whole, is not. But God has not made any difference between black and white. We must be careful not to behave as though the suffering of our enslaved ancestors makes us more esteemed in God's eyes. It doesn't. The Bible teaches that bad things happen to righteous people as well as to unrighteous people.[1] Therefore we are no better, no more spiritual, or no more favored of God due to the mistreatment of our ancestors, than any other race or nationality of people.

We must remember that not only do we have ancestors who were slaves but we also have ancestors who were slave masters. African tribes enslaved other African tribes before the Portuguese, Spanish, Europeans, and Americans took Africans captive into slavery. People of color have no less a history of enslaving people than white people do. It was the Egyptians who enslaved the Jews. Hieroglyphics uncovered from Archaeological excavations have given evidence that the ancient Egyptians were people of color with varying degrees of skin tone ranging from very dark to very light.[2] Because of this, many African Americans categorize the ancient Egyptians as black. The Egyptians did not treat the Jewish slave any better than the white man treated the black slave. Also, in both instances the atrocities committed against the slave were so wicked that God had to intervene. In the case of the Egyptian slavery of the Jews, God intervened by afflicting the Egyptians with ten consecutive plagues. In the case of the American enslavement of blacks, God intervened by orchestrating the defeat of the Confederate South by way of the Civil War.

Although it may be difficult for us to put aside any bitter feelings we may have, we must attempt to do so because if we don't, Satan

---

[1] Matthew 5:44-45 (NASB) reads, *But I say to you, love your enemies, and pray for those who persecute you in order that you may be sons of your Father who is in heaven; for He causes His sun to rise on the evil and the good, and sends rain on the righteous and the unrighteous.*

[2] In the first chapter of his book, *Before the Mayflower*, Lerone Bennett Jr. informs us that Egyptian Hieroglyphics also portray white people. However, Bennett goes on to imply that all whites who were portrayed were foreigners, not Egyptians. He argues his point by giving one example of the way whites are illustrated in one particular mural depicting a procession and quotes G.A. Hopkins as saying that these were white slaves sent to the Egyptian King as a gift. Some scholars might argue his conclusion. Despite this, Bennett nullifies the question as to whether or not there were white people who lived in ancient Egypt. According to him and Hopkins, there were.

will use it against us. One way to put aside bitterness is to pray for a forgiving heart. However, it is not easy to forgive those who have done wrong and refuse to acknowledge the wrong. But, if we are to follow the ways of Christ then we must learn to forgive. Christ forgave those who crucified him despite the fact that those who had a hand in crucifying him did not ask to be forgiven.

It may help to remember that while there were many whites who fought to maintain slavery during the antebellum years there were just as many whites fighting to abolish it. If this had not been the case then there never would have been a Civil War. There were also a great many whites who assisted in the Civil Rights movement. When we look at white people today we can not distinguish between which of them have ancestors who were pro-slavery and which of them have ancestors who were anti-slavery. We can not distinguish between which of them have forefathers who fought for Civil Rights and which of them have forefathers who fought against it. What should it matter anyhow? We should only be concerned about those who may be trying to oppress us today.

As mentioned in Chapter Three, there has been, in the American black community, a long standing infiltration of the type of thinking that says that white people are demons and that they are "blue eyed devils." Demons are demons and white people are not devils. There are plenty of literal demons (referred to as fallen angels) and there is only one devil. Satan is the devil. Of course Satan would like for blacks to think that the white man is the devil because if we, as blacks think this, then we will be blind to who the devil really is. The devil is our enemy. However, if we don't know who our enemy *really* is, then our enemy has the advantage over us and if our enemy has the advantage then the probability increases that we will be spiritually defeated as a people. It is much worse to be defeated spiritually than physically. The devil is a spiritual being whose only desire is to ensnare souls.

It must be understood that the devil wants to keep black people bitter about slavery. He wants black people to be unforgiving. He wants black people to see all white people as demons. Why is this? Well, the devil knows that if blacks become entangled in feelings of bitterness and those feelings of bitterness are directly related to the historical incidences of oppressive slavery forced upon blacks, then it stands to reason that many blacks would denounce anything that is felt to uphold slavery. Hence, the Bible. If black people think (as many do) that the Bible condones the kind of slavery that was forced upon Africans of the past then blacks will not want to have anything to do with the Bible. However, by rejecting the Bible, those same blacks would have turned away from the only true God thus putting their spiritual lives and afterlives in jeopardy and consequently bringing Satan closer to his goal: spiritual genocide.

Think about it. Why would Satan attack the people of a nation, race, or ethnic group one by one when he can try to annihilate them altogether? If he can enrage black people to the point where we refuse to pick up a Bible and read it then he has made his job easier. Satan has done the same with other ethnic groups. Look at the historical account of the holocaust. Six million Jews were murdered. The Jewish religion does not acknowledge the deity of Christ. In looking at the atrocities of the Jewish holocaust we can clearly see that the holocaust was just another one of Satan's attempts at spiritual genocide. His idea is to kill as many Jews as possible before they discover the truth. Satan is using the same strategy towards blacks and any other group of people who might fall for his clever tricks. Remember, 1 Peter 5:8 tells us that the devil is as a roaring lion walking about seeking whom he may devour. Satan does not want mankind to worship God but instead wants mankind to worship him and he will attempt to accomplish this goal *by any means necessary.*

We must remember that God is responsible for putting an end to slavery in America. The irony of the Civil War is that the very people who the Confederates fought to keep enslaved were the very people who contributed most to the North's defeat of the South. The following quote[3] supports the previous statement:

> The 200,000 blacks who made their way into the ranks of the Northern army, the 29,000 blacks in the navy (one-fourth of the entire navy enrollment), and the tens of thousands of others who worked for the army as laborers and teamsters, played a crucial role in the winning of the war. In a letter to Lincoln, General Grant wrote, "By arming the Negro we have added a powerful ally. They will make good soldiers and taking them from the enemy weakens him in the same proportion they strengthen us." Toward the end of the war, Lincoln, too, came to believe that the participation of the blacks was the blow that defeated the South.

---

[3] The American Slave: From Sundown to Sunup, George Rawick, © 1972 by Greenwood Publishing Company. Reproduced with permission of Greenwood Publishing Group, Inc., Westport , CT., p. 117

Epilogue

God uses similar strategies when handling similar situations. In the case of the Jews he gave them power to rise up over the Egyptians. He did the same with black slaves. He also gave them power to rise up over the Confederates. It was not a mistake that blacks were able to take arms and fight for their freedom. It was an act of God. It is this same God that is indirectly and unjustly criticized when a person refuses to follow his word because of his or her own misconceptions and preconceived notions surrounding God's stand on slavery.

As Black people in America and abroad, many of us and most of our African ancestors have lived a *hell on earth* because of the history of the enslavement of black people and its after effects. However, to deny Christ out of a lack of knowledge as to what the Bible really says about slavery, or for any reason, is to guarantee one's place in a *literal hell* for all of eternity. If we allow this to happen then the devil has won and his plan has worked. One hellish experience per lifetime is enough. We must turn away from anything that gets in the way of us securing the gift of salvation no matter how comfortable it is for us not to turn away. Many blacks who have misgivings and bitter feelings about the Bible, because of the misinformation they've absorbed about the Bible as it pertains to slavery, have become comfortable with these feelings and misgivings and have allowed the same to turn them away from the Gospel of Jesus Christ. But we must put aside our bitterness, do away with our misgivings, embrace the Bible as the Word of God, and accept Jesus Christ as our Lord and Saviour. In doing so we are promised eternal life in God's kingdom which has no end.

APPENDIX:
SCRIPTURAL VERSES REFERENCED IN THE TEXT

CHAPTER ONE

Hebrews 3:7-19

⁷Wherefore (as the Holy Ghost saith, To day if ye will hear his voice,
⁸Harden not your hearts, as in the provocation, in the day of temptation in the wilderness:
⁹When your fathers tempted me, proved me, and saw my works forty years.
¹⁰Wherefore I was grieved with that generation, and said, They do always err in their heart; and they have not known my ways.
¹¹So I sware in my wrath, They shall not enter into my rest.)
¹²Take heed, brethren, lest there be in any of you an evil heart of unbelief, in departing from the living God.
¹³But exhort one another daily, while it is called To day; lest any of you be hardened through the deceitfulness of sin.
¹⁴For we are made partakers of Christ, if we hold the beginning of our confidence stedfast unto the end;
¹⁵While it is said, To day if ye will hear his voice, harden not your hearts, as in the provocation.
¹⁶For some, when they had heard, did provoke; howbeit not all that came out of Egypt by Moses.
¹⁷But with whom was he grieved forty years? Was it not with them that had sinned, whose carcases fell in the wilderness?
¹⁸And to whom sware he that they should not enter into his rest, but to them that believed not?
¹⁹So we see that they could not enter in because of unbelief.

Hebrews 4:1-11

¹Let us therefore fear, lest, a promise being left us of entering into his rest, any of you should seem to come short of it.
²For unto us was the gospel preached, as well as unto them: but the word preached did not profit them, not being mixed with faith in them that heard it.
³For we which have believed do enter into rest, as he said, As I have sworn in my wrath, if they shall enter into my rest: although the works were finished from the foundation of the world.

⁴For he spake in a certain place of the seventh day on this wise, And God did rest the seventh day from all his works.

⁵And in this place again, If they shall enter into my rest.

⁶Seing therefore it remaineth that some must enter therein, and they to whom it was first preached entered not in because of unbelief:

⁷Again, he limiteth a certain day, saying in David, To day, after so long a time; as it is said, To day if ye will hear his voice, harden not your hearts.

⁸For if Jesus had given them rest, then would he not afterward have spoken of another day.

⁹There remaineth therefore a rest to the people of God.

¹⁰For he that is entered into his rest, he also hath ceased from his own works, as God did from his.

¹¹Let us labour therefore to enter into that rest, lest any man fall after the same example of unbelief.

CHAPTER TWO

Matthew 26:62-66 (NIV)

⁶²Then the high priest stood up and said to Jesus, "Are you not going to answer? What is this testimony that these men are bringing against you?" ⁶³But Jesus remained silent.

The high priest said to him, "I charge you under oath by the living God: Tell us if you are the Christ, the Son of God.

⁶⁴"Yes, it is as you say," Jesus replied. "But I say to all of you: In the future you will see the Son of Man sitting at the right hand of the Mighty One and coming on the clouds of heaven"

⁶⁵Then the high priest tore his clothes and said, "He has spoken blasphemy! Why do we need any more witnesses? Look, now you have heard the blasphemy. ⁶⁶What do you think?"

"He is worthy of death," they answered.

⁶⁷Then they spit in his face and struck him with their fists. Others slapped him ⁶⁸and said, "Prophesy to us, Christ. Who hit you."

Matthew 27

¹When the morning was come, all the chief priests and elders of the people took counsel against Jesus to put him to death:

²And when they had bound him, they led him away, and delivered him to Pontius Pilate the governor.

Appendix

[3]Then Judas, which had betrayed him, when he saw that he was condemned, repented himself, and brought again the thirty pieces of silver to the chief priests and elders,

[4]Saying, I have sinned in that I have betrayed the innocent blood. And they said, What is that to us? See thou to that.

[5]And he cast down the pieces of silver in the temple, and departed, and went and hanged himself.

[6]And the chief priests took the silver pieces, and said, It is not lawful for to put them into the treasury, because it is the price of blood.

[7]And they took counsel, and bought with them the potter's field, to bury strangers in.

[8]Wherefore that field was called, The field of blood, unto this day.

[9]Then was fulfilled that which was spoken by Jeremy the prophet, saying, And they took the thirty pieces of silver, the price of him that was valued, whom they of the children of Israel did value;

[10]And gave them for the potter's field, as the Lord appointed me.

[11]And Jesus stood before the governor: and the governor asked him, saying, Art thou the King of the Jews? And Jesus said unto him, Thou sayest.

[12]And when he was accused of the chief priests and elders, he answered nothing.

[13]Then said Pilate unto him, Hearest thou not how many things they witness against thee?

[14]And he answered him to never a word; insomuch that the governor marvelled greatly

[15]Now at that feast the governor was wont to release unto the people a prisoner, whom they would.

[16]And they had then a notable prisoner, called Barabbas.

[17]Therefore when they were gathered together, Pilate said unto them, Whom will ye that I release unto you? Barabbas, or Jesus which is called Christ?

[18]For he knew that for envy they had delivered him.

[19]When he was set down on the judgment seat, his wife sent unto him, saying, Have thou nothing to do with that just man: for I have suffered many things this day in a dream because of him.

[20]But the chief priests and elders persuaded the multitude that they should ask Barabbas, and destroy Jesus.

[21]The governor answered and said unto them, Whether of the twain will ye that I release unto you? They said, Barabbas.

[22]Pilate saith unto them, What shall I do then with Jesus which is called Christ? They all say unto him, Let him be crucified.

[23]And the governor said, Why, what evil hath he done? But they cried out the more, saying, Let him be crucified.

[24]When Pilate saw that he could prevail nothing, but that rather a tumult was made, he took water, and washed his hands before the multitude, saying, I am innocent of the blood of this just person: see ye to it.

[25]Then answered all the people, and said, His blood be on us, and on our children.

[26]Then released he Barabbas unto them: and when he had scourged Jesus, he delivered him to be crucified.

[27]Then the soldiers of the governor took Jesus into the common hall, and gathered unto him the whole band of soldiers.

[28]And they stripped him, and put on him a scarlet robe.

[29]And when they had platted a crown of thorns, they put it upon his head, and a reed in his right hand; and they bowed the knee before him and mocked him, saying, Hail, King of the Jews!

[30]And they spit upon him, and took the reed, and smote him on the head.

[31]And after that they had mocked him, they took the robe off from him, and put his own raiment on him, and led him away to crucify him.

[32]And as they came out, they found a man of Cyrene, Simon by name: him they compelled to bear his cross.

[33]And when they were come unto a place called Golgotha, that is to say, a place of a skull,

[34]They gave him vinegar to drink mingled with gall; and when he had tasted thereof, he would not drink.

[35]And they crucified him, and parted his garments, casting lots: that it might be fulfilled which was spoken by the prophet, They parted my garments among them, and upon my vesture did they cast lots.

[36]And sitting down they watched him there;

[37]And set up over his head his accusation written, THIS IS JESUS THE KING OF THE JEWS.

[38]Then were there two thieves crucified with him, one on the right hand, and another on the left.

[39]And they that passed by reviled him, wagging their heads,

[40]And saying, Thou that destroyest the temple, and buildest it in three days, save thyself, If thou be the Son of God, come down from the cross.

[41]Likewise also the chief priests mocking him, with the scribes and elders, said,

[42]He saved others; himself he cannot save. If he be the King of Israel, let him now come down from the cross, and we will believe him.

[43]He trusted in God; let him deliver him now, if he will have him: for he said, I am the Son of God.

[44]The thieves also, which were crucified with him, cast the same in his teeth.

[45]Now from the sixth hour there was darkness over all the land unto the ninth hour.

[46]And about the ninth hour Jesus cried with a loud voice, saying Eli, Eli, lama sabach'tha-ni. That is to say, My God, my God, why hast thou forsaken me?

[47]Some of them that stood there, when they heard that, said, This man calleth for Elias.

[48]And straightway one of them ran, and took a sponge, and filled it with vinegar, and put it on a reed, and gave him to drink.

[49]The rest said, Let be, let us see whether Elias will come to save him.

[50]Jesus, when he had cried again with a loud voice, yielded up the ghost.

[51]And, behold, the veil of the temple was rent in twain from the top to the bottom; and the earth did quake, and the rocks rent;

[52]And the graves were opened; and many bodies of the saints which slept arose,

[53]And came out of the graves after his resurrection, and went into the holy city, and appeared unto many.

[54]Now when the centurion, and they that were with him, watching Jesus, saw the earthquake, and those things that were done, they feared greatly, saying, Truly this was the Son of God.

[55]And many women were there beholding afar off, which followed Jesus from Galilee, ministering unto him:

[56]Among which was Mary Magdalene, and Mary the mother of James and Joses, and the mother of Zebedee's children.

[57]When the even was come, there came a rich man of Arimathaea, named Joseph, who also himself was Jesus' disciple:

[58]He went to Pilate, and begged the body of Jesus. Then Pilate commanded the body to be delivered.

[59]And when Joseph had taken the body, he wrapped it in a clean linen cloth,

[60]And laid it in his own new tomb, which he had hewn out in the rock: and he rolled a great stone to the door of the sepulchre, and departed.

[61]And there was Mary Magdalene, and the other Mary, sitting over against the sepulchre.

⁶²Now the next day, that followed the day of the preparation, the chief priests and Pharisees came together unto Pilate,

⁶³Saying, Sir, we remember that that deceiver said, while he was yet alive, After three days I will rise again.

⁶⁴Command therefore that the sepulchre be made sure until the third day, lest his disciples come by night, and steal him away, and say unto the people, He is risen from the dead: so the last error shall be worse than the first.

⁶⁵Pilate said unto them, Ye have a watch: go your way, make it as sure as ye can.

⁶⁶So they went, and made the sepulchre sure, sealing the stone, and setting a watch.

Matthew 28

¹In the end of the sabbath, as it began to dawn toward the first day of the week, came Mary Magdalene and the other Mary to see the sepulchre.

²And, behold, there was a great earthquake: for the angel of the Lord descended from heaven, and came and rolled back the stone from the door, and sat upon it.

³His countenance was like lightning, and his raiment white as snow:

⁴And for fear of him the keepers did shake, and became as dead men.

⁵And the angel answered and said unto the women, Fear not ye: for I know that ye seek Jesus, which was crucified.

⁶He is not here: for he is risen, as he said, Come, see the place where the Lord lay.

⁷And go quickly, and tell his disciples that he is risen from the dead; and, behold, he goeth before you into Galilee; there shall ye see him: lo, I have told you.

⁸And they departed quickly from the sepulchre with fear and great joy: and did run to bring his disciples word.

⁹And as they went to tell his disciples, behold, Jesus met them, saying, All hail. And they came and held him by the feet, and worshipped him.

¹⁰Then said Jesus unto them, Be not afraid: go tell my brethren that they go into Galilee, and there shall they see me.

¹¹Now when they were going, behold, some of the watch came into the city, and shewed unto the chief priests all the things that were done.

¹²And when they were assembled with the elders, and had taken counsel, they gave large money unto the soldiers,

¹³Saying, Say ye, His disciples came by night, and stole him away while we slept.

¹⁴And if this come to the governor's ears, we will persuade him, and secure you.

¹⁵So they took the money, and did as they were taught: and this saying is commonly reported among the Jews until this day.

¹⁶Then the eleven disciples went away into Galilee, into a mountain where Jesus had appointed them.

¹⁷And when they saw him, they worshipped him: but some doubted.

¹⁸And Jesus came and spake unto them, saying, All power is given unto me in heaven and in earth.

¹⁹Go ye therefore, and teach all nations, baptizing them in the name of the Father, and of the Son, and of the Holy Ghost:

²⁰Teaching them to observe all things whatsoever I have commanded you: and lo, I am with you always, even unto the end of the world. A-men.

CHAPTER FOUR

Genesis 27: 1-41

¹And it came to pass, that when Isaac was old, and his eyes were dim, so that he could not see, he called Esau his eldest son, and said unto him, My son: and he said unto him, Behold, here am I.

²And he said, Behold now, I am old, I know not the day of my death:

³Now therefore take, I pray thee, thy weapons, thy quiver and thy bow, and go out to the field, and take me some venison;

⁴And make me savoury meat, such as I love, and bring it to me, that I may eat; that my soul may bless thee before I die.

⁵And Rebekah heard when Isaac spake to Esau his son. And Esau went to the field to hunt for venison, and to bring it.

⁶And Rebekah spake unto Jacob her son, saying, Behold I heard thy father speak unto Esau thy brother, saying,

⁷Bring me venison, and make me savoury meat, that I may eat, and bless thee before the LORD before my death.

⁸Now therefore, my son, obey my voice according to that which I command thee.

⁹Go now to the flock, and fetch me from thence two good kids of the goats; and I will make them savoury meat for thy father, such as he loveth:

¹⁰And thou shalt bring it to thy father, that he may eat, and that he may bless thee before his death.

Appendix

[11]And Jacob said to Rebekah his mother, Behold, Esau my brother is a hairy man, and I am a smooth man:

[12]My father peradventure will feel me, and I shall seem to him as a deceiver; and I shall bring a curse upon me, and not a blessing.

[13]And his mother said unto him, Upon me be thy curse, my son: only obey my voice, and go fetch me them.

[14]And he went, and fetched, and brought them to his mother; and his mother made savoury meat, such as his father loved.

[15]And Rebekah took goodly raiment of her eldest son Esau, which were with her in the house, and put them upon Jacob her younger son.

[16]And she put the skins of the kids of the goats upon his hands, and upon the smooth of his neck:

[17]And she gave the savoury meat and the bread, which she had prepared, into the hand of her son Jacob.

[18]And he came unto his father, and said, My father; and he said, Here am I; who art thou, my son?

[19]And Jacob said unto his father, I am Esau thy firstborn; I have done according as thou badest me: arise, I pray thee, sit and eat of my venison, that thy soul may bless me.

[20]And Isaac said unto his son, How is it that thou hast found it so quickly, my son? And he said, Because the Lord thy God brought it to me.

[21]And Isaac said unto Jacob, Come near, I pray thee, that I may feel thee, my son, whether thou be my very son Esau or not.

[22]And Jacob went near unto Isaac his father; and he felt him, an said, The voice is Jacob's voice, but the hands are the hands of Esau.

[23]And he discerned him not, because his hands were hairy, as his brother Esau's hands: so he blessed him.

[24]And he said, Art thou my very son Esau? And he said, I am.

[25]And he said, Bring it near to me, and I will eat of my son's venison, that my soul may bless thee. And he brought it near to him, and he did eat: and he brought him wine, and he drank.

[26]And his father Isaac said unto him, Come near now, and kiss me, my son.

[27]And he came near, and kissed him: and he smelled the smell of his raiment, and blessed him, and said, See, the smell of my son is as the smell of a field which the Lord hath blessed:

[28]Therefore God give thee of the dew of heaven, and the fatness of the earth, and plenty of corn and wine:

Appendix

²⁹Let people serve thee, and nations bow down to thee: be lord over thy brethren, and let thy mother's sons bow down to thee: cursed be every one that curseth thee, and blessed be he that blesseth thee.

³⁰And it came to pass, as soon as Isaac had made an end of blessing Jacob, and Jacob was yet scarce gone out from the presence of Isaac his father, that Esau his brother came in from his hunting.

³¹And he also had made savoury meat, and brought it unto his father, and said unto his father, Let my father arise, and eat of his son's venison, that thy soul may bless me.

³²And Isaac his father said unto him, Who art thou? And he said, I am thy son, thy firstborn Esau.

³³And Isaac trembled very exceedingly, and said, Who? Where is he that hath taken venison, and brought it me, and I have eaten of all before thou camest, and have blessed him? yea, and he shall be blessed.

³⁴And when Esau heard the words of his father, he cried with a great and exceeding bitter cry, and said unto his father, Bless me, even me also, O my father.

³⁵And he said, Thy brother came with subtilty, and hath taken away thy blessing.

³⁶And he said, Is not he rightly named Jacob? For he hath supplanted me these two times: he took away my birthright; and, behold, now he hath taken away my blessing. And he said, Hast thou not reserved a blessing for me?

³⁷And Isaac answered and said unto Esau, Behold, I have made him thy lord, and all his brethren have I given to him for servants; and with corn and wine have I sustained him; and what shall I do now unto thee, my son?

³⁸And Esau said unto his father, Hast thou but one blessing, my father? Bless me, even me also, O my father. And Esau lifted up his voice, and wept.

³⁹And Isaac his father answered and said unto him, Behold, thy dwelling shall be the fatness of the earth, and of the dew of heaven from above;

⁴⁰And by thy sword shalt thou live, and shalt serve thy brother; and it shall come to pass when thou shalt have the dominion, that thou shalt break his yoke from off thy neck.

⁴¹And Esau hated Jacob because of the blessing wherewith his father blessed him; and Esau said in his heart, The days of mourning for my father are at hand; then will I slay my brother Jacob.

Appendix

Daniel 3

[1]Nebuchadnezzar, the king made an image of gold, whose height was threescore cubits, and the breadth thereof six cubits; he set it up in the plain of Dura, in the province of Babylon.

[2]Then Nebuchadnezzar the King sent to gather together the princes, the governors, and the captains, the judges, the treasurers, the counsellors, the sheriffs, and all the rulers of the provinces, to come to the dedication of the image which Nebucchadnezzar the king had set up.

[3]Then the princes, the governors, and captains, the judges, the treasurers, the counsellors, the sheriffs, and all the rulers of the provinces, were gathered together unto the dedication of the image that Nebuchadnezzar the king had set up and they stood before the image that Nebuchadnezzar had set up.

[4]Then an herald cried aloud, To you it is commanded, O people, nations, and languages,

[5]That at what time ye hear the sound of the cornet, flute, harp, sackbut, psaltery, dulcimer, and all kinds of musick, ye fall down and worship the golden image that Nebuchadnezzar the king hath set up:

[6]And whoso falleth not down and worshippeth shall the same hour be cast into the midst of a burning fiery furnace.

[7]Therefore at that time, when all the people heard the sound of the cornet, flute, harp, sackbut, psaltery, and all kinds of musick, all the people, the nations, and the languages, fell down and worshipped the golden image that Nebuchadnezzar the king had set up.

[8]Wherefore at that time certain Chaldeans came near, and accused the Jews.

[9]They spake and said to the king Nebuchadnezzar, O king, live for ever.

[10]Thou, O king, hast made a decree, that every man that shall hear the sound of the cornet, flute, harp, sackbut, psaltery, and dulcimer, and all kinds of musick, shall fall down and worship the golden image:

[11]And whoso falleth not down and worshippeth, that he should be cast into the midst of a burning fiery furnace.

[12]There are certain Jews whom thou hast set over the affairs of the province of Babylon, Shadrach, Meshach, and Abednego; these men, O king, have not regarded thee; they serve not thy gods, nor worship the golden image which thou hast set up.

[13]Then Nebuchadnezzar in his rage and fury commanded to bring Shadrach, Meshach, and Abednego. Then they brought these men before the king.

¹⁴Nebuchadnezzar spake and said unto them, Is it true, O Shadrach, Meshach, and Abednego, do not ye serve my gods, nor worship the golden image which I have set up?

¹⁵Now if ye be ready that at what time ye hear the sound of the cornet, flute, harp, sackbut, psaltery, and dulcimer, and all kinds of musick, ye fall down and worship the image which I have made; well: but if ye worship not, ye shall be cast the same hour into the midst of a burning fiery furnace; and who is that God that shall deliver you out of my hands?

¹⁶Shadrach, Meshach, and Abednego, answered and said to the king, O Nebuchadnezzar, we are not careful to answer thee in this matter.

¹⁷If it be so, our God whom we serve is able to deliver us from the burning fiery furnace, and he will deliver us out of thine hand, O king.

¹⁸But if not, be it known unto thee, O king, that we will not serve thy gods, nor worship the golden image which thou hast set up.

¹⁹Then was Nebuchadnezzar full of fury, and the form of his visage was changed against Shadrach, Meshach, and Abednego: therefore he spake, and commanded that they should heat the furnace one seven times more than it was wont to be heated.

²⁰And he commanded the most mighty men that were in his army to bind Shadrach, Meshach, and Abednego, and to cast them into the burning fiery furnace.

²¹Then these men were bound in their coats, their hosen, and their hats, and their other garments, and were cast into the midst of the burning fiery furnace.

²²Therefore because the king's commandment was urgent, and the furnace exceeding hot, the flame of the fire slew those men that took up Shadrach, Meshach, and Abednego.

²³And these three men, Shadrach, Meshach, and Abednego, fell down bound into the midst of the burning fiery furnace.

²⁴Then Nebuchadnezzar the king was astonished, and rose up in haste, and spake, and said unto his counsellors, Did not we cast three men bound into the midst of the fire? They answered and said unto the king, True, O king.

²⁵He answered and said, Lo, I see four men loose, walking in the midst of the fire, and they have no hurt; and the form of the fourth is like the Son of God.

²⁶Then Nebuchadnezzar came near to the mouth of the burning fiery furnace, and spake, and said, Shadrach, Meshach, and Abednego, ye servants of the most high God, come forth, and come hither. Then

Shadrach, Meshach, and Abednego, came forth of the midst of the fire.

²⁷And the princes, governors, and captains, and the king's counsellors, being gathered together, saw these men, upon whose bodies the fire had no power, nor was an hair of their head singed, neither were their coats changed, nor the smell of fire had passed on them.

²⁸Then Nebuchadnezzar spake, and said, Blessed be the God of Shadrach, Meshach, and Abednego, who hath sent his angel, and delivered his servants that trusted in him, and have changed the king's word, and yielded their bodies, that they might not serve nor worship any god, except their own God.

²⁹Therefore I make a decree, That every people, nation, and language, which speak any thing amiss against the God of Shadrach, Meshach, and Abednego, shall be cut in pieces, and their houses shall be made a dunghill: because there is no other God that can deliver after this sort.

³⁰Then the king promoted Shadrach, Meshach, and Abednego, in the province of Babylon.

Daniel 6

¹It pleased Darius to set over the kingdom an hundred and twenty princes, which should be over the whole kingdom;

²And over these three presidents; of whom Daniel was first: that the princes might give accounts unto them, and the king should have no damage.

³Then this Daniel was preferred above the presidents and princes, because an excellent spirit was in him; and the king thought to set him over the whole realm.

⁴Then the presidents and princes sought to find occasion against Daniel concerning the kingdom; but they could not find none occasion nor fault; forasmuch as he was faithful, neither was their any error or fault found in him.

⁵Then said these men, We shall not find any occasion against this Daniel, except we find it against him concerning the law of his God.

⁶Then these presidents and princes assembled together to the king, and said thus unto him, King Darius, live for ever.

⁷All the presidents of the kingdom, the governors, and the princes, the counsellors, and the captains, have consulted together to establish a royal statute, and to make a firm decree, that whosoever shall ask a

petition of any God or man for thirty days, save of thee, O king, he shall be cast into the den of lions.

[8]Now, O king, establish the decree, and sign the writing, that it be not changed, according to the law of the Medes and Persians, which altereth not.

[9]Wherefore king Darius signed the writing and the decree.

[10]Now when Daniel knew that the writing was signed, he went into his house; and his windows being open in his chamber toward Jerusalem, he kneeled upon his knees three times a day, and prayed, and gave thanks before his God, as he did aforetime.

[11]Then these men assembled, and found Daniel praying and making supplication before his God.

[12]Then they came near, and spake before the king concerning the king's decree; Hast thou not signed a decree, that every man that shall ask a petition of any God or man within thirty days, save of thee, O king, shall be cast into the den of lions? The king answered and said, The thing is true, according to the law of the Medes and Persians, which altereth not.

[13]Then answered they and said before the king, That Daniel, which is of the children of the captivity of Judah, regardeth not thee, O king, nor the decree that thou hast signed, but maketh his petition three times a day.

[14]Then the king, when he heard these words, was sore displeased with himself, and set his heart on Daniel to deliver him: and he laboured till the going down of the sun to deliver him.

[15]Then these men assembled unto the king, and said unto the king, Know, O king, that the law of the Medes and Persians is, That no decree nor statute which the king established may be changed.

[16]Then the king commanded, and they brought Daniel, and cast him into the den of lions. Now the king spake and said unto Daniel, Thy God whom thou servest continually, he will deliver thee.

[17]And a stone was brought, and laid upon the mouth of the den; and the king sealed it with his own signet, and with the signet of his lords; that the purpose might not be changed concerning Daniel.

[18]Then the king went to his palace, and passed the night fasting: neither were instruments of musick brought before him: and his sleep went from him.

[19]Then the king arose very early in the morning, and went in haste unto the den of lions.

[20]And when he came to the den, he cried with a lamentable voice unto Daniel: and the king spake and said to Daniel, O Daniel, servant

of the living God, is thy God, whom thou servest continually, able to deliver thee from the lions?

21Then said Daniel unto the king, O king, live for ever.

22My God hath sent his angel, and hath shut the lions' mouths, that they have not hurt me: forasmuch as before him innocency was found in me; and also before thee, O king, have I done no hurt.

23Then was the king exceeding glad for him, and commanded that they should take Daniel up out of the den. So Daniel was taken up out of the den, and no manner of hurt was found upon him, because he believed in his God.

24And the king commanded, and they brought those men which had accused Daniel, and they cast them into the den of lions, them, their children, and their wives; and the lions had the mastery of them, and brake all their bones in pieces or ever they came at the bottom of the den.

25Then king Darius wrote unto all people, nations, and languages, that dwell in all the earth; Peace be multiplied unto you.

26I make a decree, That in every dominion of my kingdom men tremble and fear before the God of Daniel: for he is the living God, and stedfast for ever, and his kingdom that which shall not be destroyed, and his dominion shall be even unto the end.

27He delivereth and rescueth, and he worketh signs and wonders in heaven and in earth, who hath delivered Daniel from the power of the lions.

28So this Daniel prospered in the reign of Darius, and in the reign of Cyrus the Persian.

Exodus 21: 7-11 (NIV)

7If a man sells his daughter as a servant, she is not to go free as menservants do. 8If she does not please the master who has selected her for himself, he must let her be redeemed. He has no right to sell her to foreigners, because he has broken faith with her. 9If he selects her for his son, he must grant her the rights of a daughter. 10If he marries another woman, he must not deprive the first one of her food, clothing and marital rights. 11If he does not provide her with these three things, she is to go free, without any payment of money.

Appendix

Deuteronomy 21: 10-14 (NIV)

[10]When you go to war against your enemies and the LORD your God delivers them into you hands and you take captive, [11]if you notice among the captives a beautiful woman and are attracted to her, you may take her as your wife. [12]Bring her into your home and have her shave her head, trim her nails [13]and put aside the clothes she was wearing when captured. After she has lived in your house and mourned her father and mother for a full month, then you may go to her and be her husband and she shall be your wife. [14]If you are not pleased with her, let her go wherever she wishes. You must not sell her or treat her as a slave, since you have dishonored her.

Deuteronomy 17:17

Neither shall he multiply wives to himself, that his heart turn not away: neither shall he greatly multiply to himself silver and gold.

(The above verse of scripture specifically applies to Israelite leaders)

CHAPTER FIVE

Books of the Old Testament:

Genesis	Psalms	Haggai
Exodus	Proverbs	Zechariah
Leviticus	Ecclesiastes	Malachi
Numbers	Song of Songs	
Deuteronomy	Isaiah	
Joshua	Jeremiah	
Judges	Lamentations	
Ruth	Ezekiel	
1 Samuel	Daniel	
2 Samuel	Hosea	
1 Kings	Joel	
2 Kings	Amos	
1 Chronicles	Obadiah	
2 Chronicles	Jonah	
Ezra	Micah	
Nehemiah	Nahum	
Esther	Habakkuk	
Job	Zephaniah	

Appendix

Books of the New Testament:

Matthew	1 Timothy
Mark	2 Timothy
Luke	Titus
John	Philemon
Acts	Hebrews
Romans	James
1 Corinthians	1 Peter
2 Corinthians	2 Peter
Galatians	1 John
Ephesians	2 John
Philippians	3 John
Colossians	Jude
1 Thessalonians	Revelation
2 Thessalonians	

Genesis 16:1-11

[1]Now Sarai[1] Abram's wife bare him no children; and she had an handmaid, an Egyptian, whose name was Hagar.

[2]And Sarai said unto Abram, Behold now, the Lord hath restrained me from bearing: I pray thee, go in unto my maid; it may be that I may obtain children by her. And Abram hearkened to the voice of Sarai.

[3]And Sarai Abram's wife, took Hagar her maid the Egyptian, after Abram had dwelt ten years in the land of Canaan, and gave her to her husband Abram to be his wife.

[4]And he went into unto Hagar, and she conceived: and when she saw that she had conceived, her mistress was despised in her eyes.

[5]And Sarai said unto Abram, My wrong be upon thee: I have given my maid into thy bosom; and when she saw that she had conceived, I was despised in her eyes: the LORD judge between me and thee.

[6]But Abram said unto Sarai, Behold, thy maid is in thy hand; do to her as it pleaseth thee. And when Sarai dealt hardly with her, she fled from her face.

[7]And the angel of the Lord found her by a fountain of water in the wilderness, by the fountain in the way to Shur.

---

[1] The Hebrew spelling of the name Sarah is *Sarai*. Both refer to Abraham's wife.

[8]And he said, Hagar, Sarai's maid, whence camest thou? And whither wilt thou go? And she said, I flee from the face of my mistress Sarai.

[9]And the angel of the Lord said unto her, Return to thy mistress, and submit thyself under her hands.

[10]And the angel of the Lord said unto her, I will multiply thy seed exceedingly, that it shall not be numbered for multitude.

[11]And the angel of the Lord said unto her, Behold, thou art with child, and shalt bear a son, and shalt call his name Ishmael; because the Lord hath heard thy affliction.

Job 31 (NASB)

[1]"I HAVE made a covenant with
my eyes;
How then could I gaze at a
virgin?
[2]"And what is the portion of
God from above
Or the heritage of the Almighty
from on high?
[3]"Is it not calamity to the
unjust,
And disaster to those who
work iniquity?
[4]"Does He not see my ways,
And number all my steps?

[5]"If I have walked with
falsehood,
And my foot has hastened
after deceit,
[6]Let Him weigh me with
accurate scales,
And let God know my
integrity.
[7]"If my step has turned from
the way,
Or my heart followed
my eyes,
Or if any spot has stuck to
my hands,

[8]Let me sow and another eat,
And let my crops be uprooted.,

[9]"If my heart has been enticed
        by a woman,
Or I have lurked at my
        neighbor's doorway,
[10]May my wife grind for
        another,
And let others kneel down
        over her.
[11]"For that would be a lustful
        crime;
Moreover, it would be an iniquity
        punishable by judges.
[12]"For it would be fire that
        consumes to Abaddon,
And would uproot all my
        increase.
[13]"If I have despised the claim
        of my male or female
        slaves
When they filed a complaint
        against me,
[14]What then could I do when
        God arises,
And when He calls me to
        account, what will I answer
        Him?
[15]"Did not He who made me in
        the womb make him,
And the same one fashion us
        in the womb?

[16]"If I have kept the poor from
        their desire,
Or have caused the eyes of
        the widow to fail,
[17]Or have eaten my morsel
        alone,
And the orphan has not shared it

[18](But from my youth he grew
up with me as with a father,
And from infancy I guided her),
[19]If I have seen anyone perish
    for lack of clothing,
Or that the needy had no
    covering,
[20]If his loins have not thanked
    me,
And if he has not been
    warmed with the fleece
    of my sheep,
[21]If I have lifted up my hand
    against the orphan,
Because I saw I had support
    in the gate,
[22]Let my shoulder fall from the
    socket,
And my arm be broken off at
    the elbow.
[23]"For calamity from God is a
    terror to me,
And because of His majesty I
    can do nothing.
[24]"If I have put my confidence
    in gold,
And called fine gold my
    trust,
[25]If I have gloated because my
    wealth was great,
And because my hand had
    secured so much;
[26]If I have looked at the sun
    when it shone,
Or the moon going in
    splendor,
[27]And my heart became
    secretly enticed,
And my hand threw a kiss
    from my mouth,
[28]That too would have been an
    iniquity calling for judgment,

For I would have denied God above

²⁹"Have I rejoiced at the
    extinction of my enemy,
Or exulted when evil befell
    him?
³⁰"No, I have not allowed my
    mouth to sin
By asking for his life in a
    curse.
³¹"Have the men of my tent not
    said,
Who can find one who has
    not been satisfied with
    his meat?
³²"The alien has not lodged
    outside,
For I have opened my doors
    to the traveler.
³³"Have I covered my
    transgressions like Adam,
By hiding my iniquity in my
    bosom,
³⁴Because I feared the great
    multitude,
And the contempt of families
    terrified me,
And kept silent and did not
    go out of doors?
³⁵"Oh that I had one to hear me!
Behold, here is my signature;
Let the Almighty answer me!
And the indictment which
    my adversary has
    written,
³⁶Surely I would carry it on my
    shoulder;
I would bind it to myself like
    a crown.
³⁷"I would declare to Him the
    number of my steps;
Like a prince I would approach Him.

Appendix

> ³⁸"If my land cries out against
>   me,
> And its furrows weep
>   together;
> ³⁹If I have eaten its fruit
>   without money,
> Or have caused its owners to
>   lose their lives,
> ⁴⁰Let briars grow instead of
>   wheat,
> And stinkweed instead of
>   barley."
> The words of Job are ended.

Philemon (NIV)

[1] Paul, a prisoner of Christ Jesus, and Timothy our brother,

To Philemon our dear friend and fellow worker, [2]to Apphia our sister, to Archippus our fellow soldier and to the church that meets in your home.

[3]Grace to you and peace from God our Father and the Lord Jesus Christ.

[4]I always thank my God as I remember you in my prayers, [5]because I hear about your faith in the Lord Jesus and your love for all the saints. [6]I pray that you may be active in sharing your faith, so that you will have a full understanding of every good thing we have in Christ. [7]Your love has given me great joy and encouragement, because you, brother, have refreshed the hearts of the saints.

[8]Therefore, although in Christ I could be bold and order you to do what you ought to do, [9]yet I appeal to you on the basis of love. I then, as Paul—an old man and now also a prisoner of Christ Jesus—[10]I appeal to you for my son Onesimus, who became my son while I was in chains. [11]Formerly he was useless to you, but now he has become useful both to you and to me.

[12]I am sending him—who is my very heart—back to you. [13]I would have liked to keep him with me so that he could take your place in helping me while I am in chains for the gospel. [14]But I did not want to do anything without your consent, so that any favor you do will be spontaneous and not forced. [15]Perhaps the reason he was separated from you for a little while was that you might have him back for good—[16]no longer as a slave, but better than a slave, as a dear brother.

He is very dear to me but even dearer to you, both as a man and as a brother in the Lord.

[17]So if you consider me a partner, welcome him as you would welcome me. [18]If he has done you any wrong or owes you anything, charge it to me. [19]I, Paul, am writing this with my own hand. I will pay it back—not to mention that you owe me your very self. [20]I do wish, brother, that I may have some benefit from you in the Lord; refresh my heart in Christ. [21]Confident of your obedience, I write to you, knowing that you will do even more than I ask.

[22]And one thing more: Prepare a guest room for me, because I hope to be restored to you in answer to your prayers.

[23]Epaphras, my fellow prisoner in Christ Jesus, sends you greetings. [24]And so do Mark, Aristarchus, Demas and Luke, my fellow workers. [25]The grace of the Lord Jesus Christ be with your spirit.

Isaiah 10: 22-23 (NIV)

[22]Though your people, O Israel, be like the
sand by the sea,
only a remnant will return.
Destruction has been decreed,
overwhelming and righteous.
[23]The Lord, the LORD Almighty, will carry out
the destruction decreed upon the whole land.

Ezekiel 12: 8-16 (NIV)

[8]In the morning the word of the LORD came to me: [9]"Son of man, did not that rebellious house of Israel ask you, 'What are you doing?'

[10]Say to them, 'This is what the Sovereign LORD says: This oracle concerns the prince in Jerusalem and the whole house of Israel who are there.' [11]Say to them, 'I am a sign to you."

"As I have done, so it will be done to them. They will go into exile as captives.

[12]"The prince among them will put his things on his shoulder at dusk and leave, and a hole will be dug in the wall for him to go through. He will cover his face so that he cannot see the land. [13]I will spread my net for him, and he will be caught in my snare; I will bring him to Babylonia, the land of the Chaldeans, but he will not see it, and there he will die. [14]I will scatter to the winds all those around him—his staff and all his troops—and I will pursue them with drawn sword.

[15]They will know that I am the LORD, when I disperse them among the nations and scatter them through the countries. [16]But I will spare a few of them from the sword, famine and plague, so that in the nations where they go they may acknowledge all their detestable practices, Then they will know that I am the LORD."

Romans 9: 27-28 (NIV)

[27]Isaiah cries out concerning Israel:

"Though the number of the Israelites be
like the sand by the sea,
only the remnant will be saved.
[28]For the Lord will carry out
his sentence on earth with speed and
finality.

2 Kings 25:1-30

[1]And it came to pass in the ninth year of his reign, in the tenth month, in the tenth day of the month, that Nebuchadnezzar king of Babylon came, he, and all his host, against Jerusalem, and pitched against it; and they built forts against it round about.

[2]And the city was besieged unto the eleventh year of king Zedekiah.

[3]And on the ninth day of the fourth month the famine prevailed in the city, and there was no bread for the people of the land.

[4]And the city was broken up, and all the men of war fled by night by the way of the gate between two walls, which is by the king's garden: (now the Chaldees were against the city round about:) and the king went the way toward the plain.

[5]And the army of the Chaldees pursued after the king, and overtook him in the plains of Jericho: and all his army were scattered from him,

[6]So they took the king, and brought him up to the king of Babylon to Riblah and they gave judgment upon him.

[7]And they slew the sons of Zedekiah before his eyes, and put out the eyes of Zedekiah, and bound him with fetters of brass, and carried him to Babylon.

[8]And in the fifth month, on the seventh day of the month, which is the nineteenth year of king Nebuchadnezzar king of Babylon, came Nebuzaradan, captain of the guard, a servant of the king of Babylon, unto Jerusalem:

⁹And he burnt the house of the LORD, and the king's house, and all the houses of Jerusalem, and every great man's house burnt he with fire.

¹⁰And all the army of the Chaldees, that were with the captain of the guard, brake down the walls of Jerusalem round about.

¹¹Now the rest of the people that were left in the city, and the fugitives that fell away to the king of Babylon, with the remnant of the multitude, did Nebuzaradan the captain of the guard carry away.

¹²But the captain of the guard left of the poor of the land to be vinedressers and husbandmen.

¹³And the pillars of brass that were in the house of the LORD, and the bases, and the brasen sea that was in the house of the LORD, did the Chaldees break in pieces, and carried the brass of them to Babylon.

¹⁴And the pots, and the shovels, and the snuffers, and the spoons, and all the vessels of brass wherewith they ministered, took they away.

¹⁵And the firepans, and the bowls, and such things as were of gold, in gold, and of silver, in silver, the captain of the guard took away.

¹⁶The two pillars, one sea, and the bases which Solomon had made for the house of the LORD; the brass of all these vessels was without weight.

¹⁷The height of the one pillar was eighteen cubits, and the chapiter upon it was brass; and the Height of the chapiter three cubits; and the wreathen work, and pomegranates upon the chapiter round about, all of brass; and like unto these had the second pillar with wreathen work.

¹⁸And the captain of the guard took Seraiah the chief priest, and Zephaniah the second priest, and the three keepers of the door:

¹⁹And out of the city he took an officer that was set over the men of war, and five men of them that were in the king's presence, which were found in the city, and the principal scribe of the host, which mustered the people of the land, and threescore men of the people of the land that were found in the city:

²⁰And Nebuzaradan captain of the guard took these, and brought them to the king of Babylon to Riblah:

²¹And the king of Babylon smote them, and slew them at Riblah in the land of Hamath. So Judah was carried away out of their land.

²²And as for the people that remained in the land of Judah, whom Nebuchadnezzar king of Babylon had left, even over them he made Gedaliah the son of Ahikam, the son of Shaphan, ruler.

²³And when all the captains of the armies, they and their men, heard that the king of Babylon had made Gedaliah governor there came to Gedaliah to Mizpah, even Ishmael the son of Nethaniah and Johanan

the son of Careah, and Seraiah the son of Tanhumeth the Netophathite, and Jaazaniah the son of a Maachathite, they and their men.

²⁴And Gedaliah sware to them, and to their men, and said unto them Fear not to be the servants of the Chaldees: dwell in the land, and serve the king of Babylon; and it shall be well with you.

²⁵But it came to pass in the seventh month, that Ishmael the son of Nethaniah, the son of Elishama, of the seed royal, came, and ten men with him, and smote Gedaliah, that he died, and the Jews and the Chaldees that were with him at Mizpah.

²⁶And all the people, both small and great, and the captains of the armies, arose, and came to Egypt: for they were afraid of the Chaldees.

²⁷And it came to pass in the seven and thirtieth year of the captivity of Jehoiachin king of Judah, in the twelfth month, on the seven and twentieth day of the month, that Evilmerodach king of Babylon in the year that he began to reign did lift up the head of Jehoiachin king of Judah out of prison;

²⁸And he spake kindly to him, and set his throne above the throne of the kings that were with him in Babylon;

²⁹And changed his prison garments: and he did eat bread continually before him all the days of his life.

³⁰And his allowance was a continual allowance given him of the king, a daily rate for every day, all the days of his life.

Jeremiah 26

¹In the beginning of the reign of Jehoiakim the son of Josiah King of Judah came this word from the Lord, saying,

²Thus saith the LORD; Stand in the court of the LORD'S house, and speak unto all the cities of Judah, which come to worship in the LORD's house, all the words that I command thee to speak unto them; diminish not a word:

³If so be they will hearken, and turn every man from his evil way, that I may repent me of the evil, which I purpose to do unto them because of the evil of their doings.

⁴And thou shalt say unto them, Thus saith the LORD; If ye will not hearken unto me, to walk in my law, which I have set before you,

⁵To hearken to the words of my servants the prophets, whom I sent unto you, both rising up early, and sending them, but ye have not hearkened;

⁶Then will I make this house like Shiloh, and will make this city a curse to all the nations of the earth.

⁷So the priests and the prophets and all the people heard Jeremiah, speaking these words in the house of the LORD.

⁸Now it came to pass, when Jeremiah had made an end of speaking all the LORD had commanded him to speak unto all the people, that the priests and the prophets and all the people took him, saying, Thou shalt surely die.

⁹Why hast thou prophesied in the name of the LORD, saying, This house shall be like Shiloh, and this city shall be desolate without an inhabitant? And all the people were gathered against Jeremiah in the house of the LORD.

¹⁰When the princes of Judah heard these things, then they came up from the king's house unto the house of the LORD, and sat down in the entry of the new gate of the LORD's house,

¹¹Then spake the priests and the prophets unto the princes and to all the people, saying, This man is worthy to die; for he hath prophesied against this city, as ye have heard with your ears.

¹²Then spake Jeremiah unto all the princes and to all the people, saying, The LORD sent me to prophesy against this house and against this city all the words that ye have heard.

¹³Therefore now amend your ways and your doings, and obey the voice of the LORD your God; and the Lord will repent him of the evil that he hath pronounced against you.

¹⁴As for me, behold, I am in your hand: do with me as seemeth good and meet unto you.

¹⁵But know ye for certain, that if ye put me to death, ye shall surely bring innocent blood upon yourselves, and upon this city, and upon the inhabitants thereof; for of a truth the LORD hath sent me unto you to speak all these words in your ears.

¹⁶Then said the princes and all the people unto the priests and to the prophets; This man is not worthy to die: for he hath spoken to us in the name of the LORD our God.

¹⁷Then rose up certain of the elders of the land, and spake to all the assembly of the people, saying,

¹⁸Micah the Morasthite prophesied in the days of Hezekiah king of Judah and spake to all the people of Judah, saying, Thus saith the LORD of hosts; Zion shall be plowed like a field, and Jerusalem shall become heaps, and the mountain of the house as the high places of a forest.

¹⁹Did Hezekiah king of Judah and all Judah put him at all to death? did he not fear the LORD, and besought the LORD, and the LORD

repented him of the evil which he had pronounced against them? Thus might we procure great evil against our souls?

[20]And there was also a man that prophesied in the name of the LORD, Urijah the son of Shemaliah of Kirjathjearim, who prophesied against this city and against this land according to all the words of Jeremiah: [21]And when Jehoiakim the king, with all his mighty men, and all the princes, heard his words, the king sought to put him to death: but when Urijah heard it, he was afraid, and fled, and went into Egypt; [22]And Jehoiakim the king sent men into Egypt, namely, Elnathan the son of Achbor, and certain men with him into Egypt. [23]And they fetched forth Urijah out of Egypt, and brought him unto Jehoiakim the king; who slew him with the sword, and cast his dead body into the graves of the common people. [24]Nevertheless the hand of Ahikam the son of Shaphan was with Jeremiah, that they should not give him into the hand of the people to put him to death.

Jeremiah 27

[1]In the beginning of the reign of Jehoiakim the son of Josiah king of Judah came this word unto Jeremiah from the LORD, saying, [2]Thus saith the LORD to me; Make thee bonds and yokes and put them upon thy neck, [3]And send them to the king of Edom, and to the king of Moab, and to the king of the Ammonites, and to the king of Tyrus, and to the king of Zidon, by the hand of the messengers which come to Jerusalem unto Zedekiah king of Judah; [4]And command them to say unto their masters, Thus saith the Lord of hosts, the God of Israel; thus shall ye say unto your masters; [5]I have made the earth, the man and the beast that are upon the ground, by my great power and by my outstretched arm, and have given it unto whom it seemed meet unto me. [6]And now have I given all these lands into the hand of Nebuchadnezzar the king of Babylon, my servant; and the beasts of the field have I given him also to serve him. [7]And all nations shall serve him, and his son, and his son's son, until the very time of his land come: and then many nations and great kings shall serve themselves of him. [8]And it shall come to pass, that the nation and kingdom which will not serve the same Nebuchadnezzar the king of Babylon, and that will not put their neck under the yoke of the king of Babylon, that nation will I punish, saith the LORD, with the sword, and with the

famine, and with the pestilence, until I have consumed them by his hand.

⁹Therefore hearken not ye to your prophets, nor to your diviners, nor to your dreamers, nor to your enchanters, nor to your sorcerers, which speak unto you, saying, Ye shall not serve the king of Babylon: ¹⁰For they prophesy a lie unto you, to remove you far from your land; and that I should drive you out, and ye should perish.

¹¹But the nations that bring their neck under the yoke of the king of Babylon, and seve him, those will I let remain still in their own land, saith the LORD; and they shall till it, and dwell therein.

¹²I spake also to Zedekiah king of Judah according to all these words, saying, Bring your necks under the yoke of the king of Babylon, and serve him and his people, and live.

¹³Why will ye die, thou and thy people, by the sword, by the famine, and by the pestilence, as the LORD hath spoken against the nation that will not serve the king of Babylon?

¹⁴Therefore hearken not unto the words of the prophets that speak unto you, saying, Ye shall not serve the king of Babylon: for they prophesy a lie unto you.

¹⁵For I have not sent them, saith the LORD, yet they prophesy a lie in my name; that I might drive you out, and that ye might perish, ye, and the prophets that prophesy unto you.

¹⁶Also I spake to the priests and to all this people, saying, Thus saith the LORD; hearken not to the words of your prophets that prophesy unto you, saying, Behold, the vessels of the LORD's house shall now shortly be brought again from Babylon: for they prophesy a lie unto you.

¹⁷Hearken not unto them; serve the king of Babylon, and live: wherefore should this city be laid waste?

¹⁸But if they be prophets, and if the word of the LORD be with them, let them now make intercession to the LORD of hosts, that the vessels which are left in the house of the LORD, and in the house of the king of Judah, and at Jerusalem, go not to Babylon.

¹⁹For thus saith the LORD of hosts concerning the pillars, and concerning the sea, and concerning the bases, and concerning the residue of the vessels that remain in this city.

²⁰Which Nebuchadnezzar king of Babylon took not, when he carried away captive Jeconiah the son of Jehoiakim king of Judah from Jerusalem to Babylon, and all the nobles of Judah and Jerusalem;

²¹Yea, thus saith the LORD of hosts, the God of Israel, concerning the vessels that remain in the house of the LORD, and in the house of the king of Judah and of Jerusalem;

[22]They shall be carried to Babylon, and there shall they be until the day that I visit them, saith the LORD; then will I bring them up, and restore them to this place.

Deuteronomy 20

[1]When thou goest out to battle against thine enemies, and seest horses, and chariots, and a people more than thou, be not afraid of them: for the Lord thy God is with thee, which brought thee up out of the land of Egypt.

[2]And it shall be when ye are come nigh unto the battle, that the priest shall approach and speak unto the people,

[3]And shall say unto them, Hear, O Israel, ye approach this day unto battle against your enemies: let not your hearts faint, fear not, and do not tremble, neither be ye terrified because of them;

[4]For the Lord your God is he that goeth with you, to fight for you against your enemies, to save you.

[5]And the officers shall speak unto the people, saying, What man is there that hath built a new house, and hath not dedicated it? let him go and return to his house, lest he die in the battle, and another man dedicate it.

[6]And what man is he that hath planted a vineyard, and hath not yet eaten of it? let him also go and return unto his house, lest he die in the battle, and another man eat of it.

[7]And what man is there that hath betrothed a wife, and hath not taken her? let him go and return unto his house, lest he die in the battle, and another man take her.

[8]And the officers shall speak further unto the people, and they shall say, What man is there that is fearful and fainthearted? Let him go and return unto his house, lest his brethren's heart faint as well as his heart.

[9]And it shall be, when the officers have made an end of speaking unto the people, that they shall make captains of the armies to lead the people.

[10]When thou comest nigh unto a city to fight against it, then proclaim peace unto it,

[11]And it shall be, if it make thee answer of peace, and open unto thee then it shall be, that all the people that is found therein shall be tributaries unto thee, and they shall serve thee.

[12]And if it will make no peace with thee, but will make war against thee, then thou shalt besiege it:

13And when the LORD thy God hath delivered it into thine hands, thou shalt smite every male thereof with the edge of the sword:

14But the women, and the little ones, and the cattle, and all that is in the city, even all the spoil thereof, shalt thou take unto thyself; and thou shalt eat the spoil of thine enemies, which the LORD thy God hath given thee.

15Thus shalt thou do unto all the cities which are very far off from thee, which are not of the cities of these nations.

16But of the cities of these people, which the LORD thy God doth give thee for an inheritance, thou shalt save alive nothing that breatheth:

17But thou shall utterly destroy them; namely, the Hittites, and the Amorites, the Canaanites, and the Perizzites, the Hivites, and the Jebusites; as the LORD thy God hath commanded thee;

18That they teach you not to do after all their abominations, which they have done unto their gods; so should ye sin against the LORD your God.

19When thou shalt besiege a city a long time, in making war against it to take it, thou shalt not destroy the trees thereof by forcing an ax against them: for thou mayest eat of them, and thou shalt not cut them down (for the tree of the field is man's life) to employ them in the siege:

20Only the trees which thou knowest that they be not trees for meat, thou shalt destroy and cut them down; and thou shalt build bulwarks against the city that maketh war with thee, until it be subdued.

Deuteronomy 28

1And it shall come to pass, if thou shalt hearken diligently unto the voice of the LORD thy God, to observe and to do all his commandments which I command thee this day, that the LORD thy God will set thee on high above all nations of the earth:

2And all these blessings shall come on thee, and overtake thee, if thou shalt hearken unto the voice of the LORD thy God.

3Blessed shalt thou be in the city, and blessed shalt thou be in the field.

4Blessed shall be the fruit of thy body, and the fruit of thy ground, and the fruit of thy cattle, the increase of thy kine, and the flocks of thy sheep.

5Blessed shall be thy basket and thy store.

6Blessed shalt thou be when thou comest in, and blessed shalt thou be when thou goest out.

[7]The LORD shall cause thine enemies that rise up against thee to be smiten before thy face: they shall come out against thee one way, and flee before thee seven ways.

[8]The LORD shall command the blessing upon thee in thy storehouses, and in all that thou settest thine hand unto; and he shall bless thee in the land which the LORD thy God giveth thee.

[9]The LORD shall establish thee an holy people unto himself, as he hath sworn unto thee, if thou shalt keep the commandments of the LORD thy God, and walk in his ways.

[10]And all people of the earth shall see that thou art called by the name of the LORD; and they shall be afraid of thee.

[11]And the Lord shall make thee plenteous in goods, in the fruit of thy body, and in the fruit of thy cattle, and in the fruit of thy ground, in the land which the LORD sware unto thy fathers to give thee.

[12]The LORD shall open unto thee his good treasure, the heaven to give the rain unto thy land in his season, and to bless all the work of thine hand: and thou shalt lend unto many nations, and thou shalt not borrow.

[13]And the LORD shall make thee the head, and not the tail; and thou shalt be above only, and thou shalt not be beneath; if that thou hearken unto the commandments of the LORD thy God, which I command thee this day, to observe and to do them:

[14]And thou shalt not go aside from any of the words which I command thee this day, to the right hand, or to the left, to go after other gods to serve them.

[15]But it shall come to pass, if thou wilt not hearken unto the voice of the LORD thy God, to observe to do all his commandments and his statutes which I command thee this day; that all these curses shall come upon thee, and overtake thee:

[16]Cursed shalt thou be in the city, and cursed shalt thou be in the field.

[17]Cursed shall be thy basket and thy store.

[18]Cursed shall be the fruit of thy body, and the fruit of thy land, the increase of thy kine, and the flocks of thy sheep.

[19]Cursed shalt thou be when thou comest in, and cursed shalt thou be when thou goest out.

[20]The LORD shall send upon thee cursing, vexation, and rebuke, in all that thou settest thine hand unto for to do, until thou be destroyed, and until thou perish quickly; because of the wickedness of thy doings, whereby thou hast forsaken me.

[21]The LORD shall make the pestilence cleave unto thee, until he have consumed thee from off the land, whither thou goest to possess it.

22The LORD shall smite thee with a consumption, and with a fever, and with an inflammation, and with an extreme burning, and with the sword, and with blasting, and with mildew; and they shall pursue thee until thou perish.

23And thy heaven that is over thy head shall be brass, and the earth that is under thee shall be iron.

24The LORD shall make the rain of thy land powder and dust: from heaven shall it come down upon thee, until thou be destroyed.

25The LORD shall cause thee to be smitten before thine enemies; thou shalt go out one way against them, and flee seven ways before them: and shalt be removed into all the kingdoms of the earth.

26And thy carcase shall be meat unto all fowls of the air, and unto the beasts of the earth, and no man shall fray them away.

27The LORD will smite thee with the botch of Egypt, and with the emerods, and with the scab, and with the itch, whereof thou canst not be healed.

28The LORD shall smite thee with madness, and blindness, and astonishment of heart:

29And thou shalt grope at noonday, as the blind gropeth in darkness, and thou shalt not prosper in thy ways: and thou shalt be only oppressed and spoiled evermore, and no man shall save thee.

30Thou shalt betroth a wife, and another man shall lie with her: thou shalt build an house, and thou shalt not dwell therein: thou shalt plant a vineyard, and shalt not gather the grapes thereof.

31Thine ox shall be slain before thine eyes, and thou shalt not eat thereof: thine ass shall be violently taken away from before thy face, and shall not be restored to thee: thy sheep shall be given unto thine enemies, and thou shall have none to rescue them.

32Thy sons and thy daughters shall be given unto another people, and thine eyes shall look, and fail with longing for them all the day long: and there shall be no might in thine hand.

33The fruit of thy land, and all thy labours, shall a nation which thou knowest not eat up; and thou shalt be only oppressed and cursed always:

34So that thou shalt be mad for the sight of thine eyes which thou shalt see.

35The LORD shall smite thee in the knees, and in the legs, with a sore botch that cannot be healed, from the sole of thy foot unto the top of thy head.

36The LORD shall bring thee, and thy king which thou shalt set over thee, unto a nation which neither thou nor thy fathers have known; and there shalt thou serve other gods, wood and stone.

³⁷And thou shalt become an astonishment, a proverb, and a byword, among all nations whither the LORD shall lead thee.

³⁸Thou shalt carry much seed out into the field, and shalt gather but little in; for the locust shall consume it.

³⁹Thou shalt plant vineyards, and dress them, but shalt neither drink of the wine, nor gather the grapes; for the worms shall eat them.

⁴⁰Thou shalt have olive trees throughout all thy coasts, but thou shalt not anoint thyself with the oil; for thine olive shall cast his fruit.

⁴¹Thou shalt beget sons and daughters, but thou shalt not enjoy them; for they shall go into captivity.

⁴²All thy trees and fruit of thy land shall the locust consume.

⁴³The stranger that is within thee shall get up above thee very high; and thou shalt come down very low.

⁴⁴He shall lend to thee, and thou shalt not lend to him; he shall be the head, and thou shalt be the tail.

⁴⁵Moreover all these curses shall come upon thee, and shall pursue thee, and overtake thee, till thou be destroyed; because thou hearkenedst not unto the voice of the LORD thy God, to keep his commandments and his statutes which he commanded thee:

⁴⁶And thy shall be upon thee for a sign and for a wonder, and upon thy seed forever.

⁴⁷Because thou servedst not the LORD thy God with joyfulness, and with gladness of heart, for the abundance of all things;

⁴⁸Therefore shalt thou serve thine enemies which the LORD shall send against thee, in hunger, and in thirst, and in nakedness, and in want of all things: and he shall put a yoke of iron upon thy neck, until he have destroyed thee.

⁴⁹The LORD shall bring a nation against thee from far, from the end of the earth, as swift as the eagle flieth; a nation whose tongue thou shalt not understand;

⁵⁰A nation of fierce countenance, which shall not regard the person of the old, nor shew favour to the young:

⁵¹And he shall eat the fruit of thy cattle, and the fruit of thy land, until thou be destroyed: which also shall not leave thee either corn, wine, or oil, or the increase of thy kine, or flocks of thy sheep, until he have destroyed thee.

⁵²And he shall besiege thee in all thy gates, until thy high and fenced walls come down, wherein thou trustedst, throughout all thy land: and he shall besiege thee in all thy gates throughout all thy land, which the LORD thy God hath given thee.

⁵³And thou shalt eat the fruit of thine own body, the flesh of thy sons and of thy daughters, which the LORD thy God hath given thee, in

the siege, and in the straitness, wherewith thine enemies shall distress thee:

[54]So that the man that is tender among you, and very delicate, his eye shall be evil toward his brother, and toward the wife of his bosom, and toward the remnant of his children which he shall leave:

[55]So that he will not give to any of them of the flesh of his children whom he shall eat: because he hath nothing left him in the siege, and in the straitness, wherewith thine enemies shall distress thee in all thy gates.

[56]The tender and delicate woman among you, which would not adventure to set the sole of her foot upon the ground for her delicateness and tenderness, her eye shall be evil toward the husband of her bosom, and toward her son, and toward her daughter.

[57]And toward her young one that cometh out from between her feet, and toward her children which she shall bear: for she shall eat them for want of all things secretly in the siege and straitness, wherewith thine enemy shall distress thee in thy gates.

[58]If thou wilt not observe to do all the words of this law that are written in this book, that thou mayest fear this glorious and fearful name, THE LORD THY GOD;

[59]Then the LORD will make thy plagues wonderful, and the plagues of thy seed, even great plagues, and of long continuance, and sore sicknesses, and of long continuance.

[60]Moreover he will bring upon thee all the diseases of Egypt, which thou wast afraid of; and they shall cleave unto thee.

[61]Also every sickness, and every plague, which is not written in the book of this law, them will the LORD bring upon thee, until thou be destroyed.

[62]And ye shall be left few in number, whereas ye were as the stars of heaven for multitude; because thou wouldest not obey the voice of the LORD thy God.

[63]And it shall come to pass, that as the LORD rejoiced over you to do you good, and to multiply you; so the LORD will rejoice over you to destroy you, and to bring you to nought; and ye shall be plucked from off the land whiter thou goest to possess it.

[64]And the LORD shall scatter thee among all people, from the one end of the earth even unto the other; and there thou shalt serve other gods, which neither thou nor thy fathers have known, even wood and stone.

[65]And among these nations shalt thou find no ease, neither shall the sole of thy foot have rest: but the LORD shall give thee there a trembling heart, and failing of eyes, and sorrow of mind:

[66]And thy life shall hang in doubt before thee; and thou shalt fear day and night, and shalt have none assurance of thy life:

[67]In the morning thou shalt say, Would God it were even! and at even thou shalt say, Would God it were morning! For the fear of thine heart wherewith thou shalt fear, and for the sight of thine eyes which thou shall see.

[68]And the LORD shall bring thee into Egypt again with ships, by the way whereof I spake unto thee, Thou shalt see it no more again: and there ye shall be sold unto your enemies for bondmen and bondwomen, and no man shall buy you.

CHAPTER SIX

Job 2: 1-6 (NIV)

[1]On another day the angels came to present themselves before the LORD, and Satan also came with them to present himself before him.

[2]And the LORD said to Satan, "Where have you come from?"

Satan answered the LORD, "From roaming through the earth and going back and forth in it."

[3]Then the LORD said to Satan, "Have you considered my servant Job? There is no one on earth like him; he is blameless and upright, a man who fears God and shuns evil. And he still maintains his integrity, though you incited me against him to ruin him without any reason."

[4]"Skin for skin!" Satan replied. "A man will give all he has for his own life. [5]But stretch out your hand and strike his flesh and bones, and he will surely curse you to your face."

[6]The LORD said to Satan, "Very well, then, he is in your hands; but you must spare his life."

END NOTES

INTRODUCTION

1   Columbus Salley and Ronald Behm, What Color is Your God?
     (Secaucus, NJ: Citadel Press, 1988) p. 14

2   Ibid., p.35,

CHAPTER ONE

1   Jerome H. Smith, Editor, *The New Treasury of Scripture Knowledge* (Nashville,
     TN: Thomas Nelson Publishers, Inc., 1992), p. 1188,

CHAPTER TWO

1   Josh McDowell and Bill Wilson, *A Ready Defense* (Nashville, TN: Thomas
     Nelson Publishers, Inc., 1990), p.30, used by permission of Thomas Nelson
     Publishers, Inc.

2   Ibid., p. 210, used by permission of Thomas Nelson Publishers, Inc.,

3   Leslie B. Flynn, *The Twelve* (Wheaton, IL: Victor Books, 1988), p. 22

4   McDowell and Wilson, *A Ready Defense*, p. 245, used by permission
     of Thomas Nelson Publishers Inc.

CHAPTER THREE

1   Taken from *Defending Black Faith* by Craig S. Keener and Glenn Usry. © 1997
     by Craig S. Keener and Glenn Usry. Used with permission of Intervarsity Press,
     P.O. Box 1400, Downers Grove, IL 60515, p. 25

CHAPTER FOUR

1   Erick McKitrick, *Slavery Defended: The Views of the Old South*
     (Englewood Cliffs, NJ: Prentice –Hall Incorporated, 1963), P.69-70

2   Larry Pierce, *The On-line Bible Lexicon* (Elmira, Ontario: Woodside
     Bible Fellowship, 1988), used by permission.

3   Ibid., used by permission

4   Albert Barnes, *An Inquiry into the Scriptural Views of Slavery* (Philadelphia:
     Parry and McMillan, 1855; republished by Negro History Press, Detroit, MI)
     p.67

5   Trent C. Butler, Ph.D., *Holman Bible Dictionary* (Nashville, TN Holman Bible
     Publishers, 1991), p. 1286, all rights reserved, used by permission.

6   Barnes, *An Inquiry into the Scriptural Views of Slavery*, p.120

7   George P. Rawick, *The American Slave From Sundown to Sunup* (Westport, CT: Greenwood Publishing Company, 1972), p.57, used by permission

8   Ibid., p.58, used by permission

9   Ibid., p.64, used by permission

10   Ibid., p.62, used by permission

11   Ibid., p.55, used by permission

12   McKitrick, *Slavery Defended*, p. 22-23

CHAPTER FIVE

1   William Jay, *Miscellaneous Writings on Slavery* (Freeport, NY: Books For Library Press, 1853; reprinted 1970) p. 130

2   Ibid,. p. 130

3   James D. Essig, *Bonds of Wickedness* (Philadelphia PA: Temple University Press, 1982), p. 10-11

5   Butler, *Holman Bible Dictionary*, p. 674, all rights reserved, used by permission

CHAPTER SIX

1   William Dwight McKissic Sr., *Beyond Roots: In Search of Blacks in The Bible* (Woodbury, NJ: Renaissance Productions, Inc., 1990) p. 51, used by permission

2   Ibid., p. 64, used by permission

3   Butler, *Holman Bible Dictionary*, P. 539-540, all rights reserved, used by permission.

4   Declaration of Independence

BIBLIOGRAPHY

The Holy Bible, *King James Version*, 1611

The Holy Bible, *New International Version* (Grand Rapids MI: Zondervan Bible Publishers, 1996 Thinline Bible)

The Holy Bible, *New International Version, 10th Anniversary Edition* (Grand Rapids MI: Zondervan Publishing House, 1995)

The Bible, *New American Standard Bible* (Nashville, TN: Thomas Nelson Publishers and the Lockman Foundation, 1985)

Columbus Salley and Ronald Behm, *What Color is Your God*, (Secaucus, NJ: Citadel Press, 1988)

Jerome H. Smith, *The New Treasury of Scripture Knowledge* (Nashville, TN: Thomas Nelson Publishers, Inc., 1992)

Josh McDowell and Bill Wilson, *A Ready Defense* (Nashville, TN: Thomas Nelson Publishers, Inc., 1990)

Lerone Bennett Jr., *Before the Mayflower: A History of Black America*, Sixth Edition (New York, NY: Penguin Books, 1993)

Leslie B. Flynn, *The Twelve* (Wheaton, IL: Victory Books, 1988)

Kevin Shillington, *History of Africa*, Revised Edition (New York, NY: St. Martins Press, 1989, 1995)

Eric L. McKitrick, *Slavery Defended: The Views of the Old South* (Englewood Cliffs, NJ: Prentice-Hall Incorporated, 1963)

Larry Pierce, *The On-line Bible Lexicon* (Elmira, Ontario: Woodside Bible Fellowship, 1988)

Albert Barnes, *An Inquiry into the Scriptural Views of Slavery* (Philadelphia: Parry and McMillan, 1855; republished by Negro History Press, Detroit MI)

Trent C. Butler, Ph.D., *Holman Bible Dictionary* (Nashville, TN: Holman Bible Publishers, 1991)

George P. Rawick, *The American Slave from Sundown to Sunup* (Westport, CT: Greenwood Publishing Company, 1972)

James D. Essig, *Bonds of Wickedness* (Philadelphia, PA: Temple University Press, 1982)

William Dwight McKissic Sr., *Beyond Roots: In Search of Blacks in the Bible* (Woodbury, NJ: Renaissance Productions Inc., 1990)

Dale Taylor, *Everyday Life in Colonial America* (Cincinnati Ohio: Writer's Digest Books, 1997)

INDEX